NINE ETCHED FROM LIFE

NINE ETCHED FROM LIFE

BY EMIL LUDWIG

NANSEN · MASARYK · BRIAND
RATHENAU · MOTTA · LLOYD GEORGE
VENIZELOS · MUSSOLINI · STALIN

Essay Index Reprint Series

BOOKS FOR LIBRARIES PRESS
FREEPORT, NEW YORK

First Published 1934
Reprinted 1969

STANDARD BOOK NUMBER:
8369-1225-X

LIBRARY OF CONGRESS CATALOG CARD NUMBER:
70-90658

PRINTED IN THE UNITED STATES OF AMERICA

To

HENDRIK VAN LOON

whose books I should like to have written

CONTENTS

SERVANTS OF THE PEOPLE

RULERS OF THE PEOPLE

FOREWORD

THE nine biographical portraits presented in this book have been etched directly from life. This is the feature that makes the present work quite different from the various biographical studies I have published since 1920—*Napoleon, Bismarck, Goethe,* etc. All the men whose lives and characters are described here were personally known to me. With some of them I have had a prolonged acquaintance and others I have met only from time to time. With Masaryk, Mussolini and Rathenau I have had a long series of systematic discussions extending over a considerable period. The others I have met occasionally during their public careers. Stalin is the only member of the group with whom I have had but one conversation.

The German edition of this book, together with that of another I have recently written, is being published in Holland. Arrangements have been made for its simultaneous appearance in twelve different foreign languages. That is my reply to the funeral pyre which they made of my writings in Germany last year. In Germany alone my books had reached a circulation of 1,200,000. Of these about a thousand were burned at the public bonfire—among them my book on Goethe, which had reached a larger German circulation than any other book hitherto written on the great poet. When the whole conflagration will have played itself out, and the impartial critic comes to assess the ob-

jective historical importance of our contemporary Aryan heroes,
I believe that the men whose lives and achievements I have
endeavoured to describe here will be found to have held their
ground unshaken.

It may be questioned whether the nine statesmen presented
in this book can justly be called the leaders of their respective
nations. I should certainly answer in the affirmative except in
the cases of England and France. So far as the other seven
countries are concerned, the leader whose name I have chosen
undoubtedly represents his country's most important statesman
in our time. If it be objected that the policy of European unification which Briand and Rathenau pursued has failed, the
answer is that this is true only in the eyes of people who live
for the moment and take their thoughts only from the newspapers. In relation to the basic trends of European development
the work of these two men is far more significant than is that
of those who succeeded them in France and Germany. When
we talk of leaders of Europe we do not think of passing dema-
gogues, but rather of the men who come into an historical perspective and whose lives are significant for Europe as a whole.

Of the group that I have presented here all except Nansen
and Rathenau are examples of self-made men. They have risen
from the rank and file. All except Nansen and Motta were
journalists at one time or other. Five are authors. Two are professors. Two are lawyers and two are philosophers by profession.
Not one of the group was a professional soldier.

Although the distinction between Autocrat and Democrat is
no longer very clear, those whom I have allocated to the first
part of my book and styled *Servants of the People* undoubtedly
deserve that title. Those whose names I have grouped together
in the second part of the book have been called *Rulers of the
People*. But that is only a relative designation, because it includes

those whom the British and the Greeks chose from their own midst because they alone possessed the necessary ruling qualities.

In the development of history we often find two distinct phases which succeed each other and are of such a nature that they may respectively be called the masculine phase and the feminine phase. During the masculine phase the people are vigorously active and creative, to achieve their freedom if they be in subjection or, if their free destiny be in their own hands, they will be daring and venturesome and creative. During the feminine phase the people are passive. They look for a leader to protect them and make their decisions for them. Virile nations do not look for a dictator. They would oppose anybody who might try to assume that rôle. An epoch that is persistently talking about the problem of leadership thereby acknowledges its incapacity for the direction of its own affairs. Hand in hand with this incapacity goes the trend towards the deification of the state. This idea is entirely foreign to the mind of the free citizen freely accepting and asserting his share of responsibility for public affairs. Where the state is endowed with the divine attributes of omnipotence and omniscience there is no other aim in life for the individual except to serve blindly. The service of this idol, which is expressed today in racial and national rivalries, in the grading of citizens into various orders and levels of merit, in the training of the young as mere numerical items in the roll of citizenship—all this shows the lack of a creative vision and a degeneration of religion, which in its pristine stage lays emphasis on the individual soul. The idea of the community, which is now being hammered into the heads of millions of Europeans, is meant as a substitute for the personal worth of the individual. It helps little souls. The person who needs the community in order to express his own little self feels that his place is only in the chorus.

Such a criterion of human values is entirely foreign to the

individualist. His ideal is to develop his own talents and in that way to raise himself up towards God or the Ideal in his own soul. The national community is to him something natural, like the colour of his eyes or his own physique. The idea of a National Standard Bearer, which has led to the mysterious word "patriotism" has nothing in common with the feeling for one's native land, which one loves without boasting about it. Europe is steadily becoming smaller in extent year by year, thanks to modern development in trade, transport, etc. Nationalism, therefore, blows its trumpet all the more stridently, because it fears to face its allotted end. The obscuration of our cosmopolitan ideal at the present moment is due to the fact that the nations insist on having the display lights turned on themselves, as if they were public monuments or the domes of government buildings, so that the passers-by may see them in the night. But the Citizen of Europe stands indifferently in the shadow and gazes on the stars.

My children have been born and grown up in Switzerland. For that reason it is easy for me to teach them love for their native land, because here the problem of nationality was long ago solved practically. But if they belonged to another country I should teach them, too, that there is no such thing as a chosen nation, that the achievements of the mind are common to all the nations, and only by these is the greatness of a people to be estimated, not by the growth of its armed power, its extent of territory or the number of its inhabitants. The discovery of a serum which would make mankind immune from some disease is a matter of far more importance than the question of who shall have the political mastery of Europe. If I were to compare with one another the different ways and degrees in which the state is deified in the various countries, I should not hesitate to say that the Russian system seems to have the best chance of a future; because the fact of taking political power out of the hands of finance and the throwing open of all opportunities to those who had hitherto been disfranchised must necessarily have important moral results, while it matters nothing from the standpoint of the future of humanity whether a certain province or certain oil wells pass from the control of one racial motley—which they call a state—to that of another.

The question of how to govern is not so important as: Who shall govern? For the past twenty years and more I have devoted all my time to the study of individual genius and the presentation of it to the public in biographical and dramatic form. To one who has conceived world history as definitely based on the work of individual personalities, government by four hundred mediocrities must seem much less acceptable than the rule of a competent dictator. I should readily take part in the hero-worship which holds the youth of Europe in its fanatical grip today if only I could see a few more heroes to worship. Personally I should far prefer to be ruled dictatorially by Masaryk than democratically by the Palais Bourbon.

It is too late now for hoping. The idea of a United Europe has been cast into the outer darkness by brute force. The old-fashioned nationalist rivalry is being developed anew. While statesmen meet in conference and waste time on ridiculous discussions as to what differentiates defensive from offensive armament all the nations are forging the same kinds of weapons. Whether they are defensive or offensive is not a problem of calibre, but rather a question of the ideals that are being taught in the schools and propagandized publicly by the state. The next war will not merely be annihilating. It will be empty of results even for itself. That is to say, it will bring victory to none of the belligerents.

Meanwhile Fate is preparing the final doom of nationalism. When the great struggle for the mastery of the races and the nations is finished, nobody will ask whose flag is that which flies from the towers of a conquered city. All national problems will have been obliterated. The victims will turn on their leaders and betrayers and will take from them the last remnants of that money and property around which the national conflicts have raged. But the ideal of a World Citizenship will tower above the waters of this final deluge and towards it our impoverished successors will reach out for succour in their common distress.

February, 1934.   EMIL LUDWIG

NINE ETCHED FROM LIFE

PART ONE

SERVANTS OF THE PEOPLE

NANSEN

THE NORDIC PHILANTHROPIST

IT WAS in the Autumn of 1899, at a banquet given by the
Munich Naturalists' Congress, that I first saw Fridtjof Nansen.
The hall was thronged with distinguished guests. Medals and
decorations glittered from every table. Waiters moved hurriedly
to and fro. Dishes clanged and wine flowed. At one end of the
hall there was a raised platform on which about a dozen ladies
and gentlemen were seated, dining apart, like Gunther and
his family in the *Götterdämmerung*. I was then a young student
eighteen years of age. I sat beside my father in the body of the
hall; but my face was turned all the time towards the raised
platform at the end, and my eyes were fixed on one guest who
sat at table there. When the toasts began the whole hall became
lively. Chairs were drawn back from the tables. The guests
smiled on one another and clinked their glasses. But I was
thinking all the time how much better it would be to be sitting
up there on the platform.

For there sat the man whose book I had recently read. It bore
the dedication "To her who baptized the ship and had the
courage to wait." I had repeated that dedication to myself a
hundred times. At the end of the festive ceremonies my father
conducted me to the table on the platform. A magnificent-look-

ing man rose to greet us. He was in evening dress and wore his decorations; a slim figure, looking as if it were all made of sinew. From a long narrow face two steel-grey eyes gazed at us as if searching for something in the distance. This was Fridtjof Nansen, then a man in the late thirties. My heart went out to him.

It remained with him as we returned to our table and sat among the professors. I kept constantly turning towards Nansen, believing that I knew him better now, because I had shaken hands and spoken with him. I watched the restrained movements of his hands, and noticed the sharp look in the eyes, as if searching for something in the distance. Once in a while a smile played over his face. And I now recognized something that was quite new to me. I can only describe it by saying that it expressed some sort of inner certainty, such as one has only in a dream. It obviously sprang from a perfect balance of temperament and character and intellect, which seemed to be wanting in our own explorers and men of learning. It was just this singular characteristic that marked out the Nordic hunter and sailor from the purely academic bearing of the other guests. I had never before come face to face with any living being whose appearance expressed such a perfect inner balance.

My imagination clothed him in his furs. I saw the colossal gloves on his hands, gripping the gun and harpoon just as I had so often seen him in photographs. In the picture that now sketched itself on my imagination I saw the professors around me as Nordic hunters or polar bears. I saw Virchow's spectacled face on one of the great white dogs drawing the sledge. My father's head and white beard decorated a penguin. A row of these birds stood awaiting the stranger with a curious but fearless gaze. And above them all I saw Nansen himself, sparing of speech, in a commanding attitude, searching all round through his long field glass for a path between the ice floes.

A moment later I imagined him beside his wife—she who had the courage to wait. I pictured the tragic leave-taking when he went on that first expedition and the romantic meeting when he returned. At this moment he had just raised his champagne glass and as I saw him in the flesh once again I realized how perfect a gentleman was this man of genius whose fame had now filled the world. Comparing him with the academic men of learning around me, he seemed rather to be a poet who had dreamed a pathway through the Arctic night.

When all was over and the guests began to leave I followed him to the cloakroom and watched the lithe, athletic figure draw the heavy fur coat over the evening dress. Then he vanished from my sight. Thirty years passed before I saw him again.

2

This man who was a painter in his youth, a fisherman and a hunter and a scientist in his university days, had developed into a geographer and explorer and a great organizer. Such an evolution would have been only one of several other interesting cases were it not for the fact that in the depths of his being two main forces—which in most other men are found in conflict with each other—here operated in harmony and strengthened each other. For Nansen was an adventurer and a philanthropist; and he was passionately devoted to both. Yet he did not develop the second interest after he had outgrown the first, as is the case with so many men. Both threads were interwoven in the basic pattern of his life; for at thirty he was already a philanthropist and at sixty he was still an adventurer. On his first exploratory trip he became sad and sorrow-stricken when he discovered a distant people living in such need as he had never believed to exist. When he went out on his last journey it was to help a distant people in dire necessity. But this last journey too was a dangerous adventure which demanded the same stamina of will and body.

One had to see Nansen in the flesh in order to understand him. His body showed how the balance of the two inner forces I have spoken of gradually changed within twenty years. This tall sinewy man, with a sallow complexion and a skin which appeared to be salted by the sea air, seemed from his youth upwards, and even well into the forties, to observe man and beast with searching eyes, not assailing them but rather in a spirit of watchfulness and expectancy. The nose was large. The brow was bare and high above the temples. The fair moustache was cropped short. The lips were narrow and the mouth well shaped. Here was a man who seldom allowed himself to be as romantic as his nature was. He was not devoted to women, but yielded his whole soul to one. Among men he was sparing of words, almost to brusqueness. He had a booming voice that reminded one of the traditional old sea captains. And at table he had a manly laugh that was never loud.

This disposition may be explained by the mixture of aristocratic blood which came to him from his mother's family and that which came from the pioneering and professional forbears on his father's side. Athletic sports and games and hard bodily schooling from his early childhood helped to develop this disposition. Although the Nansen boys were the sons of a well-to-do lawyer, they were brought up in Spartan fashion. They lived in the family home at the edge of the forest and had to walk three kilometres daily to school in Christiania and the same distance back. In summer they walked ten kilometres to and from their swim. As children, they were taught carpentry and several other handicrafts; and they had to serve at table in turn. Their mother was one of the first women in Norway to cultivate the sport of ski-running. The first snow-shoes which she gave to young Fridtjof were a cast-off pair and were of unequal length. Then a friend donated him a good pair which lasted him for ten years. Before he was twenty years old he won first prizes for running and jumping and at the age of eighteen he broke the world's speed record in ski-running. In this he held the Norwegian championship for twelve years. Then he gave up sports competitions permanently.

From his boyhood he had been a magnificent yachtsman and swimmer and a first-class rifle shot. His favourite pastime was to wander alone in the forests and go sailing on the fjords. In order to harden himself and accustom his body to feats of endurance, he took all sorts of athletic exercises and ate sparingly. "For journeys lasting over a week," he says, "I often equipped myself with nothing more than a piece of bread and some matches and a fishing rod; and I cooked my own fish on the fires I used to kindle in the forest."

Even during those hunting days of his boyhood the dual nature of his character was already noticeable. He loved animals but he hunted them and shot them. He avoided human company and went alone into the forest for weeks on end, yet he was kind-hearted and devoted to his companions. At sixteen he rescued his brother from drowning and at sixty he jumped in to save a drowning man; for fearlessness was inherent in him, always one of the essentials of his success. On the farm at home he became acquainted with the horses and the cattle, the poultry and the pigs. His whole life was passed in intercourse with animals and in studying them, from infusoria under the microscope to the polar bears of the frozen wilderness. But at the same time he was passionately devoted to game-hunting. On one occasion in his old age I drew his attention to what I considered a certain inconsistency between pacifism and game-hunting. He looked at me in astonishment and said:

"Oh! no. To work with dogs like that . . ."

Such stability of temperament, based on traditions of blood and country and not influenced by anything in the nature of Tolstoian theoretics, gives to the lover of mankind and nature the steadfastness and resource which made Nansen's whole career possible. I should say of him that he was the manliest man I ever met.

In town he seemed always shy and retiring and gave the impression of being somewhat distrait in the midst of streets and shops. One of his comrades states that it was possible really to understand him only when one knew him in the country. "There he becomes quite another person, simple and yet with many nuances, a child with open and trustful blue eyes, enjoying every hour and moment of the day. Yet he was always fearless and independent, modest and steadfast, honourable, upright and clean-minded."

In his youth he wrote poetry and painted pictures. For several years he kept up his work as an artist; but he had to study physics at the University. In order to live as much as possible in the fresh air and to be able to travel while carrying out his professional studies, he gave up physics and turned to zoölogy. At twenty-one he became Curator of the National History Museum in Bergen.

About this time Nordenskjöld had undertaken a journey across Greenland. Nansen, who at the age of twenty had spent several weeks on a sealing ship, was much interested in this expedition. "I was sitting and listening indifferently," he says, "as the day's paper was being read. Suddenly my attention was aroused by a telegram stating that Nordenskjöld had come safely back from his expedition to the interior of Greenland, and that he had found no oasis but only endless snowfields on which the

Lapps were said to have covered, on their skis, an extraordinary distance in an astonishingly short time. The idea instantly flashed upon me of an expedition crossing Greenland on skis from coast to coast. Here was the plan in the same form in which it was afterwards laid before the public and eventually carried out." But he had to wait for five years.

He now began to travel. In pursuit of his zoölogical studies he went to Naples; but he spent much more time sketching and painting than in scientific work. When he came home he pursued his investigations on the central nervous system, with the intention of becoming a university tutor. But the flash of that telegram had struck his heart as if it had been lightning. The skis allured him and he read books about Greenland. He applied for a subsidy to undertake an expedition similar to that of Nordenskjöld, but people thought him mad and refused. When at last he received 5,000 kronen from abroad and set about making preparations for his undertaking, one of the comic papers wrote: "In June Dr. Nansen will give an exhibition in skiing and long distance jumping on the ice in the interior of Greenland. Seats bookable in crevasses. Return tickets unnecessary."

He was twenty-seven years old when he set out, with five companions, on the Greenland expedition. The preparations he made for this undertaking show that he was much more than an adventurer. He proved himself a practical and skilled mechanic. He designed and constructed with his own hands the most important articles of his equipment. In making general plans his practical experience in skiing and his knowledge of sailing came to his aid. Everything was carefully thought out. "If we had taken woollen sleeping bags with us," he wrote, "instead of ones made of reindeer skin, we should never have reached the west coast." The expedition was a success. These modern Vikings were the first to traverse Greenland on skis, at 65 degrees latitude, from east to west. But when they reached the west coast the last ship for that season had already left. They were accordingly forced to remain at Godthaab, on the south-west coast of Greenland, until the following spring.

This apparent misfortune proved to be a decisive factor in the shaping of Nansen's career. He was now for the first time brought into intimate touch with a primitive and downtrodden people. In this Norwegian, who had always been more attracted to the life of the forest and companionship with animals rather than men, who did not read newspapers and had given no time to the study of national questions or questions of state either at home or abroad, political feelings were for the first time awakened by the moral shock he received when he saw how the Eskimos lived. These feelings soon grew into a problem. He did not make a merely theoretical study of the Eskimos. He shared their lot and their hardships and from that experience he became a practical champion of their rights. That this feeling should have been awakened in him only in the Arctic North, and that he should have acquired his first knowledge of a foreign people on a skiing excursion, was a fitting confirmation of Nansen's mission in life. Of the Eskimos he wrote in his diary as follows:

"In Greenland the Eskimos came to know the Europeans. When we brought them Christianity and the products of our civilization they were forced to recognize us as their masters and since then they have been steadily deteriorating. Every time I saw one of these people suffering from or falling a victim to the vices that we brought them the feeling of justice was awakened in me—a feeling of which most of us still preserve a remnant. If that feeling of justice were fully alive among ourselves then we should all feel urged to put right the wrong. Poor young man! You can put forward nothing that has not already been said. The unhappy fate of the Greenlanders, as well as of other aborigines, has often been brought to the knowledge of civilized

nations; but no change has come of it. Nevertheless I will un-
burden my conscience. Moreover, it seems to me to be a sacred
duty to raise a voice in protest. It is true that this expression
of feeling on my part will be like a cry across a boundless plain
and will awaken no echo from the mountains. My sole hope is
that perhaps in one single bosom I may awaken a feeling of grief
and sympathy for the lot of the poor Eskimos."

Towards the end of his book he cries out against the Christian
missions as the messengers of a false culture, and says: "Will our
eyes never be opened to what we are doing there? Will the real
friends of mankind never unite from pole to pole in a single
protest against this whole work of wickedness, this self-righteous
and scandalous treatment of other civilizations and other be-
liefs?" The only hope for the Eskimos, as Nansen sees it, is that
little by little Europeans should withdraw from Greenland.

When Nansen began and ended that earnest book of his
with such pathetic words he well knew how unpopular one
makes oneself with the Governments of countries that rule over
foreign colonies if one pleads for the emancipation of the latter.
He hated the pious missions and missionary societies. At the
very moment that this zoölogist had developed into a geographer
he set people wondering about his new rôle by becoming at the
same time a champion of political and moral rights. At that time
he can scarcely have realized that this was to be his mission in
later life.

3

Eva Sars was the daughter of a well-known zoölogist and marine
explorer. She became a singer; and Nansen married her soon

after his return from the Greenland expedition. He was then thirty-one years old. Both his artistic and explorative instincts found a sympathetic echo in the character of his bride. She went with him on skiing excursions. She went swimming and hunting with him in the summertime. She fasted with him and learned to endure bodily privations. She is said to have been proud and gay. She named her first daughter *Liv*, which means *Life*. She certainly faced life with a steady nerve and a stout heart. When they became engaged Nansen's first ejaculation was: "But—I must go to the North Pole."

For twenty years this couple remained perfectly devoted to each other. She came under the influence of his poetic fancy. She shared in his work and underwent the same privations in the cold winter. Only one day after the wedding he took her out to study nature with him. And while he was building himself a home he spent the first winter with her in a shed where no human being had yet lived and where the water in the basins froze night after night. She declared afterwards that in this first winter he accustomed her to the experience of being frozen. But he sat there steadfastly in his hut and wrote a book of seven hundred pages on Greenland and the Eskimos. Long before the dwelling was finished they went to live in it.

The house was called *Good Hope*. It stood alone on a small tongue of land, from which meadows and woods reached the Christiania Fjord. He himself designed the house and made the furniture in the Scandinavian style. He carved the mantelpiece himself. He had already learned lithography and was able to make the blocks for the sketches he used in his study of the nervous system. Later he was able to make all the drawings and blocks for his zoölogical and histological charts.

Why did he not remain in his new home with the wife he adored and with his child? What was it that called him away? It was his dream, the kind of dream that has driven so many men on so many adventures. He wanted to be off again. Day after day the phrase kept recurring to his lips: "But I must go to the North Pole."

The lure of this adventure fascinated him. The hunter and sailor, the explorer and ski-runner, the champion of Eskimo rights, felt the inexorable urge to press forward. Hence he named his ship *Fram* which means *Forward*. The Government built this ship for him, according to his own designs. His idea was to leave the ship at a certain latitude and press forward to the pole on sledges. He intended to be away for a year, perhaps even two. But it finally turned out to be three. And then it seemed a miracle that he returned at all. Thus he wrote in his diary:

"And now, alas, farewell to home. Yonder it lies on the point; the fjord sparkling in front, pine and fir woods around, a little smiling meadow-land and long wood-clad ridges behind. Through the telescope I could descry a summer-clad figure by the bench under the fir tree. That was the hardest moment of the whole journey."

Such expressions clearly reveal the Nordic nature of the man, reserved and devoted. Again he was sailing away of his own free will, obeying his own inner compulsion, to explore distant coasts, leaving behind him a young and much loved wife after only two years of wedlock and a child only a few months old. And for what? To earn fame and wealth? Of both his simple nature already had enough. To prove some theory? He had advanced none. Nor was he an Arctic explorer by profession. Fearlessness. Deep down in his nature the urging motive was to overcome dangers, like his ancestors, the Vikings.

How these moods came repeatedly to the surface of his consciousness, and sometimes seemed to overwhelm him during the long Arctic night on the ice, is strangely revealed in his diary. When the voyage had lasted six months he wrote as follows, on New Year's Eve: "It has been a long year and has brought much of both good and bad. It began with good by bringing little Liv, such a new strange happiness that at first I could hardly believe it. But hard, unspeakably hard, was the parting that came later; no year has brought worse pain than that. And the time since has been one great longing."

Three days later he wrote: "And I? Yes, I am happy too. It is an easy life, nothing that weighs heavy on one, no letters, no newspapers, nothing disturbing; just that monastic out-of-the-world existence that was my dream when I was younger and yearned for quietness in which to give myself up to my studies. Longing, even when it is strong and sad, is not unhappiness. A man has truly no right to be anything but happy when fate permits him to follow up his ideals."

On March 26, 1894, he wrote: "Still I must wait and watch the drift: but should it take a wrong direction I will break all the bridges behind me and stake everything on a northward march over the ice. I know nothing better to do. It will be a hazardous journey, a matter, it may be, of life or death. But have I any other choice?

"It is unworthy of a man to set himself a task and then give in when the brunt of the battle is upon him. There is but one way and that is *Fram*—Forward."

In October of the same year he wrote: "Sometimes that devouring longing comes on with all its old strength, as if it would tear me to pieces. But this is a splendid school of patience. Much good it does to sit wondering whether they are alive or dead at home. It only drives one mad. . . .

"All the same I never grow quite reconciled to this life. It is really neither life nor death, but a state between the two. It means never being at rest about anything or any place—a constant waiting for what is coming; a waiting in which, perhaps, the best years of one's manhood will pass. . . . Every night I am at home in my dreams; but when the morning breaks I must again, like Helge, gallop back on the pale horse by the way of the reddening dawn, not to the joys of Valhalla, but to the realm of eternal ice." Meanwhile he often sat up late at night working with his microscope.

The dual world in which this seafarer lived is shown in a drawing wherein he is sketched sitting in his cabin, a man now thirty-four years old, with sterner features and a harder look than before. Above him on the left hangs a picture of his wife and child and on his right a map of the polar seas. In these month-long icy nights he was sometimes stern and ill-tempered. He could storm at the whole crew because a bottle of beer was missing. Later, when he was leaving the ship for ever, he begged the crew to forgive him for these fits of anger.

It was during the second long night of winter that Nansen decided to leave the ship and push forward on sledges with one of his men, Johansen. There was nothing of the daredevil kind of adventure about this undertaking. He set up his tent on the ice at some distance from the ship and lived there for two weeks for the purpose of scientifically testing his equipment and his own capacity to push forward in that way. Thus he was able to reckon how much food he and his companion could take with them. They returned to the ship and added to their wardrobe, using wolfskin as clothing and deerskin for the making of sleeping bags. Then towards the middle of March they set out northwards—two men, with their dogs, sledges and guns, in a northern latitude where no human being had yet set foot, alone in the immense stillness, exposed to the rigours and dangers of the ice and also in danger of being attacked by unknown beasts. They reached latitude 86° 14'. In his diary he tells of some of their experiences on this sledge journey.

"During the course of the day," he writes, "the deep exhalations from our bodies had little by little become condensed in our outer garments, which were now a mass of ice and transformed into complete suits of ice-armour. They were so hard and stiff that if we had only been able to get them off they could have stood by themselves; and they crackled audibly every time we moved. These clothes were so stiff that the sleeve of my coat actually rubbed deep sores in my wrists during our marches, When we got into our sleeping bags in the evening our clothes began to thaw slowly, and on this process a considerable amount of physical *heat* was expended. We packed ourselves tight into the bag and lay with our teeth chattering for an hour, or an hour and a half, before we became aware of a little of the warmth in our bodies which we so sorely needed. At last our clothes became wet and pliant, only to freeze again a few minutes after we had turned out of the bag in the morning. There was no question of getting these clothes dried on the journey so long as the cold lasted, as more and more moisture from the body collected on them.

"How cold we were as we lay there shivering in the bag, waiting for the supper to be ready! I, who was the cook, was obliged to keep myself more or less awake to see to the culinary operations. At last the supper was ready, was portioned out, and always tasted delicious. These occasions were the supreme moments of our existence, moments to which we looked forward the whole day long. But sometimes we were so weary that our eyes closed and we fell asleep with the food on its way to our mouths."

Although the obstinacy with which the ice lasted made them turn back sooner than they had planned, these two men spent a whole year camping on the ice and completely alone in an ice-hut. They survived the third polar night only by hunting for their food and finally had to sacrifice most of the dogs. The experiences of modern explorers cannot be compared to the destitution which these men endured. Their souls suffered some of the agonies of solitary confinement. As the weeks and months passed each became lonelier in himself. "All day long we are both silent," wrote Johansen, "and if we speak at all it is usually of how to get ahead, or of home and how glorious it would be if we could finally arrive there." In spite of these moods Nansen took three-quarters of a year before he decided to address his comrade in the familiar second-person-singular. This was on New Year's Eve. "The portioning of the food," writes Johansen, "was always just. One of us turned away and chose right or left. Nansen, who was bigger than I and probably needed more food, made no difference in the rations. At the moment we are pushing forward thus: Nansen reconnoitres a little way ahead and I follow stage by stage with the sledges until I reach him again. Then each takes his own sledge. Often we both have to lift our sledges over walls of ice."

When he found good ice Nansen spoke of it as "The land of Canaan." When later on they began to kill their dogs because of having no food for them Nansen became quite sad. To shoot a bear seemed all right to him. But to kill a four-footed friend? "Yesterday Pan was slaughtered," writes Johansen, "who used to pull hard enough for three; and Koik, who at last ate even her sailcloth harness, has had to go the same way. The night that Koik had to be slain Nansen seemed quite different from his usual self. She was the only one of our dogs that hailed from Norway. Nansen had her in his home; and everybody there loved her. I speared her secretly, before he was fully aware of what was happening."

And so the months passed during this life of camping on the ice as smoothly as if they were idyllic hours. But it was a devilish idyl. "Our clothes," writes Johansen, "which were greased through and through, stuck to our bodies. Hair and beard grew wild. Our faces and hands were black and greasy. We had become savages. It was terrible to have to cope with all that grease and never to have a thing with which to wipe one's hands thoroughly. Nansen's thighs became sore and raw from all this dirt. Sometimes he had to melt a cupful of water, take a bandage from our medical supplies and wash himself with it."

4

But the day of their home-coming dawned at last. The world welcomed the seafarers whom they had long given up for lost. Eva alone had kept up her faith in Fridtjof's star. She had been giving concerts in Norway; and, as if to compensate for the impossibility of having news from her husband, she insisted on daily telegraphic reports of her little daughter's health. Today it is possible in a moment to send home news by radio from airships or distant vessels; but forty years ago that was impossible. And this woman remained for a long three years without news of her husband. She could read in the eyes of the strangers she met that they were striving to conceal their conviction that he had either been shipwrecked or had died of starvation. Now at last he stood before her. And beside her stood their four-year-old daughter.

In this hour, after having put his courage and manliness to such severe tests, will he decide never to gamble with them again? He is now forty. Will he devote himself to science or to some work at home in his own country and give up these terrible dreams of adventure? Soon after the return of the two men the *Fram* drew slowly into harbour. When Nansen's glance fell on the ship and when he sat again with his comrades, is it conceivable that the ship which had pushed through the dangers just as he had and the men who had given their trust to him—is it conceivable that these should not in due course secretly incite him to a new adventure? Did not his forbears, the Vikings, do likewise?

He immediately became famous all over the world. A professorship at home and honorary degrees in other countries were conferred on him. He was invited to hundreds of meetings to read papers. He had to write the story of his adventure. And all this held him for the moment. The field of his activities was constantly increasing. He found it necessary to have a bigger house to live in. In the mountains above Lysaker he purchased for himself and his wife a portion of the pine forest. Here he lived from the age of forty until his death, and he never thinned the trees; except sometimes when the road became too narrow he would cut some of the limbs with his own hands. There was a large hall, two storeys high, tall windows and doors, views of forest or ocean on all sides, no gates between the courtyard and garden and forest, and inside a few rooms overstocked with books and pictures, the quietest of all being reserved for himself high up in the tower.

Here he worked for the next few years, during which he contributed some important discoveries to the science of oceanography. At the same time he attended to his duties as professor and also delivered lectures in various cities at home and abroad. But all the time the seafaring blood was warming up and he was pondering and hesitating whether he should not set out again to the North Pole in the reconditioned *Fram*. It seems that he never said much about these plans to his wife. At any rate he lived with her during this period, from the age of forty to forty-five, more like a scholar in the tranquil home circle. It seemed as if he were now destined to be a research worker for the rest of his life, as he had dreamed in youth.

But in the year 1905 an excited nation knocked at the door of his room in the tower. And although he had not hitherto been politically active, nor even interested, he at once took his stand beside Björnson, the most popular man in that small nation. The passionate desire of Norway to be independent of Sweden should now, he claimed, be carried into effect by men who were not politicians. For, as he said, "in the life of a nation, just as in the life of an individual, come moments when everything must be risked. The least compromise, the least deviation from the straight path at such times, injures the very soul of the nation." But a character such as his could never desire war. Therefore he took his stand against the hotheads of his own country. In speeches and articles and in a pamphlet he supported the movement for a peaceful solution of the national question. As he was so well known all over the world he was chosen to visit the Foreign Offices of some of the great powers. For a time it looked as if either he or Björnson would become President of Norway. But they were both sensible enough to leave that rôle to the so-called experts.

When the King of Sweden had renounced his claim to the throne of Norway the nation sent Fridtjof Nansen "as private secretary of the Norwegian Government" to the Danish Prince Karl to bring him as King to Christiania. For the new state it was very important to make use of Nansen's universal fame. He was sent to London as the first diplomatic representative of an independent Norway. This office he held for three years. While in London he learned the ropes of European diplomacy in a fashion and for a purpose which was still concealed from himself and everyone else.

While at home on leave and occupied with his scientific work, Roald Amundsen, his countryman and colleague and companion on the polar voyage, came to him and asked for the *Fram*, with which he wished to make an expedition to the South Pole. Nansen hesitated. The other was eleven years younger. That was his sole advantage. Otherwise? And he himself? With a youthful physique that nobody would have credited in a man of forty-six,

was he too old for adventure? There was information on geographical conditions which suggested that the conquest of the
South Pole would be easier than that of the north. We must remember that up to this time, 1907, nobody had yet claimed to
have reached the North Pole. A natural feeling of pride must
have urged him to try himself out once again. Had he not
planned and carried out the building of the ship himself? What
tang of life had this humdrum existence, poring over political
documents, scientific charts and books, even at home with wife
and child? Why should one not draw in the clean air once more
in the midst of the ice and the polar bears and long again with
one's whole heart to be at home?

When Amundsen returned eight months later Nansen was
still undecided. Why he could never like the other man becomes
clear if we study their portraits. Nansen admired Amundsen's
energy. Before going down to the hall to meet his visitor on this
second occasion he went into his wife's room.

"I know what's coming now," she said. "You are going to
leave me again." He himself declares that on hearing this he
went down at once to the hall, greeted Amundsen and promised
him the vessel. A few months later Eva Nansen died suddenly.
She was only about forty years old. Had she suffered from some
illness of which neither she nor her husband was aware? Or
was the shock too great for her? After twenty years was even
the thought of such another adventure too difficult for her to
bear? Now that she was gone for ever, why did he not board
ship again and seek once more the far horizon, seeing that everything at home had lost interest for him? No. He merely left
London and gave up politics. He returned home and resumed
his duties as professor at the university in Christiania, lecturing
on oceanography to ten or twenty listeners.

In the meantime he assisted Amundsen in preparing for the
new expedition. These preparations lasted over a year. Probably

his own heart rebelled in secret when, three years after giving the ship to his colleague, Nansen stood at the window in his tower and watched the *Fram* depart with Amundsen on the bridge.

Several years later he said to his son: "That was the bitterest hour of my life." But between one pole and the other lay the equator. With a sort of magic insight this man, who was familiar with earth and sea through natural instinct and long years of study, felt himself called toward that symbolic line in the region of which he would make new researches and put his courage and stamina to the test under conditions so different from those at either pole.

He soon heard of the discovery of both poles, by Amundsen and Peary respectively. Well, he had frozen all his life. Why not go for once into the burning sun? Eva was dead. He need now not even dread that biting longing for home. Nansen decided on a voyage of discovery to the equator. That was in 1914.

5

"What a mountain of madness! And no one seems to call a halt. No one. The nations of Europe, the torchbearers of civilization are devouring one another. . . . By the mere fact of donning a uniform, a suit of some particular colour or cut, or perhaps even only a decoration, a man seems to acquire the right to commit every kind of crime. He may hurl bombs from the air into peaceful towns, in the midst of hard-working citizens who are going about their daily duties and not dreaming of danger. He may destroy property, homes and life. It makes one's blood boil. But the greatest nations see no evil in it; or, if they do, they do not raise their voices in protest. This world calls for a man who will bring in a new epoch. He must be a man of strong simple mind, a man all of one piece, a man without the depraved vision of a double moral outlook."

Only one who meditates on his own nature could have written thus in his diary. But what could he do? Could he go round the world on a preaching crusade? That was not Nansen's way. To take active part in the war would have had meaning for him if he could see any meaning in the war; but he could see nothing in it but madness. In other parts of his diary he speaks of the wives and mothers whose husbands and children and brothers are dying on the battlefield. As the war progressed this feeling of protest grew stronger with Nansen. Instead of becoming used to the war, he became gradually more horrified at the spectacle of it. His horror was not that of a frightened scholar, nor was it in the warning of a prophet or priest. In his diary we recognize a man who is as Nature made him, who has sought danger since his boyhood, who has suffered and overcome more hardships than any of his contemporaries, who is horrified at the spectacle of a modern war because it has lost the heroic features of former times, because it has been reduced to a mechanical technique which forces most soldiers to suffer but not to fight and in which the part of the individual is entirely submerged when the final issue is being decided. Among all the outcries that arose in the various countries during the war and since, not one has the force and weight of Nansen's protest. From the outbreak of the war until his death this protest grew stronger and stronger. Its great value lay in the fact that no other man was in a similar position to judge of fear and courage, of heroism and heroic adventure.

The next mission which he undertook was on Norway's behalf. He went to Washington on a special mission and there he learned something that was quite new to him. He had to buy grain for his people and in doing so had to deal with farmers, shipowners, traders, bankers and lawyers. He tried to deal through a committee which was made up of one delegate from each of these categories. But he found the negotiations impossible and the delegates had to go home. He then took the matter into his own hands and bought directly what he wanted, his Government giving him full power of attorney to sign agreements in its name. This experience helped him well afterwards. When the idea of the League of Nations was launched a little group of philanthropists who had kept an open mind and heart during the war seized upon it and clung to it as if it were a safety rope thrown out to a world which was being engulfed in its own crime and folly. In April 1919 Nansen came to Paris to negotiate for Norway's entry into the League that was to be founded. At that time there was a world uproar against the Soviets; but Nansen turned a kindly ear towards Russia. What reached him from there was not the war cry of the Bolsheviks but the moan of the starving. He realized that he alone understood what he heard and he wrote a letter to each of the four leaders of the great Conference. The letter to Wilson began thus:

"The present commissariat conditions in Russia, where thousands are dying every month of starvation, constitute a problem that must affect the heart of mankind. Up to now it seems that no solution of this food and health problem has been found. Therefore, from a purely neutral point of view and for philanthropic reasons only, I take the liberty of making a proposal for the amelioration of this frightful need."

The arrow struck the centre of the problem but not the one the marksman had aimed at. The political panjandrums in Paris postponed the hunger problem for another two years, because starving people are not dangerous. But there was the problem also of the prisoners of war. That was a direct political issue; and the politicians in Paris said that Nansen was just the man who could arrange for them to be sent home. And so they called on Nansen to undertake this task. At first he refused, for he was occupied with many new tasks. Then a British representative, Mr. Baker, came to him and begged him to give up one or two months to the cause of the prisoners. Nansen agreed. The League of Nations could not inform him as to how many war prisoners were held in Russia, nor could the League suggest any way whereby they could be transported home. The League could not tell whether the Soviet Government would help, nor could it give him any money. The League gave him just the same kind of mandate as Bennett gave to Stanley when he said "Go and find Livingstone."

"One Sunday," Nansen told me later, "a telegram came to Lysaker. The League of Nations asked me if I would go and bring back half a million prisoners who were detained in Russia. But why ask me? I had no idea. Hoover seems to have told them something. I had done some business with him over there during the war. They wanted a neutral and possibly they thought that a diplomat would not have the courage to go, even though in reality no courage was necessary. When I reached Moscow Chicherin at once refused to recognize the right of the League of Nations to meddle in the affair. Within two hours I had sent a special train back to the frontier. Then he calmed down and agreed that I should obtain special authority from each of the countries concerned. Perhaps these credentials arrived within six months or so and perhaps they never came. However, I had completely fulfilled my mission in the meantime."

When Nansen arrived in Russia that country was being ravaged by famine and revolution. The Russians had neither ships nor trains nor clothing nor food nor the necessary sanitary disinfectants for the prisoners. Within a few months Nansen had organized a Baltic fleet of fourteen vessels. He got together railway rolling stock and by the end of the year three hundred thousand men had been sent to their homes in a dozen different nations. Nansen carried out this work as a philanthropist and political thinker; for he wished its success to redound to the credit of the League of Nations, in whose name he acted. He was then sixty years old. Of the three helpers who went with him, two died of typhus and another fell seriously ill. But Nansen went through it all without flinching. He made three further journeys into Russia within the next three years. This whole undertaking, which originally had been forced upon him on the understanding that he would devote a couple of months to it, lasted for a decade—until his death. Prisoners of war and refugees throughout the world were not in possession of any official papers. Nansen called a meeting of the various Governments at Geneva and proposed a new kind of passport which the League of Nations should be empowered to grant. Thirty-one Governments accepted the proposal. It was called the "Nansen pass" and still bears his portrait. This passport, which is now issued for fifty-two nations and recognized all the world over, is a novelty in international history. It is a symbol of a supernational bond; and instead of the usual imprint, which generally bears the sign of an eagle or a lion, to proclaim the pugnacious majesty of a single state, it bears the head of a private individual who has an open, manly and courageous look. Never did the work of a single man find a more excellent memorial.

6

Thus the geographer and zoölogist, the explorer on skis and sledges, became at the age of sixty "High Commissioner for Refugees and for Relief Work in Russia." In the summer of

1921, when Nansen had returned from the mountains to his
home, he found a telegram from Geneva asking him to go again
to Russia, this time to save the starving. Two years earlier he had
pleaded this cause in vain. Now he was enraged at being torn
away from his work again. This time he intended to refuse and
stick by his refusal. His friend and neighbour, who was with
him at the time, tells how Nansen declared: "If I take it on, it
means the renunciation of all my scientific work, of everything
for which I live."

It is extraordinary how this elderly man could still be mistaken
as to the lifework which God meant him to do. His friend knew
better and said to him: "If you refuse you will never have any
peace of mind again."

Five days later Nansen was on his way to Riga. On a conservative estimate, four million tons of wheat were needed to
feed the victims of the Russian famine. This meant a thousand
trains of fifty cars each. The harvest had been terribly bad in
Russia, so that it yielded less than half this amount. The problem
now confronting Nansen was much more difficult than that of
the war prisoners, which he had faced a year before. Now he
needed not only plenipotentiary authority from the various nations; he needed the actual assistance of the outside world, which
hated the Bolshevik régime. For the first time in his life the
philanthropist came up against the diplomats and had a taste
of their malice and cynicism; for many of them felt, though they
did not express it, what a Serbian representative said in Geneva:
"If they [the starving Russians] continue to die, then the régime
will crash all the sooner."

That was the phrase which greeted Nansen at Geneva, where
he had come to beg for bread and credit. The air was thick with
hatred and calumny. This Nansen, they said, is at heart a Bolshevik. That is why he got on so well with Lenin last year. He
stood there in one of the halls of that labyrinthine building in

Geneva, where there are hundreds of staircases and corridors and unexpected exits and entries, all giving a clear indication of the back-stair politics practised in the place—there he stood, lithe and tanned, still the seafarer and adventurer, before a correctly dressed, pale and mostly bespectacled body of European delegates. He addressed them:

"At this moment twenty to thirty million people are threatened by famine. Should no help be forthcoming within the next two months we are lost. Transport is possible, control assured. Do you wish to throw the whole responsibility on the shoulders of voluntary charity? Even that will be hindered by the calumnies that are being circulated. I believe I know what the feeling at the back of all this is. You are afraid that our help might strengthen the Soviet rule. That is a mistaken notion. We do not strengthen the Russian Government by showing the Russians that human hearts beat in Europe. There are people ready to help these Russians who are now threatened with death by starvation. But the Governments of these same people state that they are unable to produce the necessary five million pounds. That is to say, all of you together, cannot produce half the amount required for the building of one battleship. If you were asked to produce the expenses necessary for the formation and maintenance of half a battalion of soldiers the money would be there immediately. Do you say that you cannot? Then say it outright and be done with it. But cut out the trick of offering to set up committees and conferences and debates lasting for months at a time, while the people are dying.

"We have to start upon a terrible race with the Russian winter, which approaches silently and mercilessly from the north. The Russian seas will soon be frozen over. Soon there will be an end of transport by water. Must we permit the winter to smother for ever the voice of those millions who are crying to us for help? There is still time, you say. But we have not a moment to lose. In the name of humanity, in the name of everything noble and everything that we hold sacred, I call upon you who have wives and children yourselves to consider what it really means to leave women and children to die of starvation. I appeal to the Governments and to the nations of Europe. I call upon the world for help. Act before it is too late for repentance."

What was the answer to this cry for help? Committees, sub-committees, excuses, objections, warnings and finally calumny. To look over the minutes of one of these meetings is to feel one's heart slowly and piteously freezing over, like the Russian seas. The account of one of the meetings runs thus: "Dr. Nansen attended two of the sessions, in which the following resolutions were passed:

"(1) The gravity of the famine cannot be denied. The problem which Dr. Nansen has brought before the meeting is of the highest importance, both from the humanitarian and the economic points of view.

"(2) It cannot be denied that speedy action also is required."

And so on. And so on. Expressions of confidence, appeals, the unhappy people, etc., etc., until we come to resolution 6, which runs thus:

"(6) From many statements made by members of the Committee it seems that, on behalf of their Governments, they do not feel prepared at this moment to agree to the granting of official credits."

At the following session Nansen refuted all their calumnies; but we have no direct account of what he said, except in the mechanical language of the official report: "Dr. Nansen appears to think that some central organization seeks to make use of the terrible misery of the Russian famine for political ends. If it be the intention in some quarters to allow twenty million people to starve to death this winter, in the hope of obtaining thereby some political change in Russia, he declares such an intention to be monstrous. If this terrible tragedy itself be not sufficient to open all eyes, so that the world may act unanimously, what is the use of making appeal after appeal? To do nothing would be disastrous for Europe. He said that he could quote many of the stories that were being circulated but that he would content himself with mentioning only two. Then he proved that a relief train which was said to have been sent by Hoover and plundered by Soviet soldiers never existed at all."

The politicians remained indifferent and got rid of this enthusiastic philanthropist for the time being by sending him to the Red Cross and other such institutions. Nansen travelled from one European capital to another in an effort to awaken public opinion. "I happen to know," he said, "what it is to have to fight winter conditions, but the struggle now raging in Eastern Russia is more terrible than I dare think of." Thus spoke the man who had spent twelve months camping on the ice at latitude 86° North.

At last he succeeded. He got the money together and once more started off to Russia and fed the multitude. He travelled through the country in any kind of railway wagon that he could get and ate his meals out of a bowl. Everywhere he helped the hungry with his own hands. He was personally active in every detail and would have scorned the rôle of unseen organizer sitting among documents and secretaries and travelling in a private train, as we hear that Hoover did in Russia. "At a meeting in Moscow," one of Nansen's companions told me, "he, as chairman, listened to a debate in which Germans and Russians upheld contradictory political aims over a question of exchange of prisoners. Nansen did not understand a word of it. But on long journeys he could hold forth eloquently on the characteristics of a forest or a marsh and the conditions of life therein, but never with the air of a lecturer."

What he meant to the Russian population became clear to me

later on when I spoke with a peasant woman on the southern
Volga. Three years after Nansen had been there I mentioned
his name to an old woman on the steamer. She made the sign
of the Cross and asked me with wide-open eyes whether I knew
him. When I nodded she touched my chest with her hand, in a
gesture which meant that I was to convey her blessing to him.

The press of half the world accused him of being a Bolshevik
and a spy, who had sold himself for money. Nansen, however,
continued his work and his heart was so much in it that he did
not speak of anything else. He knew the amount of food that
he had brought with him and the length of the winter months.
And so he drew up a plan from which he did not depart. Every
auxiliary centre had its list of men and women to be fed. When
people dragged themselves thither from far away parts, because
they had heard of this saviour, he turned them away because, as
one of his companions explained, he did not wish to risk a second time the lives of those he had saved. "We had to refuse
them help and let them die." No report, no diary, tells of the
suffering of this man who came to help and had to pronounce
such sentences of death.

In his book *Russia and the Peace* he vents his anger at the indifference of the political authorities in Geneva. "We had hoped,"
he writes, "for a disarmament of souls; but the spirit of hostility and national hatred is growing worse than ever between
former enemies and even before former allies. Everything that
happens seems to hasten the catastrophe. We have decided for
a policy of words. We have made most problems more difficult
by postponing their solution, because of laziness or fear of accepting responsibility. . . .

"The innumerable conferences were not under the direction
of unprejudiced authorities and experts who would be anxious
to find solutions that suited all parties. The negotiators were
nearly all diplomats and politicians. They were far more con-

cerned about their own positions, or those of their party or country, than they were with the sufferings of Europe or the problem
of how these sufferings could be healed. And so, with oppor-
tunist resolutions, they only increased the evil; or they simply
ignored the most vital questions. The political life of Europe
today gives a depressing impression of uncertainty and indeci-
sion, of incapacity and, above all, of bluff."

Among all those who held responsible positions at that international centre in Geneva Nansen is the only one who spoke out
fearlessly and critically and directly from his own experience.
He wrote bitterly about Europe and he succeeded in being fair
to Russia, although he saw it during its worst years. After long
consideration he came to the conclusion that the establishment of
a moderate constitutional government there was a psychological
impossibility. "It was in the nature of things inevitable," he
writes, "that the pendulum should swing from the completely
reactionary right wing of Czarism to the extreme left, that is,
to Communism. Anyhow we have no right to say of any particular social institution that it is the only good and perfect
one. . . . I felt strongly that European equilibrium would be
tragically upset by the exclusion of Russia from all European
interests. And so I hailed with joy the opportunity offered by
my activities to study conditions there *sine ira et studio*."

In 1920 and 1921 Nansen restored nearly half a million prisoners to their people and rescued several millions from famine in
Russia. In 1922 he conducted the exchange of a million Greek
and Turkish refugees. In 1923 he organized the transport of the
Bulgarian deportees to Trakim. And he arranged the return
home of three hundred thousand persecuted Armenians.

No wonder all these experiences made him disgusted with
politics. In 1926 he received a mandate to become Prime Minister and form a Government in Norway; but he refused. In the

same year he extended his activities to the task of founding an organization to take care of political refugees all the world over.

7

During the Great War the Turks had exterminated more than one-third of the Armenian people. As an Englishman, Lord Curzon had less need to bother himself about the fate of his enemies than had their allies, the Germans. Speaking of the Turks, Curzon called their action one of the greatest scandals of history. Nansen said that in history there are few instances of such unfathomable baseness. In virtue of the Treaty of Sèvres, between the Turks and the Entente, Armenia was recognized as a free and independent country and was soon afterwards allotted 55,000 square miles of territory. But in 1920 a treaty was forced on the Armenians from Angora which reduced by one-half the territory originally allotted to them by the great powers. In 1921 this remnant joined other Transcaucasian republics in a union under the auspices of the Soviets. In the year 1923 the Treaty of Lausanne, between Turkey and the European nations, made no mention of Armenian territory. Not one of the Powers took a single step to assure to the Armenians the land that had been allotted to them by the Treaty of Sèvres. "The whole affair," writes Nansen, "gave the impression of a sorry farce. The Powers kept quiet. They allowed Armenian blood to be shed on their behalf and then, after 1918, they repaid them with worthless paper. The most astonishing feature of the whole business is that it was just those Powers who had neglected to fulfil their own undertakings that reproached the Armenians for joining the Soviets in order to save their land and lives.

That reproach will now have to do duty as an excuse for making no further move in favour of the Armenians. The Powers have lost interest in the Armenian nation as completely as they have forgotten their own promises."

Nansen threw himself heart and soul into this problem. He travelled the country, with a commission from the League of Nations, and wrote a large book about it. The book is entitled *A Cheated People*. It illustrates how he always remained an ethnographer and a geographer. For three years he laboured at Geneva to obtain justice and funds for the Armenians.

The meaning of these struggles of his can be realized only when we remember that Nansen was alone in speaking the language of humanity at that very spot where it should have been the mother tongue. In the League of Nations he was looked upon as a curiosity, a sort of wonderland prophet who was unable to understand the "hard necessity of international reason." He was talked of as a romantic who desired to save the nations rather than exploit them as make-weights in maintaining the balance in the game played by the powers. Among this crowd of so-called statesmen he was a strange figure. And what was strangest of all to the Geneva delegates was the sight of one whose actual aim was to help suffering humanity. One must bear this antagonism in mind to understand Nansen when, as High Commissioner for the League of Nations, he addressed the whole world in the pages of that book on Armenia:

"Why does the League of Nations set up committees to investigate the question of whether something can be done for the homeless Armenian refugees? Is it only for the purpose of lulling its own uneasy conscience to rest? Has it a conscience? The very name of Armenia awakens memories of a tragic chain of broken promises for the fulfilment of which they have not raised a finger. After all, it was only a culturally gifted nation, possessing no oil wells or gold mines."

For a moment it seemed as if England would stand by him
and give him help. In 1924 he influenced Mr. Baldwin and Mr.
Asquith to send a memorandum to Ramsay MacDonald, who
was then Prime Minister. In this memorandum they demanded
a large sum for the Armenian refugees and based their demand
on moral grounds. The Armenians had been encouraged by
pledges of independence to fight for the Allies and suffer for
them. After the Armistice these pledges were confirmed by new
obligations. England was responsible for the Armenians being
driven out after the sack of Smyrna. Even the £5,000,000 of
Turkish gold which the conquerors seized was money that belonged entirely to the Armenians.

MacDonald did not remain long in power. Baldwin took over
the reins of government once again. Nansen was sure the Armenian claim would now be recognized. But Baldwin's Government refused to move an inch in favour of the Armenians whose
claims had been recognized as based on such important moral
principles. In bewilderment one asks what could have been
the purpose of the memorandum which Baldwin had so recently
addressed to MacDonald? Did it represent merely empty words
without meaning? And the League of Nations? Is there no sense
of responsibility even there?—So Nansen wrote. "Woe to the
Armenian people for allowing themselves to become involved in
European politics. Better far if the name of their country had
never come to the lips of a European diplomat. But the Armenians have never given up hope. In struggle and endurance
they have waited long. And they are still waiting today."

Nansen lost his battle for Armenian rights. At the end of 1929
he got a final refusal from the great powers. Then he returned
home. Once again he decided to devote himself entirely to his
scientific work. Only a year before his death (1930) he stated
that it would take him another decade to wind up his relief
work. He still saw a glimmer of hope afar off. And he recog-

nized that it was not so important to reach the North Pole or help the Armenians as it was to set an example.

8

I have said that thirty years elapsed between the time I first saw him and when I next met him at Geneva. Of course he was changed. But he looked hale and hearty, as if he were certain of living into the eighties. He took us in a little steamer to have lunch in a vineyard on the southern side of the lake. During the trip across he stood at the bow of the boat, without any coat, his broad-brimmed hat turned up. His moustache had become a greyish yellow. The glint in the blue eyes was still piercing, but kindly. Only the veins on his temples seemed slightly swollen. He was so much of a sailor that his personality standing there at the bow seemed to transform the little water omnibus into a vessel bound on some daring adventure.

After discussing the fish and the wine set on the table he began to tell stories. He sat a little back from the table, with the legs crossed, holding the stem of his wine glass firmly. As he recalled something to mind his gaze was directed over the bright-red liquid in the glass and the sun reflected the colour on his face. Behind him the blue waters of the lake sparkled in the sunshine. A poet might have found a symbolic theme in that picture. More than thirty years had passed since he had gone on that polar voyage; and now when he talked of the long winter night there it was like Othello telling his tale in old age.

"The only things we lacked on board," he said, "were clean linen and books. But we had a Bible and we were thus able to learn it by heart. Nowadays the other fellows refuse to take an old nutcracker like myself with them into the Siberian ice-fields. Next spring they are going in a Zeppelin. That will be just an excursion. The whole trip in a week! No, nothing can go wrong. I would naturally take dogs and sledges with me in case of emergency. But everything now seems so sophisticated and pre-arranged and specialized. Wonderful. But romance has gone. Never to return. When I, a newly married man, started off for the pole my wife pulled a sad face. Later when I declared that the turn of the South Pole had come she struck the table with her fist—so. And I had to look on with envy as Amundsen brought the plan to success. It is over. *Passé. Skaal!*"

He clinked glasses and drank. His second wife, whom he married when he was fifty, watched him with a surprised look on her face. I knew what she was thinking. Whenever he talked about his polar voyage he became thoughtful, even dreamy, and lost himself in detailed monologue, like a respectable and well-to-do father of a family recalling the escapades of his youth. Then he emptied his glass and said:

"And when I look back I see now that my whole life has been built up of coincidences. No real plan. One always grew out of the other—driven on only by an unconscious urge."

When he reviewed all his work of recent years he wavered between disappointment and hope. But the confident, manly voice—like the tone of an organ and always indicative of Nansen's character—triumphed in the end. "In spite of all failings," he wrote in his last note, "it can be said that something has been done to mitigate suffering and need in the world. Perhaps the result will be that thousands of families in various countries will be glad to know that the work of the League of Nations has not been in vain." Nansen believed that he would be able to teach Western Europe how to look upon Russia impartially and understand it. The fact that the idea of a war of intervention in Russia today seems so ridiculous is largely due to Nansen;

because he was the only non-Russian and non-Communist whom the Russians trusted.

He placed a great deal of value on the pioneer work of the Soviet Government. And he gave practical expression to this appreciation by donating the money he got from the Nobel Prize for the establishment of Russian model farms. He was a veritable Christ in the love of his neighbour. He always gave away more than his moderate means could afford. He was content to wear old clothes and old shoes and needed only thin flannel to protect his steel-hard body.

Urged by a natural moral sense he sacrificed his own health and time and money, in the truest sense. But he had long ceased to belong to any church. That was why he was chosen as chairman of a meeting summoned to organize a world congress of all religions. In Geneva and in Norway many people laughed at this; but they did not interfere. And it is significant that on the occasion of his death the leading Norwegian church paper wrote of him as follows: "Nansen's honest conviction led him out of the national church. But it cannot be denied that of all our generation it was he who contributed the greatest share of Love." In political ethics Masaryk approaches him; but as an active worker for peace Nansen has no peer. *The Patron Saint of the Refugees* was the title the Greeks gave him. When he received the Nobel Peace Prize he had the courage to proclaim his undying faith in the ideals to which he had devoted his hardest work and of which he has given the world an example:

"No more War! What does that mean? Does it mean: No more World War, but perhaps little private wars for the sake of national honour? No, it means: Never again War. All my life I have cherished the idea that in all the great decisions and undertakings of life it is of the utmost importance to leave no lines of retreat. The Governments in the League of Nations must not think of lines of retreat."

When the University of St. Andrews elected him as their Rector he delivered an address which is a magnificent *apologia pro sua vita.*

"The first important matter in life," he said, "is to find oneself. For that you need solitude and introspection, at any rate from time to time. . . . Redemption will not come from the noisy centres of civilization. It will come from the lonely places. The great reformers who have made their mark in human history came from the wilderness. . . . Many of us have not sufficient time on our hands to reflect even on the meaning of life. What is the meaning of your own lives? Are you searching for happiness? Many people are. But, believe me, it is loss of time to bother about it. The important thing is to do one's best and to make oneself independent of wants. I will reveal to you the secret of my so-called success and give you good advice. The secret was that I always burned the boats behind me. No time is then lost in looking backward, when there is plenty to do ahead. Then there is no choice for you and your men but to go forward. You must do or die."

Here we have the man of energy who gives help, not the pitying man who only longs for help. That was the indomitable part of Nansen. He always fought forward and rejoiced in the struggle, whether it led him into the close-packed ice-fields or to the burning steppes of the Volga. He was always doing, sometimes almost without any object ahead and sometimes for the sake of a million souls. When he had reached middle age he confided the following thoughts to his diary:

"Those who consciously brood on their sorrows were committed by Dante to the deepest pit of Hell. They are in love with trouble. They like to gaze on shadows. . . . When all comes to all, what we call the game of life is just what makes life worth living. The capacity for enjoyment and for care, for work, thirst, rest, effort, love, wild life and art. Life's enemies are not cares and worries, deprivations and misfortunes. They are its greatest allies. Its enemies are the damp fogs of the spirit, where there are neither shadows nor light."

In his last years he had attained perfect equilibrium of soul. He went only rarely to administer some of the duties of his high office in Geneva, because he was carrying on research work at which he did not wish to be interrupted for too long. In the big house on the fjord there were now a crowd of children and grandchildren. The captain of the *Fram* used to come to meals there sometimes, and Nansen's neighbour, Mahr, and a colleague from the Institute of Geophysics in Bergen. But the mighty ones of the League of Nations hardly ever came—scarcely anyone except Lord Robert Cecil, the best of them all.

MASARYK

THE SLAV PHILANTHROPIST

"Mundus vult decipi,
ergo non decipiatur."

MASARYK

THE SLAV PHILANTHROPIST

O N ONE of the big estates of a mighty Emperor there once lived a coachman and a maid who loved each other and wished to get married. But they did not do so until they had received the permission of their master. For they were serfs. This meant that though they could not be slaughtered or sold as slaves they were not free to make any important decision in regard to their own lives. They could not move their place of residence from one part of the country to another or change their occupation without the sanction of their overlord.

Such was the law and custom in Eastern Europe ninety years ago. It was not changed until 1849, the very year in which this marriage took place. And the change was brought about only under the pressure of the revolutionary movement which spread over Europe at that time.

The young couple called their first son Thomas, not realizing how aptly the name suited the character of the child. For he was to grow up a doubting believer, with a critical turn of mind that would accept nothing handed down by human tradition without first scrutinizing its inner worth. Yet he believed in God and accepted His law without question. When his mother taught him to pray and imparted to him the little share of knowledge that was hers she prayed that she might one day see him raised above the lowly conditions under which he was born. And perhaps she dreamed that he might yet become a master, like the steward of the farm.

But no soothsayer told her that when the hairs would have turned grey on his head he would drive out the Apostolic Emperor who ruled in Vienna and take his seat in the imperial castle at Prague as ruler of the country and the head of the Czech nation. Yet this prophecy became true without the intervention of miracle. Indeed, the most miraculous thing about it is that it became true without the hero having foreseen or willed the end. It was in reality the work of Providence. If we do not acknowledge the intervention of this Providence in directing Masaryk's career, we shall find ourselves in the hopeless confusion of having to attribute its chief events to blind chance. Perhaps the most beautiful of all legends are those in which the miraculous agency behind the progress of events does not become apparent until the end is reached. And this because the author of the tale has so carefully thought out and prepared his plan that he has kept it secret until the narrative has reached its completion. The story of Masaryk's career is like a narrative of that kind.

By descent he is both Czech and Slovak. He was born in Southern Moravia, close to the dividing line between those two peoples. But he looks almost entirely a Slovak. He is tall and thin, wiry and lightly built, agile and quick in his movements. The quality of his mind is in harmony with his physical build, pliable and alert and not at all obstinate. Even though traces of both racial stocks may be found in him, the characterizing strain is Slovak. As a boy he must have been of a critical turn of mind, inquisitive and fearless in his thought; for in his conversation today he is always turning to those earliest days and from what he tells of them one is led to conclude that he was a bold-spirited

official believe in this young fellow? The integrity of his character found its response in the mind of the policeman and eventually turned out to be the means of his salvation. It happened
in this way:

In the bilingual city of Brunn young Masaryk experienced for
the first time the traditional racial envy and rivalry between
the Czechs, who were numerically in the majority, and the
Germans, who held the ruling power in their hands. Quarrels
and fist-fights used to take place between these two races. In
the school there were quarrels about the pronunciation of classic
Greek. Masaryk insisted on the Czech pronunciation, but the
German teacher demanded that the German pronunciation
should be used. Both were wrong. But anyhow Masaryk came
to be looked upon with suspicion. Then he lost his temper over
a love intrigue and the result was that they expelled him from
the school. Being utterly without means, nothing was left for
him but to return to his village and the forge. But the policeman interceded. He knew human nature well and he knew that
it would not be easy for him to get such another boy as a companion for his own son. At that very moment the Chief of
Police was about to be transferred to Vienna. And so it was
that the son of the coachman came from the imperial farm to
the imperial metropolis.

What a significant chain of accidents. At the age of twenty-
two he became a university student. It was rather late to begin
his university career, but this was because his education had
not been continuous from the time he first left the primary
school. Now he was given a chance to learn much of the world
and the various kinds of people who make it up. He learned
to differentiate between the characteristics of people belonging
to the various professions and classes and he came into daily
contact with people speaking different languages. Referring to

his life in the home of his patron, he said to me: "In that home I became acquainted with the various duties which a police director finds himself bound to carry out and in this way I was introduced into the world of politics at an early age. Then I began to take an utterly different attitude towards political matters from that which I had at school."

He was now introduced into the home of a wealthy family belonging to a race with which he had not yet been in touch. It was the home of a Jewish merchant who employed young Masaryk as tutor to his son. He kept his eyes open and noticed the little foibles of these new acquaintances, but at the same time he was able to grasp and appreciate their great qualities. Some time previous to this young Masaryk happened to be in the company of a Jewish boy when they went out to take part in some country sports. After the game it was sundown and he noticed his Jewish companion devoutly praying. This made a profound impression on Masaryk's mind, an impression which probably was the foundation of the great sympathy he has for the Jewish race. As a Czech he knew what it meant to belong to an oppressed people.

As the son of a proletarian he also knew what it meant to be a member of the downtrodden classes. The coachman's livery, with the polished buttons, which his father wore used to be cut up and remade for the boy when it had become too shabby for service. This had the effect of arousing a spirit of derision in the coachman's son, sometimes even to tears of bitterness. When the gentry were returning from hunting parties on the imperial estates they sometimes threw to his mother fleece-coats that they had used at the hunt. But once the doors were closed and the family was alone the boy used to hear his father mutter curses between the teeth. At an early age this youth had had more experience than most other people of the contrast

between individuals who are free and those who are bondsmen
and between nations that are free and nations that are enslaved.

2

The lure of knowledge beckoned to him. In the Vienna university he attended lectures in philosophy and economics. He
became acquainted with ancient classical literature. He was
keenly interested in the study of biology and physiology. But
his studies were carried on at the same time as he gave lessons
himself, in order to earn his own expenses. He was determined
not to be tied down to mere thinking by rote, and when pedantic polemics on the rendering of certain passages from classical
authors became too boring he packed up his books and ran off
to the Vienna Prater where the big World Exposition was going on.

He yearned to travel and see the world in order that he might
verify with his own eyes all that he had read in books. This
would help him better to understand the problems that are
involved in the affairs of nations that dominate and nations
that have to obey. He would also better understand the different
forms of political rule. And so he decided to enter the diplomatic
service. He started learning Arabic so as to prepare himself for
entry into the Academy for Oriental Studies. He did not for a
moment envisage himself as achieving the right to be called
"Your Excellency" and wearing the stars and ribbons of various
orders on his ambassadorial uniform. But he forgot that this
was the leading idea of those who become ambassadors and that
for over five hundred years the Hapsburg rulers had been accustomed to send only gentlemen of commanding mien and

knightly bearing, or very clever men with pensive and penetrating eyes, as their emissaries to foreign lands. Must this son of a manual labourer learn to descend grand staircases with majestic step? He soon came to realize that only men of noble birth could enter those august halls. And so he went back to his Plato.

But in the mental make-up of this youth the sense of reality was so strong that he was eminently a practical person. And such he has always remained. This young Doctor of Philosophy came to learn in a fragmentary way the secret causes that were undermining the political and social foundations of the Austrian metropolis, though the rulers vainly tried to hide this untoward state of things. At the age of twenty-six Masaryk published his first essay on Plato and at the same time he wrote a series of articles on political theory and practice the general aim of which was to show that politics must be looked upon as a science. The first of these was an article which criticized Schopenhauer adversely. It was returned by the review to which it had been sent first. Masaryk's attitude towards life was directly opposed to every form of fatalistic passivity and it was Plato's active valuation of human existence that gave the necessary practical balance to his own theories. Thus from the very outset of his career this young thinker was able to grasp and understand the modern spirit of the times while fully appreciating the value of those things that are eternal. In this way the theoretical side of his mind became perfectly balanced by the practical.

He made few friends. He has been a great walker all his life. Throughout eighty years he has spent several hours daily in the open air. In the open country and the woods he has always sought the counterpoise for his hours of study indoors. He has always liked to move among men and to put his book learning to the test of facts and actual personalities. While his knowledge of literature steadily grew wider and more profound, he kept it living and real through his habit of always bringing it close to facts and always seeking for new relations between fact and theory.

The first book he wrote dealt with the fact of death and the questions to which that fact gives rise. He treated the subject from the standpoint of the general principles of health and dealt in detail with the question of how the average span of human existence may be lengthened and how the causes of death may be lessened. He also discussed the phenomenon of suicide. Masaryk looks upon this book today as fundamentally an expression of his own character and philosophy of life. For, though the portrait of the author which it presents is rather bizarre, yet it is in keeping with his character and reflects his upbringing and education. Interspersed with emotional outbursts are long columns of figures. Social statistics are intermingled with moral appeals. When he wrote the book the young author's mind was afire with indignation against the evils of the social structure within which he lived. The way he blazons forth his rhapsodies in numerical scales reminds one of the Overture to *Tannhäuser*. He inveighs against war and alcoholism, capitalism and sexual aberrations. But all this medley is unified under one leading motif which may be described as a passionate feeling of astonishment at the idea that a man should be capable of extinguishing the flame of life with his own hand. No kind of suicide, even that which claims to be inspired by the purest motives, finds any justification whatsoever at the hands of the young author. In confirmation of this attitude Masaryk himself once said to me: "The man who yearns for Death is morbid and deranged in his mind; for he refers everything to his own ego."

Masaryk thought this book would open the way to his appointment as a professor. Naturally no university would accept it. Here was a man who dealt with the significance of figures and made intricate calculations; he was not a mathematician,

however, but a thinker without any system of thought whatsoever, a believer without a stereotyped religion. And he remains
the same today.

So the learned professors at the university rightly objected
that throughout the book the author was constantly wandering
away from the subject he had set out to deal with. A man
of such an inconsequential turn of mind would be of no use
to them on the professorial staff in Vienna. They had chairs
of philosophy and sociology but the professor's chair could not
be exploited to serve the ethical notions of its incumbent. The
ethical views expressed in Masaryk's book belonged rather to
that part of the university course presided over by the theolo-
gians; but these looked with horror at this Christian who was
the sworn enemy of dogma. And yet today, after fifty years, this
book is being regularly quoted by the two faculties I have mentioned.

Masaryk came to Leipzig for a year to follow the lectures of
Fechner and Wundt. One day, after bearing a lecture on suicide,
a young pale-faced student came to him and stated that he
intended to take his own life. After some discussion the young
fellow regained his common sense and abandoned his former
purpose. This man whose life had been thus saved from his
own hand lived to be an old and honoured citizen. The incident
gives a good insight into Masaryk's character. It is a typical
example of his capacity for turning his theoretical knowledge
to practical ends and at the same time it is an instance of the
personal confidence he aroused in those with whom he came in
contact. Here was a young fellow whose fate seemed almost
doomed. Yet he did not approach a physician or a pastor but
merely a thinker pure and simple. And the result is an illustration of the kind of influence Masaryk has exercised throughout
his whole life. In his political activities it comes out in the grand

style; for here we have Platonic idealism going hand in hand with practical statesmanship.

It was during this stay of a year in Leipzig that Thomas Masaryk met his future wife. This was Charlotte Garrigue, who had come from Brooklyn to Germany to study music. She belonged to an old New England family of Puritan tradition, partly of French and partly of Danish descent. Her mother was a highly accomplished woman. And her father, who clearly showed the Viking strain in his character, could trace his pedigree back to the family of St. Louis of France. Even today there is a French town which bears the family name. If you buy winter oranges in Paris you will see the name written in blue letters on the skin of the orange. It is a rather attractive family symbol more in harmony with human instincts than shields and coats-of-arms.

Miss Garrigue's father was a bookseller and a democrat. He gave his eleven children full freedom to follow their own religious leanings. The result was that eight or nine sects were represented at the family table. Charlotte, who was the third eldest, was a Unitarian. This meant at once a spiritual affinity between herself and young Masaryk. A photograph taken when she was seventeen shows a girlish look which is at once timid and hopeful. At the age of seventy the expression on the countenance is a blend of hope and faith.

At the age of seventeen she was not so handsome as when she had grown to be twenty-six. It was then that Masaryk met her. They were both of the same age. She had the reputation of energetically striving after the higher ideals of life. And from the little that he now tells of their first acquaintanceship one can readily infer that the meeting with this foreigner at Leipzig at once struck a sympathetic chord in his heart. She responded to the yearnings of his mind. They read the English philosophers together. Then she left Leipzig. He wrote her a letter which contained a proposal of marriage. But her answer was indecisive. He took a fourth-class ticket on the railway and followed her. Then he won her consent. That day they read nothing together. But hindrances and difficulties were soon forthcoming. Finally he had to travel to America in order to bring her home to Europe to be his bride. That was not such an easy matter in the eighteen-seventies as it is today.

They lived together for nearly fifty years. During that time each was a source of help and strength to the other, so much so that he now declares that he cannot yet realize how much she has meant in his life. "I think she had a more subtle brain," he once said to me. And then he added emphatically: "I taught her much but it was she who shaped me." They were both enamoured of the same ideals. They wished to make life as perfect as possible here on earth, while at the same time they believed in an immortal future. Neither cared for money or power or position. They had no ambition to mix up with the prominent people of their day. In some traits of character they differed from each other; but in this each was the complement of the other. He was bright and gay. She was more dreamy and musical. He was very active while she had more of mother-care. Indeed, they were very fortunate in the balance of temperaments; for she had the qualities that were the feminine counterpart of his masculine characteristics. From the very beginning or at any rate from the early years of their married life onwards there seems to have been a perfect mental balance between the two and its development was largely due to the keen sense of humour which the husband possessed.

While the pair still enjoyed the fullness of youth they had two daughters and two sons whose careers were subsequently influenced by the great task to which the father had dedicated his life. In his struggle to carry out that task, especially in its crucial phases, Masaryk received more support and driving force

from his wife than from any other person, and that especially
during the war when it was impossible for them to be together.

3

In the bloom of youth Masaryk was a magnificent-looking person. And though he never exploited his boon, he must at least
have been aware of it; for he at once made a profound impression on the people he met, especially young people. His good
looks undoubtedly contributed to bring about this effect. Even
now in his old age he still preserves this bodily grace and
elegance of manners. I have never met anyone in whom the
inner qualities of mind and soul are so graciously balanced
with the outer harmony of bodily form and movement and
gesture as in the case of Masaryk. He has already lived to be
older than Goethe. In the portraits that we have of him between
the ages of thirty and forty he has a short dark-brown beard
covering the whole chin, somewhat in the professorial fashion
of those days. Indeed, he must then have looked a typical German professor. On glancing at his figure in group photographs
I was struck by the fact that any chance onlooker would single
him out at once from his colleagues for the physical dignity
and grace of his bearing. One would not have expected it from
a workman's son, especially as he did not have sufficient money
in those days to have a finely tailored suit. In Vienna the family
lived in furnished rooms and took their meals at a small local
restaurant. Yet when Masaryk appeared some time later in the
Imperial Parliament at Vienna one of the titled dandies described him as the best dressed man in the House.

That was an expression of the practical and everyday side

of his character. He was never a Bohemian. Elegance of dress and personal appearance quickly developed as his mental faculties matured in early middle age. It was so-called chance that first brought him to Prague, into the centre of the struggle which the Czech people were then waging on behalf of their cultural and political independence. "Probably I should never have entered politics," he says, "were it not for the fact that I was thus brought of necessity into close touch with the historical problem which our nation was facing."

At this point, therefore, his career once again took a decisive turning which was in no way attributable to the philosophical studies that he had hitherto been engaged upon. In the year 1882 he happened to deliver a lecture and publish it in the shape of an article. The subject lay entirely outside the sphere of his studies. The man who was first struck by the article was a researcher in the field of music. The responsible professors of philosophy took no interest in it. The Czech university was just then being founded at Prague. Masaryk was appointed professor there. As in the case of almost every innovator, it was by mistake that the ruling powers admitted him to an official position. When it was proposed to call Masaryk to a chair in Prague the Hapsburg authorities sanctioned the call on the grounds that —"In the Czech professorial body the aforementioned Masaryk, judging by his views, will turn out to be a moderating force."

In Prague he came to know the Czech nation, his own people. He was half-German in his bringing up, almost entirely German by his education, and his first book had been written in the German language. During his years at Vienna his interest had been absorbed in problems that were above the merely national sphere. And hence it was that he had hitherto lived out of touch with the struggle his own nation was making. Here in Prague two universities, the Austro-German and the Czech,

were now competing against each other, while the two races
in the city were rivals in business and in political and municipal
administration. Masaryk's sense of moral justice was aroused
and his practical bent led him at once into action. He founded
a review and later on a newspaper. Though there was originally
no intention of entering the polemical field, because Masaryk
was not a fighter by nature, he became involved in discussions
on cultural questions which he could not possibly avoid. This
was because such questions immediately affected his own ethical
principles and appealed to his sense of justice and truth.

He introduced an entirely new manner of dealing with the
students. It amounted to a revolution in academic traditions.
The new professor was not more than ten or fifteen years older
than his students. He had an inborn nobility of character which
was in contrast to the professorial standoffishness of his colleagues. He was superior by reason of that alone and it was
thus that he became the trusted leader of the youth. They followed him because he made no attempt at subterfuges to win
their confidence but treated them openly and squarely, analyzing
their problems frankly and fearlessly for them and making no
attempt to put things across under the ægis of his professorial
authority. Did anybody in this august Hapsburg Empire ever
before hear of a professor standing beneath a student's window
and whistling to the latter to come down to take a stroll? Did
anybody ever before hear of a professor in those quarters whose
private library was open to every student who wished to come
and borrow whatever books appealed to him? And where could
one find a professor to whom the students came with their
private woes and who encouraged them and gave them advice
or even money and even sometimes a winter coat? Like the
Russians, Masaryk was always giving tea in his home. Students
came on one errand after another and took advantage of the
opportunity to discuss Kant or Hume with the professor and his

wife. When some of those young people were hard up he had them come to his home and gave them an essay or a book to translate. One of those was Edward Benes, who was then attending the Gymnasium. It was only natural that fellow professors and the academic as well as the political authorities should grow somewhat nervous at the developments that were taking place. For here was a young professor to whom the students flocked whenever and however they liked.

If only he had belonged to some party or other he would have had at least the advantage of having behind him for his defence the corporate support of that body. But Masaryk has always been a freelance and has never remained for long a member of any organization. Again and again he resigned from organizations which he had joined. Sometimes he was called to account for offences against strict party discipline and on more than one occasion legal proceedings were taken against him on this score. Even the most enthusiastic of the Czech patriots found that they could not entirely count on the whole-hearted co-operation of their new protagonist. The reason for this was that the sense of personal rectitude and personal responsibility was so dominant in his character that he had to look upon what he considered to be the truth as above and beyond all claims of external loyalty towards party or nation. He has never cared for personal honour or fame if it came from an external source, such as his professional position or his position in the party or nation. Masaryk had no constructive plan when he first began to take part in the national struggle of the Czech people. He had no idea of achieving a position for himself. He was urged on and was sustained in his effort simply and solely by his own personal sense of moral justice. "The Arithmetic of Love" is the name he gives to the administrative justice on the basis of which the affairs of the state should be managed. He did not want mere improvement or a change of policy in the statal administration of the country. He came neither as a national prophet nor as a creative spirit in the cultural life of the people. And his paradox went even so far that when he first entered the movement for Czech independence he took the side that was opposed to the popular will.

Since the beginning of the nineteenth century the Czech national movement had been inspired by a popular belief in a certain document in which the national destiny of the Czech people was proclaimed. This document was known as "The Königshofer Manuscript." It was supposed to be of mediæval origin and to have been either lost or concealed until a priest discovered it in the clock tower of an old village church. The promulgation of the contents of this document aroused the national spirit of the Czechs and for half a century they believed in its authenticity. But in 1850, just about the time of Masaryk's birth, it was denounced as a forgery. The man who denounced it, however, was indicted and convicted. One of Masaryk's colleagues, who was an expert in documentary research, now took the matter up. His analysis of the contents of the Königshofer Manuscript proved destructive of its authenticity. The article was published in Masaryk's review. And Masaryk himself proved by scientific philological examination of the text that the supposed mediæval manuscript was a forgery. The nationalists raised a storm of protest. The publisher refused to continue to bring out the review. Public rumour accused Masaryk of having taken bribes from the Freemasons and the Jews for the paper which he now founded in collaboration with the younger elements of the Czech party. One of the leading journals in Prague at the time published in the Czech language the following denunciation: "To hell with you, infamous traitor. Don't dare in future to use our holy language. Go over to the enemy whom you are serving and forget that a Czech mother gave you birth. We excommunicate you from the national body."

Thirty years later that same paper became the government organ under the presidency of the "traitor" himself. Only a few of the die-hard nationalists believe today in the authenticity of the Königshofer Manuscript.

After this incursion into the higher sphere of national politics he was elected deputy to the Imperial Parliament in Vienna. When he pleaded there for the political rights of his native Bohemia there was an uproar in the House and one of the Austro-German deputies shouted that by taking this stand Masaryk showed himself an arch-traitor to the Empire. Thus, as in the case of so many responsible statesmen, he was accused of high treason by both sides.

His first period as deputy in the Vienna Parliament lasted two years. His second lasted ten years. During each session he spent about half his time in Vienna and the other half in Prague. Here again we have an example of the balance between the development of the theoretical side of his mind and the putting of his knowledge to practical use in public affairs. He has assured me that he has never liked his ov books and that he would never have written a book had it not been in answer to some particular necessity. As a matter of fact, the most important of them are only fragmentary—his book on suicide, for instance, and that on Russian Studies. Even the book which is entitled *The World Revolution*, and was written on the basis of historical events, suffers from the fact that two books are mixed up in one. Like Lincoln, Masaryk may best be known by his speeches, his epigrammatic sayings and his recorded conversations. If the story of his life should one day be forgotten, some fragments of his books would still be known and considered of value by experts in several branches of study. If his books should become entirely neglected, or if they never had been written, the story of his life would still retain its splendour undiminished. For though his thought has always been logical, the qualities of soul rather than of mind are the determining feature in his character. "Logical analysis," he declares, "I never looked upon as an end in itself, but rather as a means. From the very beginning I have striven after synthesis and organization. Everything I have done is an illustration of that striving."

4

The process whereby he became a politician was apparently the result of one fortuitous circumstance after another. It was a slow process also and was expedited only by steps which he took almost automatically when circumstances turned up. There was no planning on his part and he did not either will or foresee the consequences of his action on those occasions. He moved only when some outer happening called for action on his part, such as a false statement published by somebody or a report which affected some public question, or because he felt called upon to defend somebody who was being persecuted or because he thought it his duty to take up a stand against somebody in power. But then he moved only under the pressure of his friends or students and when he did there was generally a public uproar.

At first he was accused of high treason against the most cherished traditions of his own country. Later on his name was bandied about as a blasphemer and he was brought before the courts on the plaint of three hundred priests who accused him of blasphemy, all this because he had called a spade a spade when dealing with the spying activities of certain Jesuit priests who were his professional colleagues in Prague. On his acquittal by the court there was a public demonstration in the Karlplatz, some of the crowd shouting against him and others cheering him.

The opposition went so far as to accuse him of countenancing ritual murder because he wrote a pamphlet in defence of a Jew named Hilsner who was charged before the courts with the crime of a ritual murder. But Masaryk had never met Hilsner and did not know him at all. Some of his colleagues on the professorial staff, together with the clergy and public officials and members of the anti-Semitic party, raised a public protest and called for his resignation. He was accused of having been bribed by Rothschild. Disturbances took place in the lecture hall when he came to deliver his lectures. On these occasions his wife accompanied him so as to be beside him and support him. His children were insulted and maltreated on the streets. And the number of those who publicly rallied around him was small. "He who looks up to Jesus as his Master," declared Masaryk publicly, "cannot be anti-Semitic. You must be either one thing or the other and if you are a Christian you cannot be anti-Semitic."

The result of these experiences was that he grew profoundly skeptical about the good faith of those fellow professors who were constantly attacking him. I was delighted to hear him use distinctly unparliamentary language when speaking of those professors after so many decades have passed. He had to wait thirteen years before being raised to the rank of an ordinary professor. And during that time there were always money questions to trouble him. Masaryk and his family had to live on 1800 gulden a year, which at the gulden value of that time amounted to seven hundred and fifty dollars. This was all he was earning at the age of forty, though he supplemented it somewhat by a little income from his writings. The Archbishop of Prague tried to prevent his appointment as Professor Ordinarius by bringing up the case of the trial for blasphemy against him. The archbishop appealed to the Austrian Emperor. The Emperor referred the matter to the Imperial Secretary of State for Public Worship and the latter reported that there was nothing in Masaryk's writings to support the charge of blasphemy.

All this did not assuage the hostility of his criticism against Austrian officials and Austrian institutions. During his sojourns in Vienna as member of the Imperial Parliament, he had the opportunity of studying the court and the nobility, the church and the bureaucracy. When speaking of them today his favourite epithet is *Sumpf*, which in English means a bog or marsh. Long before the war he had recognized that the Metternich tradition had been outmoded. In one of his speeches he said: "The diplomats have still the illusion that they are the makers of the history. . . . Abroad they seem to me to resemble Arctic explorers standing on an ice floe and allowing the drift of the sea to take them where it will. That is the mark of aristocratic pre-eminence. For myself I have no longer any faith whatsoever in this antiquated sort of diplomacy." During this period his private studies and his keen observance led him to see clearly the value of personality in political affairs and in the affairs of state.

His travels throughout Europe and in Russia brought him into close touch with the rulers and ruled of the various nations and enabled him to put to the test of practical experience that knowledge of national characteristics and problems which he had already acquired from the reading of books. He holds that the information gained through reading and study is a necessary preparation for a sound knowledge of men and nations. "One does not become a citizen of the world," he once declared, "merely by international travel but rather by a deep and sincere study of the lives of individuals and of nations and of mankind in general."

And yet, though he makes this broad avowal and though he

was quite settled in his mind as to the rottenness at the core of the Hapsburg system, he did not allow himself to express his opinion of that system in the strong language then favoured by the red-hot Czech patriots in Vienna and Prague. He preferred to endure the unenviable reputation of being a mediator with the Vienna Government, for he was willing to fill that rôle so long as he could not overthrow the Hapsburg rule or ameliorate its corruption. When he was a comparatively young man of thirty, and even afterwards as deputy at the age of sixty, he endeavoured to bring about an understanding with the Austro-Germans for the gradual transformation of the monarchy into a federal state of which the various members would be autonomous. It was thus that the term *Trialism* came into vogue, an idea out of which the tripartite monarchy had arisen.

He was sixty years old when he started his first great political fight against the foreign policy of Count Aerenthal. As a Czech he fully realized what the oppression of the Croats by the Hungarians meant—*per analogiam,* as he was fond of saying. In 1909 Bosnia was annexed by the Hapsburg Crown, one of the first fateful steps that brought about the World War. After the annexation fifty-three Serbs and Croats were imprisoned on charges of high treason. Masaryk interfered energetically and this was the beginning of his historic conflict with Austria, the conflict which eventually made world history, though Masaryk at that time had no notion of how successful the struggle would turn out for him ten years later. In 1909 and even as late as 1913 he was still working for conciliation between Austria and the Southern Slavs, for he preferred to take a safe course which might assure the avoidance of a catastrophe rather than blindly to follow the nationalist dream which would certainly eventuate in a catastrophe though it might bring freedom to his own people as a result of that upheaval. The fact that until the hour of fate had struck he had striven hard to prevent the war is an irrefutable proof that he was in no way responsible for the actual upheaval itself. His last speech in Austria was delivered before the Vienna Peace Association in November, 1913.

As parliamentary deputy he took part in the Agram trials and, as in the case of the Königshofer Manuscript, he proved that one of the essential documents used in evidence was a forgery but that it had been forged with the connivance of the Vienna Government. This was the third great historical occasion on which he brought the truth of a complicated situation out into the foreground and procured the acquittal of the accused. That situation called forth his versatile talents and knowledge. He showed himself to be a stalwart champion of truth for its own sake and a statesman at the same time, combating the enemy of his race and yet not fighting the cause of his race. He was fighting here for the Serbs and Croats.

During that historic fight he made two important contacts, one with Wickham Steed, who was then *Times* correspondent in Vienna, and the other with an American Mæcenas who brought him to Chicago in the interest of Slav culture and would have kept him there for good had not Masaryk's wife stepped in and insisted on Masaryk remaining in Austria. She had seen the danger of uprooting a personality like his from the environment in which he had grown and developed. During all these stirring events he never neglected his sociological and philosophical studies and he continued to discharge his professorial duties without a break. The secret of his success here was that he was blessed with abounding bodily health and he took care of it by living methodically and taking everything in moderation. He settled down outside of Vienna and walked daily to the Imperial Parliament and back. He developed the habit of standing up while writing. He never drank much and under the influence of Forel he gave up alcoholic drinks entirely at the age of fifty. Today the aged President always has a good supply of various delicacies on his table but he drinks no wines.

When the hour of fate struck for Europe and the world in 1914, Thomas Masaryk was in the fullness of his bodily health and vigour. His intellectual faculties had reached their highest pitch of development. His mind was well stored with the knowledge he had acquired during half a century of assiduous study. He had seen the world and had had practical experience of the various facets of human nature. Thanks to the hand of Providence which had hitherto directed his career, and also to his own indomitable character, he had come in touch with forces and men that were now to serve him well when his life's task was finally set before him. He was then in the middle sixties.

5

Masaryk's lifework embodies an extraordinary paradox: He struggled with all his might as a private individual to prevent the war and yet through the war accomplished a task that has no counterpart in the life of any other European leader. In 1912 Masaryk approached Count Berchtold with certain proposals with which he had been entrusted directly by the Serbian Premier, M. Pasic. Berchtold wanted the war to come and broke off negotiations peremptorily. Then he asserted that the professor was simply out to earn a commission. When Berchtold and Masaryk met, it was not merely two personalities but two epochs that clashed. On the one side stood the nonchalant aristocrat whose forefathers had probably cracked their whips over the forefathers of his visitor during hunting excursions on the Hapsburg estates. The aristocrat certainly did not realize how near at hand was his own doom. Nor is it likely that the serious-minded professor had any presentiment whatsoever of his own elevation in the near future. But fate had decided that within a few years to come this man should be its instrument in bringing about the downfall of the Hapsburg Monarchy with all its Berchtolds. For the work which Masaryk did during the war was not confined in its results merely to the creation of a new state whose existence or non-existence need not upset the rest of the world.

The essential significance of his achievement lies in the fact that he engineered the destruction of the last of the theocracies. The other three—the Turkish and the Prussian and the Russian —were already breaking up and doomed to disappear; but the Entente had decided to maintain the Austrian theocracy in Europe. It was the personal intervention of Masaryk that assured its downfall. Here again the unfolding of events discloses the work of that unseen agency which directed this man's life from the start. Only after he had passed his sixtieth year did he gradually come to the conviction that he would have to support the revolutionary movement as a last resort. And then when the dogs of war were let loose by Vienna it was this turn of outer circumstances that finally forced a decision on him and laid at his door the supreme task which his life was meant to accomplish. All this gives food for thought, and for revision of thought, to the skeptic who attributes such happenings to blind chance. The man of affairs may read a lesson in it too.

Here one realizes how all that Masaryk had learned from books and meditation on them throughout a long life of study, the practical experiences through which he had to pass, the strengthening and tempering of his mental faculties through his habitual exercises in logical analysis and critical judgment, the fights he waged for certain principles and against others, the shaping of his views and character through intercourse with men of the world and with world affairs—one realizes how all this was now to be of inestimable help to him in carrying through the supreme task of his life. Of course, it is a comparatively easy matter to discern the logical chain in a series of events once they have culminated in their conclusion. But it is only the eye of God that sees the whole picture beforehand and probably has planned it. At any rate, if we humans understood the inner drift of events before they have worked themselves out to their conclusion, the study of them would lose its attraction.

Masaryk now began to reap where he had sown. And the first seed that he gathered was the return which others made to him of the trust and confidence that his personality had always given out. A Member of Parliament and a professor, but by no means a political leader and least of all a revolutionary, this man went round in Prague during the first weeks of the war, calculating and pondering and deciding on plans. Then he went to Holland. In the midst of the Austrian Empire where could he find heads and hearts that might be chosen to help him? And if he found them how could he secretly bring them together in a country where every political stirring had been watched and noticed by the police up to the eve of the war. Here in Czechoslovakia there were no illegal clubs and groups, no clandestine newspapers and meetings, which otherwise might have become revolutionary instruments in his hands. He took a few individuals aside and talked to them secretly but did not disclose his plans. Through the confidence placed in him by reason of his long fight for the cause of truth and justice he now received a mandate. Like the most fundamental dictates of human nature, none of this was committed to writing or formally expressed. It was silently given to a man who was about to flee the country in order to organize the revolution from outside. He did not even confide his purpose to his wife, who was the close companion of his career; because he knew that she would eventually be interrogated and that she could not lie.

With one of his daughters, who was ill at the time, he took the train to Italy in November 1914. He was stopped at the frontier, because his passport had not been endorsed for travelling abroad by the Austrian authorities. At once, and for the first time in his life, he introduced himself as a Member of the Imperial Parliament. And then he did what he never before had done during five and sixty years of life. He did physical violence to the law, he seized his daughter and jumped with her on the departing train to the other side of the frontier and to safety. A man of weaker character might have been held back by traditional respect for the imperial uniform and a moralist who was not at the same time a man of action might have remained at the other side of the frontier out of scrupulous considerations for the sanctity of the law.

Had he dallied here Masaryk would never have obtained from the Austrian authorities the endorsement on his passport permitting him to leave the country. His whole plan had been carefully prepared. The initial stage of it was accomplished by the act of this man when he jumped on the departing railway train. On that one sudden decision the destiny of Austria depended, just as the destiny of Russia depended on the Swiss railway train that brought Lenin across another frontier three years later. In each case a born leader set his movement going by crossing the frontier. One returned to his native country to raise the revolt. The other left his native country to organize from abroad the revolt in the land he had left.

Masaryk met some leading Serbian and Croatian refugees in Rome. The confidence which he enjoyed in those countries on account of his stand at the Agram trials was now effective in helping him to bring about an agreement for concerted action with the Southern Slav nations whose aims were similar to his. At Geneva in 1915 he started to weave his slender net of intrigue out of practically nothing. His former experience in dealing with forged documents was now of advantage to him. For the first time in his life he resorted to underhand means. He arranged a system of smuggling letters across the Austrian frontiers. He learned to write his messages with invisible ink. He adopted the ruse of false bottoms in boxes of merchandise. All this was a replica of the falsifications he had unmasked at Agram and in Prague.

A man must possess a high sense of ethical rectitude to become a conspirator after the age of sixty. He must believe in a higher justice than that of the legal system under which he lives. This belief was well grounded by Masaryk on the conviction which he had carefully arrived at after his long years of quiet study and his painstaking habit of constantly putting the principles of his moral philosophy to the test of practical life and revising them accordingly. During those years the thought of being arrested by the Austrian police came to him in his dreams, with constantly recurring persistency even up to the time that he actually became President of Czechoslovakia.

What was the object of his mission abroad? To make it clear to the leaders of the Entente that it was in their best interests to demolish Austria-Hungary. But the statesmen of the Entente had a policy that was entirely contrary to this. They aimed at the severance of Austria from Germany and the maintenance of the Austrian Empire on a reconstructed plan. Through the existence of a strong Austria they hoped to keep Germany weak; for they were not opposed to the German Empire as such but rather to the militarism of Prussia, in which they thought they saw the chief cause of world unrest. If Masaryk could bring the statesmen of the Entente to abandon this fundamental principle of their policy and supplant it by another, then he might hope for the liberation of his own country; otherwise not. He could wage no direct warfare against the Central Powers and so he had to look on with patience at the ever-growing heap of political and military mistakes which the Allies were making. Their final victory was a necessary precondition to the putting of his own plan into effect. But once that victory had been obtained there would still remain the task of preventing the reconstruction of the Austrian Empire. It must be absolutely and finally wiped out. That was an essential aim of his policy. How could this end be attained?

He had a magnificent knowledge of Europe. It was a knowledge which had been acquired by actual political experience and was superadded to the great store of learning that he possessed in various branches of science. His acquaintance with ethnological, statistical, historical and cultural questions was infinitely superior to that of the Entente ministers, for they were entirely ignorant of such matters. In contrast to those English ministers who knew no language but their own and had never travelled, and the French who are an incurably stay-at-home people, and the Americans who see Europe in the bulk as if it were a mere ant-heap of nations, stood this single individual who knew the national statistics and historical data, the customs and literature, the general character and institutions of the various nations and could elucidate them all in their respective languages.

Over and above all this stood the asset of his personal qualities and experience, which worked hand in hand for him in persuading men to listen to what he had to say and in finally bringing them round to his point of view. The confidence which he universally instilled, his journalistic experience, his absolute integrity and the entire absence of any spirit of ambition or self-seeking—all these imponderabilia constituted a leading factor

of his success. He laid down the following canons of propaganda
for his helpers: "Don't vilify or disparage the Austro-Germans.
Don't underrate the enemy. Don't distort or exaggerate. Don't
give promises that cannot be backed up and don't appear as a
suppliant before the statesmen of the Entente. . . . Operate by
the force of clear ideas and sound argument and keep your own
personality in the background. Never be a burden or bore to anybody. Take money from nobody except our own people, even
though it be freely offered. To lie and exaggerate is the worst
kind of propaganda. We must also gain people who are only
indirectly interested in our cause. This can be done by dealing
with questions on art and literature in which non-politicians are
interested; for political agitation often puts off the thinking man
and leaves him indifferent. Sometimes one sentence well and
aptly used at the suitable moment will have its effect." In the
author of such maxims we can at once detect the philosopher
and man of the world, bent on avoiding mistakes. The blunder-
ing policy of the Germans in this respect probably lost them the
war. Certainly it alienated from them the sympathy of the
world.

He had to occupy himself with an immense array of details.
On the one hand, connection with Prague had to be maintained
in order to bring collaborators from there and get them in
touch with the leading men he wished to influence in the various countries. On the other hand, he had to organize all the
details of his propaganda among the Entente nations, his leading purpose here being to convince publicists and statesmen
that his policy was the sound one. "I did not approach ministers
straight away," he once said to me, "but only after they had
been talked round somewhat by their own friends who were
on my side. For more than a year in London I never saw Lloyd
George." The Agram affair turned up here again to help his
cause; for Wickham Steed, who had become friendly with

Masaryk during the Agram trials, knew Austria thoroughly and was definitely hostile to the Austrian monarchy. He was one of the most important journalists in England and his sponsorship of Masaryk helped the latter in the conquest of Fleet Street. He gradually won ten of the London newspapers for the Czech cause. His published works were instrumental in getting him a professorship in London for the teaching of the Slav languages. This furnished him with an entrée into social circles where he never would have been welcome as a fugitive and a suspected spy. The professorial position stamped him with the cache which calmed the misgivings of the political authorities.

"What a world pilgrimage!" exclaims Masaryk towards the close of this section of his memoirs. "How many visits to influential people. How many memoranda, telegrams, letters, securing the intercession of Allied ambassadors and political personalities friendly to our cause, interviews, press articles, etc."

And yet this part of his task was by no means the most difficult or the most important. Every day he had to keep in the closest touch with the changes taking place in the war-maps on all fronts. He had to keep himself informed on every political move of importance that was being made. He had to assess the influence of those moves on the respective nations they concerned. And he had to study the psychological reactions which the vicissitudes of victory and defeat produced on the populations and leaders of the different nations. He was a sort of Atlas who bore the world on his shoulders without anybody knowing it or realizing that so much of the future of the world's history depended on this man's individual effort. He had to shoulder the weight of a greater personal responsibility than any other man of his time, except such men as Clemenceau and Ludendorff; but their individual responsibilities were only temporary. In contrast to all other statesmen of the war period he was always, or nearly always, alone. He hardly slept at all and, though now in the middle sixties, he learned to ride horseback in order to maintain his physical fitness.

He used every moment of his time and every means at hand to increase his stock of knowledge and keep it up to date. He went to the cinemas so that he might learn what position the various leaders of the Allies held in the popular estimation, judging this by the applause that greeted their portraits when thrown on the screen. His daughter collaborated with him. She tells how he used to leave the city and go out into the quiet of the suburban districts when a difficult situation faced him, and it was necessary to concentrate all his mental energy on a critical decision.

In 1916 he at last succeeded in persuading Aristide Briand to support his plan for the dismemberment of Austria and the independence of the Czechoslovak nation. Other men of great weight in public affairs had already tried to persuade the French statesman to adopt this policy, but only Masaryk succeeded. The Czech National Committee in Paris was formally acknowledged. But it took a whole twelve months of hard work on the part of Dr. Benes to have introduced into the Allied Peace Note the phrase: "The Liberation of the Czechoslovaks." Looking back on this episode Masaryk says in his memoirs: "And so we were independent and free *de jure* and *de facto*." He puts half a dozen notes of exclamation after that sentence. They are the only exclamation marks in the bulky volume of his memoirs.

6

And now as layman he took up the most difficult task of all. From the beginning of the war he had the idea that a nation

which wished to be free and called for the assistance of other
nations to help it in achieving that freedom must also fight for
it. To build up an army from the tens of thousands of Czechoslovak deserters and from the thousands of nationalized Czechs
and Slovaks in France and England and America was one of
his earliest and leading ideas, though rather extraordinary in
the circumstances. It was in contrast to his pacifist principles
and his humane outlook, which urged him to spare the shedding
of more blood and in this case the blood of his fellow countrymen. But in order to win the co-operation of the Allied statesmen in the work of founding a new nation, or at least to induce
them into an attitude of benevolent neutrality towards it, he
must present these over-spoiled gentlemen with an early morning
pick-me-up in the shape of an army corps or two. The greatest
number of Czechoslovak deserters were those who had gone
over to Russia on the Austro-Russian front. Therefore Masaryk
decided that Russia was to be the ground on which he would
organize his military plan.

But the Czar objected. He feared to trust men who had run
away from the side of their companions-in-arms. But when the
Czar fell from power Miliukov entered the Government. He
and Masaryk were professional colleagues and acquaintances.
Masaryk at once set out from London for Petrograd, armed
with a forged passport, and succeeded in reaching the Russian
capital after a roundabout journey. There the two professors of
philosophy, who had never worn a uniform, sat in council together and concluded an agreement for the enrolment of forty
thousand Czechoslovak volunteers to form an army corps. A
national committee was organized. Masaryk, in his civilian dress
and wearing the usual slouch hat, stood before the assembled
officers and men who had come over from the Austrian army
and explained to them that from this moment forward they were
no longer to be prisoners of war, in danger of being retaken

should the Austro-German armies triumph over Russia, but that they were to be again on the active list and would fight for their own country on the side of the Allies, possibly in France, for which he was already negotiating. They listened to this old gentleman whom they had never known and took his word for what he said. They placed their destiny in his hands by appointing him their dictator.

It reads like a fairy tale. A moralist and philosopher who had never shot at even a rabbit and who had become a sort of king without a country is now endowed with unlimited power as commander-in-chief of an army of his fellow countrymen. He went to live with them at their billets in the villages and in their tents. He explained to them day after day in the simple language of common sense why they should fight on foreign soil for the establishment of an independent nation which as yet was only a land of dreams that existed in the imagination of a few idealists and might easily be wiped out from even that small territory of the mind if the Central Powers should win the war or even if the Allies should make a separate peace with Austria.

During the first two years of his propaganda work among the Allies he was the sole responsible representative of twelve millions of his fellow countrymen whom the destiny of history was one day to form into an independent state. Fate had now decreed that from one day to another he had to see to the needs of these forty thousand men before him who were hungry and wanted food and clothing and weapons. He came to an agreement with Albert Thomas in Petrograd whereby it was arranged to bring these troops to fight on the Franco-German front. This first treaty was signed in the name of a state not yet in existence by a private individual who had no official mandate whatsoever but who signed as a mandatory on his own responsibility.

Miliukov fell from power and Lenin took over control of

Russia. The Czechoslovak volunteer troops were housed as guests of Russia at Kiev. They were in a mood to be easily influenced by the movement around them and as a result they were won over to the radical Bolshevik side. They deposed the Czechoslovak National Government and established soviets in its place. But whom did they appoint as their new leader? The same dictator in the slouch hat who was at the moment carrying on negotiations in Moscow. I cannot find any other event in the long life of this man which demonstrates the moral force of his personality so convincingly as does this. He decided to travel around the world with his army corps, because hostile forces were holding Southern Russia and it would be difficult to break through there. It was a matter of first necessity now for this Czechoslovak army corps to put up some sort of fight in the universal welter of murder and thus bring itself to the notice of outsiders. Masaryk, who was opposed by nature to all kinds of publicity, calculated on the suggestive force of propaganda in these modern times and banked on the effect that a daredevil piece of adventure would have on the nerves of the world, especially America, which had grown rather weary of mere heroic deeds.

So he organized the march of the Czechoslovak legions through Siberia, having arranged for them a safe passage protected by a state of armed neutrality. Masaryk himself went ahead of them by train. The danger now facing him was the danger of a sudden peace. What would happen to his plans if general hostilities were now to cease? The foundation of the new state was at this juncture threatened by one of the most powerful agencies of modern times—World Labour—which wished the war to end here and now. Wilson had to be won. In his Fourteen Points nothing had been said about the dismemberment of Austria-Hungary.

On his sixty-eighth birthday Masaryk sat in that third-class railway carriage where he had provided himself with a sort of mattress on which to rest between his long hours of work. During the seventeen days that he travelled along the Japanese coast he laid down the outlines of a world programme which he intended should be read and conned by the Allied powers. These he published in *The New Europe*. In these writings he already envisages, to use his own words, "The beginnings of a free union of European nations instead of the absolute mastery of a section of the world by one of the great powers or by treaties drawn up between groups of powers inherently inimical to one another." It suggests the kind of scene that might be pictured in a ballad—this lonely man sitting on his mattress and scribbling on his writing block as he passes through the heart of Asia on a pilgrimage from Europe to America, behind him an army the purpose of whose existence was the defence of a country that was as yet only the substance of a dream, and before him another learned professor who, like himself, had become a politician by accident and who had in his hands the power to accept or reject the existence of this new state. From Tokio he sent a long letter to President Wilson as a herald to announce his mission. Only towards the end of that letter did he mention casually that following him was an army which he had organized from the ranks of his own countrymen.

On May 18, 1918, Chicago accorded him a triumphant reception. The news of his army en route round the world to reach the field of battle, the influence of the propaganda which he had organized and kept active for the previous four years, the activities of old friends, whom he had met when he was guest professor in Chicago several years before, the prestige which his wife's family enjoyed, the collaboration of various societies which had been organized at the beginning of the war for the liberation of their respective fellow nationals in Europe, the funds that had been gathered by the thousands from Czechs living in the United States, the sympathy of the Jews who were powerful in the press and who had not forgotten the stand Masaryk took in the Jewish cause on the occasion of the Hilsner trial in Prague thirty years before—all this made a national idol of a man who hated publicity for himself and forced him eventually to admit that mass suggestion through public demonstrations and the waving of flags cannot be dispensed with in a popular movement.

The story of his life continues to heap one incredibility on another. The Czechs and Slovaks of Pittsburgh, in the heart of the coal and iron section of North America, combined together for the purpose of founding their new state. Here again was the hand of a friendly destiny. The blood of each race, the Czech and the Slovak, ran half-and-half in his veins. So that he was the personal incarnation of that union which these races now formed. He spoke both their tongues and from the fundamental urge of his dual racial blood wished that both should be united in the one state.

Associations of a more distant past came to his aid. That Mæcenas who had invited him to Chicago twenty years before was a friend of Wilson's family and so Masaryk was introduced to the man on whom so much now depended, not through any political channels but through the personal intervention of mutual friends. His army at this time mustered 100,000 men. Therefore, he could speak of his new state as a belligerent power and he had in his pocket half a dozen formal recognitions of it as such when he went to see Wilson. His success in persuading the American President and gaining him over to the Czech policy was largely due to the fact that the two ex-professors talked as experts in history and philosophers of the Platonic school. Each was acquainted with the historical writings and reputation of the other. The world at large has a prejudice against professors in politics; but all depends on who the professors are. "As a thinking and honourable man," to use Masaryk's own expression, Wilson accepted without further deliberation the idea of the dismemberment of Austria and altered in this sense that part of his war aims manifesto which referred to Central Europe. As he did so he gave a nod of the head, Masaryk told me, which was like that of a king giving the royal sanction to a death sentence.

At this part of our story the duel between Masaryk and the Hapsburgs comes to an end. The Emperor Charles was at Laxenburg, in Austria, and tried to parry the stroke at the last moment by proclaiming autonomy for the constituent nationalities of the Hapsburg Empire. But at the same moment his invisible foe across the Atlantic—the man of whom Count Berchtold had said that he came to the Ballplatz to earn a commission when, as a matter of fact, he had come with a plea for the maintenance of peace—had pressed the electric button and promulgated in Paris the Declaration of Independence for Czechoslovakia which had been prepared long before. While the imperial and royal flag of the monarchy that had ruled for half a millennium was being lowered from the towers of the Vienna Hofburg the flag of the Czech nation, for the first time after three hundred years, was unfurled across the Atlantic from the roof of the hotel where Professor Masaryk had his temporary domicile. In Independence Hall, Philadelphia, where the United States of America were founded, Masaryk proclaimed the independence of the new Czechoslovak state. At the banquet which was given in his honour that day he sat at a table decked with bouquets that had been presented in sign of his triumph and during the festive proceedings a telegram was handed to him. He read it and put it aside. Later on he announced that his fellow countrymen in Europe had chosen him as first President of the new state.

Somebody asked him the childish question: Did it make him

feel happy? He answered: "I do not know. I cannot describe my feelings. I have the sensation of a responsibility and it has come without giving me time to feel pleased. No one ought to disappoint the hopes that are placed in him. That is what I feel."

7

There is a photograph of Masaryk's wife and two children which was taken about the middle of this fourth year of the war. It is what may be called an apocalyptic picture—the mother with drooping lips and obviously suffering profoundly; the daughter pale, devoted and resigned; the son as an Austrian soldier in the uniform of the enemy which his father is passionately striving abroad to overthrow. But the three faces in that picture have the same expression. They gaze outwards on the spectator. The pupils of the eyes are extended as if wondering and frightened. The look gives the impression that for the first time these three have the dawning consciousness of the possibility of losing faith in their fellow creatures. These naïve natures seem to be facing some tragic situation in a half-dazed manner, as if suddenly brought face to face with Evil.

Following the reports of her husband's activities abroad the Austrian authorities, as was natural enough, arrested the wife and brought her up for trial. "I do not know what my husband is doing," she declared. And that was the absolute truth. "But I am sure," she continued, "that whatever he does will be just. I am quite ready to go to prison in his place here." America was still neutral. The women's clubs there interceded and Madame Masaryk was allowed to go free. Unfortunately, however, she was suffering from a disease of the heart, which grew worse.

She refused to take any food beyond that allowed to her by the rationing regulations, for she would not lie or consent to accept smuggled foodstuffs. It was only after eighteen months of suffering that she received permission from the military governor to go to the seaside. Then they arrested the daughter instead of the mother and imprisoned her in Vienna together with Benes' wife. One of the sons died of typhoid which he contracted while nursing prisoners and the other son had to undergo the agony of wearing the uniform of an officer in the Austrian army for a long four years. Masaryk was kept informed of all this abroad, but he could not send or receive any message directly. These people who had lived together so closely for so many years keenly felt the absence of any communication. They missed those letters which in some mysterious sort of way make up for the absence of those whom we love and by whom we are loved in return. He had one of the two daughters by his side; but this presence probably added all the more to the bitterness of his absence from the others. Only after some years did he again see the surviving members of the family he had left in Europe.

He returned to Europe as a conqueror in triumph. On the boat he had little time to meditate on the adventure which had taken him round the world and brought about the destruction of the venerable Hapsburg Empire. He had to look to the future. There were hundreds of things to be done. They had to be done in the right way and with the means available at home. He was fully acquainted with all the preparations that had been made in silence. The group that was called the Maffia were in constant communication with the collaborators abroad; and yet they were not always unanimous about their plans. In the first place, what was called the Kramer party at home had for a long time championed the policy of union with Russia and the appointment of a Grand Duke as King of Bohemia. Others spoke of other royal families. The uncertainty was so great that General Stefanik, who was a Slovak and was fighting for the Czechoslovak cause in France, sent a despatch to Siberia protesting against founding the new state as a republic. This message had been sent two days before Masaryk promulgated the establishment of the new state of Czechoslovakia as an independent republic. No revolution had broken out in Prague. The dissolution of the Hapsburg Monarchy was accepted as a *fait accompli*. The transition took place almost in silence and without victims. The fact that though he was absent Masaryk was elected President by the first National Assembly in spite of the existing opposition shows how accurately his effective work abroad had been understood and appreciated by his countrymen at home, even though it had been impossible for them to keep in satisfactory touch with him. And so it was that on his return he received from the nation the mandate which had not been his when he left the country.

While returning across the Atlantic he had a host of problems before his mind. A Constitution for the new state had to be hastily drawn up and he would have to rule his country on the basis of it, although it would be impossible for him at first to have more than its leading provisions at his command. He had to look out for internal opposition on the part of elements that had remained hostile to him as the result of previous conflicts. The image of his suffering wife was constantly in his mind. And flitting across it were the kaleidoscopic scenes and events through which his world adventure had brought him. During that Atlantic voyage his head was constantly in a whirl of questions that insistently pressed for solution. "Through all purely personal dislikes and prejudices I drew a thick cross," he told me. "And I kept saying aloud to myself: *We are free. We have our Republic.*" When he landed in England he was received for the first time as the head of the nation. With the British foreign minister, Lord Balfour, he had a long discussion on the philosophy of religion.

He had imagined quite a different home-coming. He had reckoned on a triumphant entry of the Allies into Berlin, led by Marshal Foch, just as the Prussians had entered Paris in 1871. He thought that he himself would march at the head of his own troops directly to Prague as dictator, arrange the first necessities in connection with the administrative machinery of the new state and then hand over his authority to the National Assembly. When he was leaving America he advised Wilson to insist that the Allies should march in triumph to Berlin. Foch's adjutant assured me later that the generalissimo himself finally decided not to risk an entry into revolutionary Germany.

The picture of this out-and-out civilian entering the capital of his country alone in a motor car decorated with flowers harmonizes much better with the rest of his life's story. If we picture him on that glorious noon in December 1918, clad in dark civilian clothes and sitting alone in the open motor car which was surrounded by soldiers and military flags, and if we set over against this the hundreds of pictures which represent the last kings of our epoch as if they never had anything else to do but to take part in ceremonial processions, the difference between the old order of things and the new stands out clearly. There was no consort seated beside him to bow and smile on the multitude. His own features were grim and solemn. He lifted the slouch hat a few times; but for the most part he kept it pulled down over the face. He was peering through his spectacles as if reading and analysing the mind of the public. Men who have set their hearts on the possession of political power as the goal of their ambition generally consider such a moment as the glorification of their personal endeavour; but for this man its significance consisted in the approval he read in the faces of his people. He was studying the spirit of this resurgent generation and its fitness for the rôle which the future would call upon it to play.

An hour later he visited his wife in the sanitarium. One result of the work he had brought to its triumphant completion that day was the breakdown of his wife's health. The rôle he had played was in such tragic contrast to his philosophy of life and his humanitarian principles that it might suggest the parallel of a Greek hero in ancient drama were it not for the fact that Masaryk as a youth had implicitly chosen this lot when he made the high resolve to struggle for justice and freedom. His wife, of simple Puritan stock, was spared the duty of making a formal entry into the royal castle which her husband had to occupy— much to his disappointment. "For I thought," he declared, "that I could go to my own home. During that first night in the castle I did not sleep." So this old man of seventy had to live in a house separated from his wife the very first evening after his return to his native land. The loneliness of his years of absence seemed to crowd more heavily upon him in this castle upon the hill from which he had driven out the last of the Hapsburgs, not by the sword but by the application to politics of a statistical process, as certain ciphers disappear when a complex equation is mathematically worked out. Here he could now ponder over the mystery of human destiny and the destiny of nations, the broad river flowing beneath the walls of his residence and the panorama of one of the world's most beautiful cities visible from his windows.

Perhaps this philosopher asked himself during the watches of that sleepless night whether Kant was right when he complained that the possession of power over one's fellow men deprives the holder of the ability to form his judgments by the unhampered use of the reasoning faculty. Or was Plato, his master, right in holding that mankind could look forward to a happier destiny only if kings were to become philosophers or if the philosophers were enthroned as kings. Probably he meditated, as he had so often meditated before, on Hume's theory of probabilities, whereby the certainty of single results always definitely following from the operation of nature's laws is denied and only a statistical means of reckoning allowed. Masaryk had adopted this law of averages for the past four years in the great game of international politics. "The choice of means," he wrote, quite in the spirit of Goethe, "results from the natural bent of our own character, which has been moulded for the most part by ourselves."

He must have been overwhelmed by the force of this fabulous career through which he had passed. Those steadily flowing tides that had borne his life onwards as if in a dream engulfed the memory of smaller voices and made it impossible for him to recall the various steps he had taken and the pronouncements he had made. And so once again he must have realized that the life of even the most out-and-out realist is but the weaving of a fabric in fulfilment of a plan already fashioned by some controlling Mind.

8

In approaching the study of Masaryk's character a monumental simplicity presents itself. He may be compared with some natural spring over which a double vault has been built. From all directions there is free entrance. But the spring itself lies hidden. He who lives there, however, has a free outlook on all sides and keeps guard over the spring. This spring is his religion, in the natural sense of that word—that is to say, the bond that unites us with God, Nature or Providence. It is faith in an ordered plan of the universe of which we are a part. Masaryk has repeatedly asserted the postulate: *Jesus, not Cæsar.* But he speaks always of Jesus and never of Christ. Although he looks upon his own life as predestined, yet, to use his own words, he "repudiates the charge of fatalism absolutely and categorically." From this profound feeling the three main lines of his character are developed in a natural way, his thought and his conduct and his sympathy.

Love of one's neighbour, which is the active feature of his faith, is for him practically the same as democracy. But it is a muscular democracy which he formulates as follows, in the spirit of a healthy, militant and bold personality: "Aristocracy is a natural thing. Each one of us wants to be boss. We are all aristocrats. We are still far from being logical and practical democrats, not only on the platform but also in everyday life. My socialism is simply love of my neighbour—humanity. The aim of that socialism is to better the lot of humanity through the agency of law and order. If this is what is meant by socialism then I am a socialist."

From this human sympathy his thought is fed and from his thought his conduct springs. Therefore his words develop into acts and his conduct is always directed towards the help of humanity. Because he rejects all dogmas and parties and programmes, his thought is free to follow his own instinct and he is directed by the circumstances of each case that he has to deal with here and now. Really, therefore, all his thought has emerged from circumstances as all great poetry does, according to Goethe's definition. Thus it is that his positive opinions about women and their place in the state have been moulded by the example of his wife. And his negative opinions about the church have evolved from what he has experienced in his own circle and from the struggle in which he himself has fought for the rights of his people.

That is the foundation on which his character has been built. In it we have the love of humanity balanced by practical realism and sentiment balanced by sound reason; or rather he has learned to balance these because at a very early stage he realized his own particular danger and he struggled hard to gain the mastery of his own equilibrium. "I do not drink at all," he says, "because otherwise I might drink too much." Ambition and vanity, which have spoiled the game of life for so many men, have always been held under control. For this reason he could shuffle the cards with an easier hand. His features show two main trends; discrimination and kindness, on the one hand; tolerance and judgment, on the other.

His character is so rich in kindliness and goodness and help for others that it would be superfluous to give examples. In the days of his childhood his father and the other servants in the Emperor's castles were changed around every two years, so that they could not possibly organize plots against their masters. Masaryk now changes his servants to and fro between one place and another every two months. But he does it in a different way and for a different reason. Those who are in the city are sent to the country and vice versa; so that each in turn may enjoy the pure air and tranquillity of the forests. Sometimes a cinema is erected in the dining room at Lany. On these occasions the President and his staff and the servants and the soldiers who are not actually on duty sit together for the performance. His secretary and his typist are constantly praising his goodness and patience. To a criminal who had been condemned to death he wrote a long letter explaining the reasons why the sentence had to be carried out. He will force his ideas of reform on nobody and he is never dogmatic. The man who claims to be infallible in his judgments, Masaryk says, is merely a half-educated person.

And yet nobody has ever criticized this man as being sentimental or weak. He is a democrat who holds that "in war and generally in practical life one leader is better than a dozen." But he says that this cannot be laid down as a rule for normal times. This pacifist is opposed to the teaching of Tolstoi and Gandhi on passive resistance. Although he speaks disapprovingly of war, he holds that war is justified in the defence of liberty. He is a man of faith who is opposed to every form of deification, whether it be of idols or of opinions. When one puts an abstract question to him he likes to start his answer in some such way as this: "Not so long ago there was a practical case of this." The romantic hunger of his soul is satisfied by the continual reading of novels. But in his own life he values nothing so highly as clearly-reasoned thought leading to a corresponding line of action. He observes realities as he finds them and generally begins his description of a character by first delineating the physical features, sometimes the facial characteristics. The clarity of his handwriting has hardly changed at all during the past sixty years.

As a result of this quality of clarity one is struck by the absence of emotion. Wherever the fire of it happens for a moment to shine through he covers it immediately with a quieting gesture. He never uses superlatives in his speech and rarely in his writing, and only seldom does a philosophical expression flit across the clear line of his practical talk. There is a mechanical simplicity about the pattern of his style. He cannot suffer stupidity and often says of So-and-so curtly: "That's a stupid fellow." Immorality and human corruptibility do not disturb him. His own innocence of mind is so striking that when he used to sit in the Vienna cafés even the most vulgar-tongued person in the conversation would feel it an insult to use careless or shady language. And yet there is not the slightest hint of the goody-goody moralist in his nature or manner.

He is unable to show his feelings openly and he does not think it prudent to do so. Throughout the five hundred pages of his memoirs only ten pages are devoted to himself and the analysis that he makes there is quite fragmentary because he is hindered by his own natural shyness. The outstanding achievements in his life's struggle he states in subordinate sentences such as: "When the Republic was proclaimed in Prague on November 14th and I was elected President." Writing of his return to Bohemia he says: "Those who came home were in tears and even the earth was kissed." But he does not say who came home in tears or by whom the earth was kissed. He is looked upon as the spiritual father of Benes and between these two there is the most profound affection. Benes was not able to be in Prague when Masaryk returned there in triumph. When Benes was to arrive several months afterwards Masaryk sent other ministers to the platform of the railway station to receive him; but he was afraid to trust his own feelings to the light of day and the eyes of the public. So he awaited Benes in a dark waiting-room where nobody could witness the emotion of the first greetings.

To this suppression of his feelings, which is a consequence of his love for reality and his consideration for human nature, we may trace his lack of interest in artistic things. "Since I was sixteen years old," he told me, "I wanted to write a novel and that wish remained with me until quite recently. I wanted it to be something like *Fiction and Reality*—life in the concrete. But I did not have the courage to go on with it. I can tell a man intimate things face to face but I cannot promulgate such things broadcast. So I burned what I had written." Though over eighty years of age, he answers the most important questions by saying: "I don't know—I think—I really don't know." He loves the reality of truth more than its form. Such a man will not be attracted by the appeal of Art. But because his unemotional nature must have something to counterbalance it he seeks that counterbalance in laughter.

His humour is never jocular or cynical. It is neither bitter nor sweet. It is like his way of looking at human nature. It is a sort of provocative humour of which one can never be certain when it plays silently on his face. Probably this has some relation to his peasant extraction. But it must also have been born with him as an individual. And when I look steadily into the features of his mother I realize how the same provocative smile must have lurked behind and barely suggested itself on that firm-set face with the clear eyes.

This is the trait that gives him his power of unconsciously influencing those with whom he comes in contact. And he has made the most of these natural gifts in his struggle with the world. "A word put in at the right time," he says "or an anecdote will often have a bigger influence than a political treatise." As President he has the knack of getting on smoothly with those ministers whom he does not like but who owe their positions to the fact that they are members of the dominant party. Within the past fifteen years as head of the state he has on several occasions shown how he can assert his disagreement with a policy he does not like and yet not come into conflict with its sponsors. He often does this through the medium of a newspaper interview which is meant for the eyes of one reader or one small group. Often when he has to refuse a request he takes care to prove to the applicant that in reality the granting of the request would serve no useful purpose whatsoever.

When he enters a room his presence is felt at once. He does not open with a greeting. He first blinks a little as he looks at the visitor. If he does not find the visitor a sympathetic character, he will treat him courteously. But if he likes him at first glance, then he is at once enthusiastic and spontaneous in his manner and talk. The strong personal influence exercised by this eighty-year-old man who does not care at all for any kind of ceremonial arises from the fact that the possession of political power over his fellow men has not altered him in the least. For a long eighty years he has looked everybody he met straight in the face, as human being to human being. His strength of character and personal charm give him a certain dignity which without any expression whatsoever, either commendatory or otherwise, puts those with whom he comes in contact immediately on their best behaviour. If you look at a photograph of him conversing with farmers of his own age, you will realize at once that there is here a union of the spirit such as no other European statesman who has risen from the proletariat possesses.

Abraham Lincoln is about the only historical figure with whom I can compare him. Both rose to presidential rank from the common people. Though interested in politics at an early age, these men did not actually give their minds to the business of politics as such until late in life. Each worked his way upwards from the ranks of the people through consciousness of moral rectitude which no opponent ever called into question. Both possessed a large-minded sense of humour. And both were lean and bony, great outdoor men, hungering always for the fresh air.

Over Lincoln's mind, however, there hovered a cloud of melancholy from his youth onwards. He was never able to dispel this and the hesitancy with which he faced every emergency accounts largely for the manner of his death. Masaryk overcomes small difficulties by laughing at them. The great difficulties he overcomes by faith. He has an undying trust in Providence. And this subjective trust itself affords him a protection which Lincoln never had. "When I was a little girl," said his daughter to me once, "I rushed during a thunderstorm into my father's study because I felt that there the lightning could do me no harm." Over two years ago the same insane Russian who shot the French President afterwards approached Masaryk's car with the idea of assassinating him. He proffered a book as a feint to cover the gesture of raising the revolver. But in the act of doing so, as he confessed later, he was so struck by the friendly look in Masaryk's eyes that he could not possibly lift the weapon with which he had meant to shoot. Perhaps Lincoln, who was shot from behind by an actor, might have saved his own life if he could have given that same kind of frank and trusting look.

9

For me Masaryk is a figure of Goethian stature. His natural attitude of wonder and admiration, his enduring sense of thankfulness, the broad sweep of his mind, his practical wisdom, the inquiring spirit and his untiring activity—this whole sphere in which action springs from thought as naturally as the spearhead from the shaft is quite Goethian. Goethe loved characters of this type. Zelter, whom Goethe called a Promethean man, was such a character. And so it was natural that the career of this man, which I have tried to sketch in outline here, should harmonize with Goethe's belief in a directing Providence, an ordered plan which he speaks of in an early letter as "The beloved invisible Thing that guides and protects me and which never asked him whether or when." Masaryk's life is a brilliant example of the extraordinary way in which fate moulds a character on a definite plan, just this way and no other. The deeds of such a character respond to the demands made of it; but these demands are made by Providence at the necessary and fitting time to be fulfilled by this character because they are not demanded of and could not be fulfilled by any other. The epitaph which the Athenians carved on the tomb of Zeno the philosopher might be taken as a fitting motto to write at the head of Masaryk's biography: His life was the perfect fulfilment of his teaching.

The story of Masaryk's career seems to contradict some of the fundamental political axioms of our time. For he belonged to no party and he never designed a new badge, a new kind of flag or invented a slogan in the struggle which he waged successfully for the founding of a new state. His story proves that the study of philosophy and the accomplishment of a first-class education do not hinder, but help, the statesman. It proves also that it is not necessary to be a man of burning sympathies and heroic action in order to influence and move the multitude. Only simple faith is necessary. It proves further that neither money nor power is indispensable in raising and directing a revolution. And finally Masaryk's career proves that even in our day politics can be carried on in accordance with sound ethical principles and that a man of moral integrity need not muffle the voice of conscience when he takes over political control of the state.

Our children will read in their history books of the bloodlust and tyranny that have characterized the political movements of our time. But in that dismal narrative they will find one brilliant exception which may possibly be related to them in some such form as this:

Once upon a time the Emperor had a farm servant who was a serf. But the son of the serf went to school and learned philosophy. He sojourned in the big cities and came to know how his nation was kept in slavery. And when he had grown so old as to be in that stage of existence wherein bodily and mental powers generally begin to wane he rose up and went wandering round the world. He rallied kings to war, overturned the Old Empire and founded an independent state for his own people over whom he ruled wisely and long even unto a very advanced age.

BRIAND

THE FRENCH EUROPEAN

BRIAND

THE FRENCH EUROPEAN

As THE traveller passes through Brittany he notices everywhere the prevalence of thick hedges which divide the peasant holdings from one another and incidentally make it impossible for the wayfarer to get an open view of the landscape. This particular characteristic is an expression of the inborn French desire for seclusion, which is further emphasized in this northern sea-girt province by the natural reticence of the seafaring folk, the enveloping fog and the everlasting beat of the surf on the coast. Even the din and rush of an industrial city like Nantes have not altered the exclusive habits of the natives. These Bretons are Celts and as such they are blood relations of their neighbours in the British Isles.

Briand was born here in 1862. From his father's side he had a peculiar mixture of blood in his veins. For though belonging to the poorer classes the father was descended from the local nobility. Briand's mother was a washerwoman. Three elements, therefore, were combined in him—the peasant, the feudal aristocrat and the Breton. And when these elements became transmuted into a statesman, the composite result was bound to be a remarkable kind of statesman, unique indeed among his colleagues. The man who emerged from this amazing mixture of

strains held the reins of power longer than most of his contemporaries in Europe and probably his work will prove to
have been a more determining influence than theirs.

His Celtic origin gave him the dreamy and rather beautiful
blue eyes of the sailor. From the same source he inherited his
liking for country life, his shrinking from society and his spirit
of opposition to rule. From his peasant forbears came the stoop-
ing figure, the heavy shock of hair on the head and the hairy
hands, together with a certain instinctive shrewdness that is
characteristic of the peasant nature. From his bourgeois stock
he inherited his corpulence and his habit of taking things easy.
From the plebeian ancestry came his desire for universal human
betterment and his sureness of touch in dealing with the masses.
But he had the hands of an aristocrat and an unusually cultured speaking voice, which has often been compared to a
violoncello. He had the composure of the aristocrat and the
sensitive touch of a diplomat of the old school.

Although this kind of analysis cannot pretend to account for
the whole man, it will help to lessen our surprise at the versatile
qualities which he manifested during his career. For though we
know that most men are complex in their nature we do not
ordinarily feel that complexity in them; but when they rise to
an exalted public position we become amazed at the contradictions which manifest themselves, in contrast to the apparently
simpler characters of everyday folk.

Briand was naturally lazy. He liked nothing better than sitting
in a rowboat, eating with common people, drinking and smoking, colloguing with pretty women and talking with the dogs
he met by chance. This rustic recluse who liked the good things
of life had his genius awakened and organized by the urge of
his innate ambition to struggle for justice and moral right
against a mass of intriguing forces. And he succeeded in over-
coming them through his typically French gift of eloquence.

Some ideas which he championed in youth and laid aside at
middle age were taken up again at a later date with more determination than ever. His qualities may best be summed up
under the word: Tolerance. Everything he worked for and
accomplished was successful because he knew how to be patient
and considerate. During all the class struggles, racial conflicts,
national rivalries and religious controversies in which he took
a hand he always tried to effect a fair balance and to lift the
minds of his fellow protagonists above the merely national and
temporary contradictions of the hour to the higher and broader
humanitarian outlook of the eighteenth century.

His technique was never that of the man who says: I want
so-and-so to be done and it must be done. This man with the
pleasing musical voice generally preferred to say: We ought to
do this. Or sometimes he asked: Can we not do this? His sober
temperament made him a good loser who strove hard for power
but did not hold on to it with passionate obstinacy, and always
relinquished it before being forced to do so. A good winner is
much rarer than a good loser; but Briand always proved himself
a good winner, because he sympathized with the beaten party
and because his sensitive nature gave him a profound feeling for
the common welfare. Therefore he could bring his mind and
heart to work in harmony. And so he was always able to win
without wounding and to lose without complaint.

This man whom nobody ever saw running or in a hurry,
who seldom got angry, and who was spared through a happy
bent of character from the danger of making sudden decisions,
was often led by his easy-going nature and wide sympathy into
giving way too much in difficult negotiations. The result was
that he sometimes had to take back in writing what he had
agreed to during word-of-mouth discussions.

In speaking to the crowd, however, his fearlessness and oratorical gifts invariably triumphed. For Briand was above all

things an artist, who listened, learned and acted, as children and women do, without system and according to instinct. And, like a clever woman, he preferred to circumnavigate an obstacle rather than attempt to steer through it. Since most, and certainly the best, of his ideas came to him on the spur of the moment and as a result of his faith in his own flair, even when he held the highest and most responsible positions he had the reputation of being an improviser. His conduct certainly gave that impression. Such a type of statesman is not easily tolerated by the machinery of state, especially in France. Yet no other country would have endured Briand so long and given him such a high place.

"You are a good man," he said to Anatole France when they were first introduced.

"I am not good at all," replied France. "I always have sympathy and nothing more, and the result is that I am often deceived. But you are a good man."

"M. Briand is a good man too," said the third party who had introduced the two men and who recently told me the story. "He is only human and nothing more."

Briand bowed to the compliment and laughed. He took his departure with a merry phrase on his lips; for though he never liked to be praised on the score of his success, it always pleased him to find his good-heartedness appreciated.

2

He had a photograph taken when he was sixteen years old. In that picture he appears to be a very handsome boy with long hair and narrow eyes like a sensitive young poet, more of a prince than a plebeian, something between Mendelssohn and Chopin. In the evenings when he was summoned into his modest little home and the neighbours endearingly called him Aristide nobody then thought how aptly he had been named or how he would one day deserve to be compared with the great prototype who originally bore that name, the Greek Aristides. At school he did not learn very quickly or easily. He told me once that his teacher used to go walking with him every Sunday during the whole summer and persistently impressed this precept on the mind of the boy: "Make friends with the animals and the plants and learn from Nature. Nobody ever became wise through reading." "I took that lesson to heart," he told me, "and I have never read anything during my whole life." Of course, he was exaggerating a bit. But all that he knew had been learned from intercourse with others and, as he possessed a very strong reproductive imagination, he was able to select from conversations and experiences what his instinct told him to be of value. This he could always revitalize for his own use. That is the chief explanation of his success.

It was through the teacher I have mentioned that Jules Verne came to know Aristide Briand as a boy. The novelist took him as the model for one of his characters. In depicting a group of boys who were shipwrecked on a desert island there is one whom he named Briant and whom he described as follows:

"He was not a worker but he was very intelligent. He was often at the tail end of his class but he could make his way to the front when he set himself to do it. He was venturesome, enterprising, pugnacious, but at the same time agreeable, good-hearted and easy-going. He preached tolerance and conciliation. 'I shall not forbid anything to anybody,' he said when they were in straits in the island; 'but if each acts for the good of us all no one will have to appeal to the leader when he wishes something done that ought to be done.' "

For three years Briand acted as a public scrivener in Paris, writing letters from dictation at some street corner or other in the Latin Quarter. When people came to him afterwards and asked for his autograph he would generally say: "There are lots of them to be had over there in the shop."

Eventually he became a Doctor of Laws and went into practice as a barrister. It was here that he discovered his oratorical gifts and this apparently was the circumstance that induced him to take up politics. Anyhow it was his gift of oratory that kept him in politics so long. At the age of thirty he appeared for the first time before a critical audience at a Socialist congress in Marseilles and immediately established his reputation as a first-class orator.

Why did he make his entry into public life as a Socialist? Jaurès, the other great orator of the day, was three years older than Briand. The study of philosophy had convinced him of the truth of the Socialist teaching and made him an enthusiastic advocate of the Socialist cause. Briand arrived at the same conclusion because he happened to be the son of poor parents and to have been brought up amid the rush and confusion of a manufacturing city; but he had never studied the doctrinal side of socialism. His isolated and bohemian character was not calculated to lead him towards the final acceptance of a doctrinal position on its own merits. His indignation over an unjust verdict given against him at a trial was also a contributing force in urging him to join the ranks of the revolutionaries; for he was found guilty of a youthful indiscretion against what was called public modesty and barred for some time from practice in the law courts.

"Yes, I was an anarchist," he said to me in reply to some questions, "in the sense that I could not be forced to take orders from any school. Karl Marx's brother-in-law once got so angry over this that he shouted at me: *I'll write you a book on the eco-*

nomic principles on which the dogma of the Immaculate Conception is based."

In one of his few articles, written when he was twenty-two, he asked: "Will the future revolution be a bloody one, like those that have gone before? I do not think so. I believe it will fall from the trees like ripe fruit." That is the reason why he never promulgated the necessity of a revolution, even when he stood on a table in his shirt-sleeves and talked to the workmen. But he always believed that a general strike would be effective. In one of his later speeches he said: "I firmly believe that the general strike will bring the revolution. Of course a lot will depend on whether the public have the will to carry it through. The general strike will strengthen the self-confidence of the working classes. At the same time we must allow for human weakness. A man does not go into a revolution with a light heart. He must be ready to ignore the tears and prayers of wife and children. Very many conflicting considerations hamper him from rushing into the street at the call of the revolution."

There is only one political field in which Briand remained an irreconcilable protagonist from youth onwards. He was always against war. His tolerant, humane, rustic and animal-loving nature made him hate all military people and especially the generals. He never did military service himself. He joined the political group that was against militant nationalism and this naturally led him to champion the idea of working for a union of all the nations. It was for this reason, and not as a believer in the struggle of the classes, that he remained a Socialist all his life. His friend, Hervé, who volunteered for service in 1914, had publicly advocated desertion from the ranks twenty years before. At that time Briand defended him in court. In his speech for the defence he exclaimed: "If we receive the command to fire on an enemy whom we do not recognize as such we shall reverse arms forthwith."

He worked for several years as a barrister and then was appointed Deputy. He practised journalism on the staffs of *Lanterne* and *Humanité*; but he read little and took life easy. When his friends shut him up in an editorial office in order to make him write a leading article and returned an hour later they found him enveloped in an Olympian cloud of tobacco smoke with nothing written. He invariably left everything to the last minute, whether it was a question of passing the article of another writer for the press or writing captions. During his whole life Briand wrote about as little as he read.

3

When he entered the Chamber of Deputies at the age of forty all France was in turmoil over the conflict between church and state. Who would nominate the bishops and who would limit their control in education? That was the question at issue. Separation of church and state had been a plank in the programme of all the radical parties for over a generation. Thirteen hundred years earlier the problem would have been much easier to solve; for then the King simply ordered the Bishop of Saintes, who had been appointed without the royal consent, to be thrown into a wagonful of thorns and transported out into the country. For over a thousand years the struggle for and against the church had been a dominating factor in the history of France. Even Napoleon had to yield to the power of the church and agree to a concordat. And now once again, in the year 1903, the question of an episcopal appointment had broken out anew.

Briand was an atheist, like most of the Socialists. But he believed in the God of Nature. He at once recognized the importance of the church-and-state conflict and saw that the situation afforded possibilities for a statesman to win his laurels.

"It was pure accident," he said to me, "that first led me to attack this question. I only knew that here was a point at which the Republic was seriously threatened, and I naturally wished to consolidate its stability. It was necessary to put an end to the situation by passing some kind of law."

Did he turn to study the history of the question, with the various acts and documents that concerned it? Did he pull the hat down over his eyes when he passed a priest? What course did he take, this man who wanted to keep the Church outside the sphere of political power? He went out to the parish priests in the country districts. He drank with the oldest abbés their still older wine. He looked up Protestants and Jews. He gathered members of the different religious persuasions around one table after another and heard them discuss their respective points of view. "In four weeks," he declared, "I learned more in the countryside and in the small towns than during four years in Parliament." So he arrived at the formulation of certain proposals that hurt nobody very much and finally resulted in the kind of amicable compromise which every great lawyer aims at. What did it matter if the writings of some dilettante historian proved that the Capet dynasty had been changed for the Carlovingian dynasty or if a Pope who died in 1216 had a quarrel with a King who was not born until 1288? Though it cannot be claimed that he actually saved his country, he certainly consolidated the Republic and he was justified in stating during the course of his famous Périgueux speech that he was a staunch and devoted Frenchman.

The success of his plan for the conciliation of church and state transformed him from a party politician into a statesman. When he was nominated Minister of Education and Worship, so that his law might be carried into effect, Briand as a Socialist

was faced with the question whether or not he should accept
office in a bourgeois Cabinet. Here was a turning-point and he
faced it as such. Would he remain in the party or go over to
the government, would he stay with the Opposition for the sake
of a theoretical principle or would he take over political power?
The old dilemma, which had to be faced by a British Labour
Leader later on, now confronted this forty-three-year-old proletarian. It would be futile to try to measure how large a part
ambition played in determining his final decision. In Parisian
society at that time Socialists did not live cut away from members of the bourgeois parties, although they had sworn to cut
each other's throats. Today almost all the oldest bourgeois ministers in France were formerly Socialists. The personal bent of
Briand's character was not in the revolutionary direction—considering the revolution here under the Socialist aspect of the
struggle of the classes—and so it was not difficult for him to
break with his old political associates. Seven years after he had
delivered a scathing philippic against Millerand for having taken
office in a bourgeois Cabinet, he himself did the same.

"Do you know what I did?" he said to me when I asked him
how he came to settle with his own conscience. "I could not
remain in the party and I could not leave the party all of a
sudden. So I went on furlough from the party and I have been
on furlough ever since." Then he looked straight ahead into
the distance and said in a low voice: "Yes, that was a difficult
moment."

If he had read the philosophers, Emerson's dictum might have
come to his aid: "A foolish consistency is the hobgoblin of little
minds."

Yet this precarious step which brought him into the Cabinet
and therewith into the midst of those who were the enemies of
his youth soon led to a difficult situation. As a Socialist had he
not called upon the teaching profession to organize a trade

union of their own, even though such an act was illegal? And now as minister he had to dismiss the leaders of this movement from their positions as teachers.

But something worse happened. When the railway strike of 1910 began Briand used his political power to force the strikers back to their jobs. He read in *L'Humanité* how the leaders of the trades union were arrested and escorted away from the very halls where he himself had so often spoken and written in favour of the strike. At that time his best friends left him. And Painlevé, who at a later date became a close colleague of his in the Government, was then so hostile that for several years he refused to recognize Briand whenever the two passed in the street or elsewhere. But after the strike ended in the defeat of the workers Briand exclaimed, with a sweeping gesture from the Speaker's tribune: "Look at my hands? There is no blood on them."

About this time Briand gave up his gypsy habit of whiling away most of his time in the cafés and at card tables. He now moved to a respectable quarter of the city where he made quite a hit in the salons through the charm of his unconventional manner and dress. In his own inner nature he remained what he always had been. His happiest moments were those in which he pulled off the starched linen collar and city clothes, and donned a flannel shirt and sports suit, to escape from the din of social chatter in Paris to a little farm in the neighbourhood where he could rest and vegetate and recuperate in that kind of idyllic seclusion so dear to the Breton. The change in his political attitude must have been germinating for a long time in the subsoil of his mind, for it is obviously the voice of conscience that is speaking in his repeated outbreaks of self-justification.

The first time, for instance, that he spoke as Premier in the Chamber of Deputies, he said: "It will not be expected of me that because life and the responsibilities of government have taught me a different lesson I should therefore abandon the principles which I once held and stoutly defended. When a political or social theory which is excellent in itself comes before my mind the problem that interests me most is how far the theory can be carried out in practice. I want to see ideas carried through and brought to reality in the realm of concrete fact. We want to govern, which means that we must maintain the prerogatives of government unimpaired. We want all citizens and their affairs to hold their proper places in the community." Twelve years later he said: "In every Government there are men whose previous speeches and writings may be cited against them. In my youth I too held hot-headed opinions but I have always had a sense of responsibility towards the institutions of State. I am like a stone that has been for a long time in running water. It has lost many of its corners but has maintained its original shape."

I once asked one of Briand's friends, who is still a leading Socialist, what he thought when Briand left the Socialist ranks. The friend answered: "We were then faced with the fact that Germany was arming for war and in such circumstances a general strike would have jeopardized the independence of France. At that time I did not know what Briand officially knew; but if I did, I should have acted as he did. And today are we not in the same position?"

4

Between 1909 and 1930 Briand became Prime Minister eleven times and was twelve times Minister of Foreign Affairs. Besides

these posts he was Minister of Justice and held other Cabinet
positions also. Like Bismarck, he exercised power with the co-
operation of both Left and Right. It was easier for him, however, than for Bismarck because there are many different parties
in France that can be shuffled and regrouped in all sorts of
ways. In America or in Great Britain he would have been lost
amid the clear-cut divisions between the two or three big parties.
It is true that Briand collaborated in the founding of a party but
he had no binding affiliations with it. He always remained a
free lance, which explains how he survived the coming and
going of parties and turned up repeatedly at the head of new
combinations with his political vitality refreshed.

Only a soloist of his quality could play in one orchestra or
another equally and take the part of either the first violin or
the conductor. Only a man of highly imaginative intelligence
could keep on holding the reins of power among party men
who are constantly regrouping themselves in one political section after another. And it needed a man of his fine feeling for
the gist of a situation to be able always to save his own name
and prestige in the vicissitudes of party government. He has
been called the field marshal of political meetings, a genius at
arranging the agenda and the best navigator in France. Because
he could bring elements from the various parties into a working
combination he was a first-class leader in a coalition Cabinet.
And since he ploughed his furrow alone, and never committed
himself to the teamwork of a colleague, he escaped the consequences of decisions which his colleagues made. His political
associates always appreciated and honoured his remarkable abilities and the high respect in which he was held by them made
it possible for him to take up the reins of government so often
and hold them so long.

His freedom from outer affiliations had a big influence even
on his opponents. A man who loved nature and conserved his

mental and physical powers by living as much as possible in the country could not easily be tempted with honours and not at all with bribes. His carelessness, in the literal sense of that word, was the chief factor that brought him power. "It is a shame that my fishing holiday will have to be cut short so abruptly," he once said in the Chamber. "The moment a man becomes Premier all the fish go over to the Opposition."

Since Briand was not a good negotiator and never had an exact knowledge of his subject, he had to depend for success on his gift of eloquence. I heard him speak at Geneva and in the Paris Chamber of Deputies and at a table where a hundred people were present, and I was astonished at the simplicity and ease with which he invariably opened his discourses. There was nothing theatrical about him and yet he showed himself a perfect actor. As a speaker he had no pose and sometimes secured his best effects through a simple gesture with the arm or head, so naturally done that one imagined it must have been a habit of his since he was a child.

Poincaré once said that Briand was a strategist in the use of language. By this he meant that Briand had the art of concentrating his strongest forces against the weakest point of the enemy's front. He did not operate on a plan thought out beforehand, for he was one of the few public speakers who rely on their instinctive grasp of the situation and on their powers of seeing directly into the mind of the audience, never allowing themselves to be carried away by the catch phrases of the hour. At Geneva, before the representatives of fifty nations, he used to speak in a very different manner from that which he adopted in the Palais Bourbon before five hundred Frenchmen. He had still another manner of approach to his subject and presentation of it when speaking at a mass meeting before five or six thousand Frenchmen. Yet he did not speak pure French. And one of Briand's former colleagues, Albert Thomas, who is justly renowned for his brilliant style, once tried to demonstrate to me the number of grammatical mistakes contained in a certain speech Briand had made. But the argument made no impression on me. Of course, Briand's speeches were much more effective when spoken than when one reads them in cold print. This is not wholly due to the famous light-and-shade of his voice, which recalled the rich colour tones in a Rembrandt painting.

I once said to him: "People say of you that you speak without preparation and that no one has ever seen a sheet of paper in your hand. But have you not the plan of the speech prearranged in your head?"

"No."

"Don't you prepare even the opening paragraph or at least the first sentence?"

"No."

"Then what ideas have you in your mind when you start?"

"The goal of the argument. Listen. Most politicians spoil their utterances because they are thinking either of posterity or of the newspapers. The truth is that a speech cannot be prepared beforehand. Everything depends on the mood of the moment. I always look my audience in the face. If I see a single yawn I change the argument. Do you understand? Then if the person becomes attentive again I notice it in his eyes. When I am sufficiently acquainted with my subject matter I have a dozen different arguments at hand. If one of them does not work or does not work on everybody, then I try another and still another until I get a better effect. The whole point is never to allow your audience to become weary even for a moment. If you do you are lost."

Briand was also an adept at telling a story, which is a gift that few orators possess. At lunch one day I heard him tell stories about his own life for two hours on end and yet no one of the sixteen persons at the table felt that Briand wished to dominate the conversation. Since I was the only outsider among that group of Frenchmen, and sat next to Briand, his stories were manifestly meant for me. For that reason he chose the war as the background of his tales and with great delicacy he selected certain episodes to make it clear that France was not governed by a race of supermen at that time. Trusting to my own sense of propriety, he risked one or two anecdotes which could be excellently utilized by the German nationalists today if I were to divulge them here.

5

The position which a leading statesman has to fill in time of war is always critical. Because he is rarely, like Napoleon was, head of the State and head of the army at one and the same time, the execution of his plans depends on hands and brains which he is officially barred from controlling. No prime minister can be sure of himself when he dismisses a general. When one general suffers a defeat his rival colleagues shout for his dismissal. But what guaranty can a statesman have that the one he nominates to the vacant position will do better than the unsuccessful predecessor? In the last resort the prime minister bears the responsibility for battles that are won or lost hundreds of miles away through the ability or incompetency of professional soldiers.

When Briand became head of the French Government in 1915 he brought all his level-headedness into play at that critical juncture. Though passionately opposed to the military group and to war, he had protested against the removal of the Government to Bordeaux during the Battle of the Marne, although he was not then head of the Government. And he was the first to return to Paris. During his time in office as War Premier, Briand devised a new plan for the Allies. Since Germany was the strongest of the adversaries he put forward the idea that a weaker adversary should be attacked first and defeated. Thus he originated the scheme of assembling a new army at Salonika, and after the Dardanelles adventure had so dismally failed, of attacking Turkey, Bulgaria and Austria through Greece. That was the only strategic plan drawn up during the war by a statesman. Consequently the French generals were opposed to it, and so was Kitchener. In military circles it was dubbed the "Balkan Adventure."

But Briand, hater of the military leaders, and hated by them, tried tooth and nail to put through his plan, only to be laughed at by the so-called experts as a dilettante. It was this plan and the failure of the French offensive in 1917 that brought about his downfall from power.

But his plan was carried out soon afterwards. When finally it led to the victory over Balkan adversaries and indirectly over Austria, Briand was in Paris, dismissed from power, disgruntled and unable to have any decisive influence whatsoever on the direction which events were taking.

More than that. Clemenceau threatened him with impeachment on the charge that he wanted to cut short the war and had seemed willing to enter into a very unsafe and indirect way of treating with the enemy. But the truth is that Clemenceau did not have the grounds to go on with such a charge simply because Briand's native cautiousness and foresightedness had forestalled him. So carefully had he considered the whole question of the negotiations to which Clemenceau referred at a later date that the radicals today blame him for having espoused the cause of peace too half-heartedly on that occasion, whereas Caillaux took the risk without thinking of the consequences and was thrown into prison as a result.

"And yet," I said, "your adversaries were right that time; for what security would have been guaranteed to them by that peace of understanding which our friends in Germany were then working for as hard as you were working for it here?"

"Would the Kaiser not have gone?" he said, quite naïvely. The best brains in France at that time knew so little of the German character that some believed the Kaiser would be dismissed by his own people and that thus the way to a reasonable peace would have been cleared.

Briand had two enemies at that period. One was hidden; the other was in the open. The hidden one was Poincaré, with whom he had to collaborate. "Poincaré knows everything and understands nothing. Briand knows nothing and understands everything." That was a popular saying in Paris. But it was only half true.

A member of Briand's wartime cabinet once said to me: "Often during a cabinet meeting Poincaré was disgusted at the ignorance of his Prime Minister in regard to some official report or other. But Briand remained perfectly cool, read the despatch and altered his views accordingly." Poincaré was as different from Briand as Lorraine is from Brittany. Poincaré was a stickler for scholarly exactitude. He had a well-stored mind, but he was pedantic, legalitarian and utterly lacking in imagination. Briand was full of surprises, unsystematic, dreamy and relying chiefly on the imaginative powers of his mind.

Clemenceau was his enemy in the open. Day after day he sat in his editorial office devising one charge after another and launching it in his paper for the purpose of bringing about the downfall of his old enemy. He rushed at the refined and mobile Briand as a bull rushes at a toreador. This was a duel between

a natural hater and a natural lover, between a malicious misan-
thrope and a lover of humanity.

And yet these two had one quality in common. During the
closing years of the war Clemenceau showed tremendous courage and inspired the whole of France with the same spirit. In
this respect Briand did practically the same. During the Battle
of Verdun he bore the terrible responsibility of the situation
with extraordinary fortitude and saved those around him from
giving way to doubt and despair. Nobody would have expected
this quality in such an inveterate hater of war.

Only the results were different. Clemenceau was a physical
force man and born to war. He would sup revenge to the
dregs of his enemy's skull, like a primitive cave dweller. His
conception of peace was based on the theory that the human
spirit remains incorrigible and that no abiding system of peace
could be hoped for in Europe. But in that hour of destiny Briand
saw another way into the future. Ten years after the Battle of
Verdun he was speaking of himself in the third person when
he said in the Chamber of Deputies: "The man who then held
the precarious honour of public responsibility was so filled with
horror by the spectacle of such terrible slaughter that he took
an oath upon his conscience that if victory were won and if
chance ever again brought him into office, he would devote all
his efforts and his whole life to the cause of peace and the pre-
vention of such slaughter in the future."

Thus the actual spectacle of war made Briand hate war even
more profoundly than he had hated it before. His visit to the
fighting front could not help making a pacifist of this man who
had been a humanitarian since his youth, and who now clearly
recognized what a futile pack the military generals were. It was
Europe's doom that Clemenceau, and not Briand, drew up the
terms of peace. At that time Briand was forced to remain in
the background in Paris and allow what was going on to go

on without being able to make a single move to influence the course of events.

"I looked upon Wilson," he said to me, "as an honest idealist, but impractical. He placed too much importance on the question of ethnographic frontiers. As a matter of fact, each nation is composed of various races and is held together much more by common historical experiences than by kinship of blood. We French are made up of five or six different racial strains; but danger, defence and destiny have firmly welded us into one nation. The white races in America have been living together for such a short time that their divisions and differences are still clearly discernible, like geological strata. At least, they were such up to the war, but that welded them together somewhat better and strengthened their sense of national unity."

"Yet you would have supported Wilson more firmly than he was actually supported?"

"Undoubtedly, I should have struggled hand in hand with him to secure for the League of Nations those powers which he failed to secure for it and which the League so tragically lacks today. And yet, though it has not those powers, it has done so much that the complaints against it for not doing more are quite unjustified. Has it not actually prevented war on at least two, or perhaps three, occasions? The situation in Manchuria is extraordinary. There you have a country which belongs to one nation, but it is traversed by a railway which belongs to another."

"But don't you believe that every situation which arises is an extraordinary one?"

He laughed at me a little and then said in a low decisive tone: "Nevertheless, the League of Nations has grown stronger."

He had been preaching for fifty years on behalf of the cause which now at last brought him this world renown. What he came to stand for as an aged statesman represented the profoundest convictions which he held as a Socialist and made up almost half of his Socialist programme. He never denied or compromised his anti-chauvinistic, anti-militarist instincts. During war, of course, each nation has to save its own skin. But those who attacked him during the middle years of his career and called him a traitor gave him their fullest respect when they saw his political career crowned with such honourable laurels.

Yet he did not wholly succeed at Locarno or create a United States of Europe. He attacked the situation before him with such enthusiasm and used his imaginative powers so well in constructing his plan that his name has justly become a household word all the world over, like the name of Edison. A character so happy as Briand's generally meets its deserts along its way of life.

Since the Anglo-American guaranty for French security was struck out of the Versailles Treaty, owing to the opposition of Congress, French statesmen—and Briand more than any other —had looked around for a substitute. At the Cannes Conference in the beginning of 1922, when he tried to get an English guaranty of security for France by offering to accede to the English request for a more lenient attitude over German reparations, Poincaré opposed him bitterly and is generally supposed to have brought about his fall from power on that occasion. A few days after the Conference at Cannes he made a speech before the Chamber of Deputies in which he defended his policy. Even his closest friends did not know at the moment whether he meant to remain in office or resign. An expert assured me that Briand improvised his own resignation at this juncture. He listened in his own way, kept his eye on the members, watched their faces, measured the fading volume of their applause and tested the sharpness of their heckling, and then closed his speech suddenly with the statement: "All this would have been my

programme. Since I see that you do not approve of it I resign."
If this interpretation is the right one, it only serves to prove
once again that he always acted on the spur of the moment and
that he was never able to play the part of a Coriolanus.

When he succeeded Herriot as Prime Minister in 1925 he
found among the papers of his predecessor a German document
that had been there since February and that outlined a pact
between Germany, France, Belgium, England and Italy, guaranteeing security against every attack not only to France but
also to Germany. It was complete in all its details. Briand took
it up and put it through at Locarno. The manner in which he
did this, the way he spoke and acted, gave him an historical
right to the title of the Great French Conciliator. It was not
merely the tone of personal responsibility in which he always
said "I," whereas Chamberlain always spoke of "His Majesty's
Government," but rather the natural human note that he struck
which made the milk of human kindness flow. In the fishing
village of Ascona where I live, and where I am writing these
lines, he once said to a German Chancellor: "You are German.
I am French. On that ground we shall have difficulty in understanding each other. But I can be French, and at the same time
a good European, while you can be a German and a good
European. Two good Europeans must needs understand each
other."

Idealists and authors on both banks of the Rhine had been
talking in that spirit for ten years, but no statesman had dared
to talk in the same way. From that day forth the curve of his
sympathies ran upwards and with it his outer manifestation of
them. After the Locarno treaties Briand discovered what
amounted to a new language. "We spoke European," he said
in the Chamber of Deputies, "a new language that will have
to be learned." As the herald of peace returned home and all

Paris greeted him he said to a friend who met him at the railway station: "I have recaptured the days of my youth."

It is quite clear now why Briand, from that day on, fought for the idea of peace with an enthusiasm that was almost fanatic and much stronger than any that inspired the earlier stages of his career. After a long twenty years of wandering, passing many solitary hours rowing and fishing and in searchings of conscience, meditating on what he calls his youthful visions, and on the numerous hostile articles written against him by his former party associates, he now at last discovered the slogan that suited him and determined to use his great authority to extend into the region of concrete fact, far beyond the confines of France, what he had championed forty years before when he stood on the table in his shirt-sleeves: LET THE NATIONS LEARN THE WAY OF UNDERSTANDING ONE ANOTHER AND LET THERE BE NO MORE WAR. The passionate heart beats can almost be heard as he stands on the tribune in the Senate to defend the Locarno treaty against the nationalists.

"What then?" he cried. "For ever? Shall this state of affairs go on for eternity? Must we always have to fear a war between France and Germany? Shall these two nations everlastingly think only of armaments, openly or secretly? Always new wars. And do you call that a future? Go out into our towns. Seek the people in their homes. Speak with our peasants. And everyone in every walk of life will cry out to you: PEACE."

Of the hundreds of letters that Briand received on the occasion of signing the treaties in London, one, which was anonymous, said: "Permit a mother to wish you luck. Now at last I can look at my children without a sense of foreboding. At last I can love them with a feeling of security." Then followed more debates in the Senate and before various commissions. The lazy Briand had to defend himself during a debate that lasted thirty-six hours without interruption. While an attempt was being made to force his resignation the debate reached a climax, just as the morning was dawning. Briand said from the tribune: "I have never looked with fear at that exit door. But today for the first time I cling to power. If you overthrow me today I feel that you will be doing something fatal against our country." His voice was like that of a prophet, its tones on this occasion being deeper and more human than ever before.

In the autumn of 1926, when Germany was about to enter the League of Nations, a flood of articles hostile to Briand appeared in the French nationalist press. While he slept in the train on the way to Geneva, two delegates, one of whom told me the story, were chatting quietly in the corridor by the window. Suddenly there was a crash. The window pane beside them was splintered. Was it an attempt on Briand's life? Should they stop the train? It went on. The following morning they discovered that some rails protruding from a freight train had struck the window. Most of the passengers had rushed out in their night-clothes; but Briand slept on. When the train reached Geneva he asked what it was that had happened during the night, merely in a casual way. He was not in the least anxious at that very critical moment in the carrying out of his great mission. A few days later he said at the meeting in Geneva:

"The epoch of wars between us is gone. Gone are the long mourning veils, with all the suffering which will never again have to be borne by both our nations. Blood will not have to be shed again to settle whatever differences may arise between us. Henceforth there will be a judge to speak the word of justice. Away with the machine guns and the cannons. And let the ground be cleared for understanding, for arbitration and for peace."

A few days later Briand and Stresemann sat at the breakfast table together in Thoiry, near Geneva. Again it was the tone in which he said things that made this meeting historic.

"From many quarters people will try to influence me," he said to the German. "I have been handed documents miles long on Germany's shortcomings. But I throw them all into the corner."

The two leading statesmen of the two so-called historically hostile countries sat down together eight years after the last shot had been fired in the war and chatted together like two poets colloguing about ideals and abstract principles, both convinced and determined that the spirit of goodwill must prevail over all obstacles. That is why the menu cards at a dinner given later on in Geneva had pictures of European statesmen trying to knock down the statue of Mars, but Briand was represented standing beside the war god and making an endeavour to talk him into committing suicide.

That Briand and Stresemann, whose entirely different characters were depicted in the formation of their features as well as in their careers, were able to overcome the impossible and arrive at an understanding, was due solely to the powers of imagination which had transformed both and lifted them above the political ruck into the sphere of constructive statesmanship. The retrospect of this great episode which Stresemann gives in his memoirs is not in the least derogatory of the spirit under which the negotiations were carried on. Of course, almost every politician will have something to say on his side which emphasizes his own position and is calculated to reassure the skeptics in his own country. And it is true that the Thoiry conversations left much unsettled and in doubt. But what human compromise doesn't? Moreover, Stresemann always remained true to the spirit of the social milieu out of which he sprang. He was a member of the German small bourgeoisie. And when he wrote the address of the ex-Crown Prince he was careful to eliminate the "ex."

The fact that one man could bring about such an alteration

in the European outlook simply by his own individual effort and the compelling force of his personality had a rallying effect on the world at large and brought the light of hope to it once again. When the wounded ex-service men from all over the world organized an international mass demonstration in the cause of peace, a blind and armless man—only the torso of a human body—approached Briand and said: "Sir! Sir! Let nothing hinder you in your work. Four or five million men are silent for ever. Here I stand and speak in their name. Go on, sir." When I heard Briand narrating this incident a sort of mist came into the eyes as he recalled the picture of the mutilated man and remembered what he had said; but the mist dispersed quickly and a new light seemed to shine on the face of the narrator.

The pact to outlaw war had already been under consideration before Briand took it up. But it was he who developed the idea. After Kellogg had proposed a bilateral pact between America and France, Briand brought his genius into play by applying another American idea and in so doing he introduced an element of elastic expansion into the pact, so that it might include other nations. In this way he converted it into a proposal to safeguard the interests of France. The pact retained Kellogg's name and America was given full credit for having taken the initiative; but it was Briand who Europeanized the plan. It was a great tactical triumph for him, because it brought to concrete realization his passionate desire to lay the foundations of an abiding European peace, while at the same time it satisfied his keen sense of responsibility for his own country's interests.

From the Locarno's treaties to the project of a United States of Europe was only one step further, at least in principle. Here again Briand was not the inventor of the idea. It was already being canvassed in many quarters. One evening as he was chatting in his free-and-easy way with some journalists, he said:

"No real progress can be made so long as things remain at this stage. Why cannot we have a European Union? We must have it."

"Do you know Europe?" I asked him.

"Just a little," he answered. "There are three people in Germany who have been friends of mine for a long time now. They are working with some success for this idea. But the real vital cells of a United Europe must be the little nations. Look at Austria, whittled down to the bone, and yet Europe can supply it with all that it lacks. What is the significance of the word we use when we speak of a 'great power' nowadays? We have just seen the greatest navy in the world crippled and brought to a standstill by a strike among the sailors [March 1931]. If people could only throw off the incubus of historical memories when they are considering actual conditions! They are always talking with one side of the brain in the grave. When the word French is mentioned they think of Napoleon and the Grand Army; but they forget that we had to suffer a bitter war experience at the hands of two other emperors. You inquire about our army in a skeptic spirit. Have you seen how we have fought two new wars since the World War came to an end? One of those wars was in Morocco and the other in Syria. In this case we had to send out three hundred thousand for the defence of European civilization."

"And just as in the case of world peace," he continued, "the shattered economic system can be reconstructed and consolidated only by international agreement. Capitalism is not dead. It is the management of it that is bad. About forty years ago a sugar crisis occurred. The leaders of this industry from various countries forthwith went into council and agreed to act like reasonable beings and not as slaves to the blind instinct of competition, with the result that the crisis was soon overcome. For the past seven years I have championed and promoted a world-embracing policy. Most politicians realize that they will remain in power only for a short time. Therefore they set for themselves a goal that is close at hand and may be reached easily. With such a goal before their eyes they cannot see far. I have held much the same position for over twenty years and therefore I have been able to practise a long-sighted policy."

"If you are right," I said, "in thinking that the small states will form the vital cells of the new European organism, why don't you establish this Europe from the small nations first and then invite our own two big nations to come in and discuss their differences in the presence of the Union, just as two people who have been inveterate enemies are often invited into a club for the purpose of settling their differences beneath a roof where the spirit of unity prevails?"

I had made a similar suggestion to him a year earlier. On both occasions he said: "Until France and Germany clasp each other's hands in peace there will be no peace." And when in connection with Italy I praised his forbearance in the face of much provocation, he said, with an emphatic seriousness that was quite unusual in him: "Believe me, nothing is more dangerous than a policy that banks on the wisdom of the opponent."

No one in recent years showed himself such an exemplar of this wisdom as Briand. And yet it was only as the outstanding exemplar of this wisdom during the last ten years of his life that he developed into a really great statesman. At the Geneva Assembly, in the autumn of 1931, I heard him make the following statement during a moderate and carefully considered speech, without the slightest forewarning and with no trace of emotion: "So long as I am responsible for its affairs France will never make war." No statesman for over a century had dared to make such a pronouncement in the face of the chauvinists. And as a matter of fact half the French press attacked Briand

and tried to bring about his downfall because of that statement.
To me it sounded like one of the sayings of Marcus Aurelius.

6

When Briand was in France he spent his time between the
big ugly office on the Quai d'Orsay—where the officials used
to say all sorts of kind things about their boss when they woke
themselves up in their chairs—and the little farm at Cocherel,
where simplicity and comfort were the chief features. There was
no luxury. The farm grew gradually from a small holding to
rather big proportions by means of the profits made on cattle
breeding. Even his bitterest enemies never accused Briand of
profiting by his political career. On the farm there used to be
a strutting type of chanticleer who went by the name of Daudet.
But that was the only political touch about the place. Otherwise
there were only the cattle and the sheep and the steward's accounts, and nothing to do but fish and hunt and read detective
stories and yarns about sea pirates, or spend the day in a motor
boat with two sailors.

Although fond of good food, Briand ate little in the evenings.
This was largely because his stomach had never been robust.
Towards the fall of the day he would generally stroll into the
village with dog and stick. He would drink a glass of wine with
the natives and sit and talk with them late into the evening,
somewhat after the manner of Lincoln. It was thus that he
always kept close to the heart of the French people and for that
reason understood them all the better.

Briand's reputation had become so overpowering in so short
a time that it aroused a good deal of jealousy among his political

and journalistic confrères in France. When the world resounded with his name and looked to him as the great champion of their hopes to see the reign of peace firmly established, the Parisian press tried to belittle his achievement and rob him of his just meed of fame by pointing to his variegated political past, his vacillating career, and the many occasions on which his success had been temporarily achieved through compromise. Here, as in every other country, the provinces had judged more soundly and remained loyal to him to the end.

His opponents would rend to pieces the rich garland of poetry which the world had woven round the name of Aristide Briand. And thus it was that half Paris rose up in indignation when he was put forward as candidate for the presidency in 1931. For sixty years the President of the French Republic had generally been a mediocre outsider and scarcely ever a statesman. Périer was an able man and for that reason resigned from the presidency before his term of office had expired. And Poincaré remarked when his term was over: "I have lost seven years."

Here was an occasion in which Briand's easy-going and pliable nature allowed him to be influenced against his better judgment. His first instinct was to refuse; but he yielded to the persuasions of a huge deputation of the Left and agreed to become a candidate for the presidency. His friends had noticed a certain weakening in his hold over the Chamber of Deputies and were anxious to save him for his own sake. He himself thought that seven years in the safe harbour of the presidency would enable him to withstand the storm that had broken out against him and against the cause of peace generally in Europe. No one thought he would be defeated in the presidential election. Was he not the most popular Frenchman alive and had he not the whole country behind him? What could the professional politicians do against that backing? So he allowed himself to be talked into becoming a candidate, because he believed he would be victorious. A wild press campaign immediately broke out against him. His enemies wished to overthrow him finally. And with all his knowledge of human nature and the French Chamber he did not know that this had arisen from jealousy of him. In France it is not the people who elect the President, but the Deputies and Senators. Briand did not even for a moment suspect that some of the Cabinet colleagues with whom he had lunch on the very day of the election in Versailles would go at once into the palace and influence the last few wavering votes against him. Here again Briand recalls old Bismarck, who until the very last moment believed it impossible that he could be dismissed after thirty years of service in the Ministry.

"It was the saddest face that I have ever seen in my life," a friend said to me while speaking of how Briand looked when he first heard of his defeat. In that moment the cause of peace suffered a tragic set-back. It seemed that France had voted the downfall of the prophet of conciliation. But in reality it was not France. It was only a few dozen jealous politicians.

People expected that Briand would immediately resign. But he didn't; because he wished first to go through with the German negotiations at Geneva. He wanted to have a certain amount of revenge; because were it not for the Austro-German Customs Union, which had been announced on the eve of the French presidential election and which looked as if the Germans had repudiated Briand's policy, his enemies could not have prevailed against him. Therefore, he smashed the whole Austro-German plan at Geneva and returned once more with the laurels of success. Paris welcomed and cheered him. But he was determined to resign, for he knew that he would come to the fore again at the next election, as he had so often done before. This was also what the country expected. The leaders of the Left-Wing parties had already decided on the electoral constituencies in which he would speak. Suddenly, between the Friday and the Sunday evening, Briand announced that he would remain in office. What had happened?

Long before the election Senator Doumer was nominated as a candidate. His friendship with Briand extended over several decades. So he came and asked Briand frankly if he had any notion of allowing his name to go forward. In that case he himself would retire. Briand, who at that time did not intend to become a candidate, honestly replied in the negative. When he changed his mind later and announced his candidacy he placed his old friend in a delicate position. The position became more delicate still after Doumer's election. But after his election Doumer sent for the Foreign Minister and said to him:

"You must not let me down now." That put Briand on his honour and he remained in office. But this necessitated his sitting in the Cabinet with some of his bitterest enemies. They were all glad that he compromised himself by staying with them because it was for the sake of the future.

This turn of events was indeed fateful, for it led to Briand's end. It was from purely gentlemanly motives that he remained in power. But he was attacked shamelessly in an underhand way by hostile forces that wished to drive him into the political wilderness. This manœuvre affected him profoundly and contributed to the development of a heart trouble from which he had suffered for a long time. Within a few weeks he was dead. Two months after that the French electorate voted against the imperialists who had destroyed the great friend of peace and gave their support to the Left, which meant a triumph for Briand's policy. Undoubtedly he would have lived much longer had he gone back to his farm when Doumer was elected President; for then he would have returned to power with renewed vitality through the victory of his party at the general election.

This fifth act was like the climax in a Greek tragedy. Had Briand been elected President of the French Republic in place of

Doumer, he might have fallen by the hand of the same assassin that killed Doumer. And thus he could not have died a martyr for the cause to which he had devoted his life. Destiny saved him from this meaningless accident and gave him a fitting exit from the great rôle he had played on the stage of European politics.

RATHENAU

THE GERMAN EUROPEAN

For our fate moves us to its decision and when it is out of our hands, when YES and NO depend on the intelligence and the feeling of others, then we must keep quiet, control ourselves, ask ourselves if we can bear it, even if it be what men call a judgment from God to which our reason is bound to submit.

GOETHE

RATHENAU

THE GERMAN EUROPEAN

He HAD the figure of an Arabian prince, tall and slim, dark-skinned and dark-haired, gentleman and sahib in both appearance and manner, scion of a race that is perchance hyperthoroughbred. Such was the impression he gave when he began to speak. He had a deep musical voice whose tones reminded one of some delicate colour such as that of brown velvet. He invariably spoke in a subdued manner, explanatory rather than assertive, as if he wished to show his hearers the way rather than push them along it. The contemplative side of his nature, which kept the will in balance without stimulating it overmuch, was mirrored in the undulations of the voice. And in these undulations one seemed to hear the strains of a vague yearning that was in contrast with the sharp and direct expression of the face.

The analytic and melodic elements of his nature were so poorly balanced that the personality was seldom in harmony with itself. But I should not say it never was. Here was a man of first-class intellect who became skeptical of the human intellect itself as an instrument of knowledge. He put forth an enormous amount of creative activity in various and dissimilar spheres of life and was at the same time a contemplative, a leader and a follower. Having trod these various paths to their respective ends, he turned back and strove with all his might to find the ground whereon a new order of things could be constructed according to the plan he had thought out. His innermost yearnings urged him inexorably into action for the purpose of bringing his ideals and abstract plans to concrete realization. But Destiny invariably barred the way before his feet, incorporated in the form of his own racial ancestry and the circumstances of the time in which he lived. And when at last he had reached the position where he actually was able to put his ideals into practice the spirit of the German people swore vengeance against those same ideals and murdered him.

As Rathenau's tragedy recedes into the perspective of history his figure appears all the more heroic. The changes which time has wrought since his death have placed him in a clearer light, so that we can now read better than ever before the symbolic meaning of his fate. Just at the present juncture in German history, when Rathenau's countrymen have ruthlessly renounced him and covered his name with obloquy, he stands out clearer than ever as a great social reformer and practical statesman, superior to all the others who took part in the government of the German nation during the past twenty years.

2

Dr. Walther Rathenau, Civil Engineer was his entry in the telephone book. It expressed not only his profession but also a part of his nature. He may go down to posterity as a philosopher, sociologist, politician, banker, organizer, artist. For he was all these. And as he entered each sphere of activity it was not for the sake of finding some outer interest to harmonize his own inner conflict, but rather for the objective benefit of what he undertook. Like Wagner, he inherited a variety of talents from each side of his parentage. It will be remembered that Wagner's family history was a forecast of his genius. And much the same is true of Walther Rathenau. The father, Emil Rathenau, was a pioneer in the technique of modern industry and banking. Indeed, his influence was world-wide and decisive in these spheres. The home from which he had come—the grandparents of Walther Rathenau—belonged to that inner circle of Berlin culture in which Heine moved. Industrial technique and commercial organization, therefore, was the legacy young Walther got from his father; high intellect and culture he inherited from his grandparents.

Emil Rathenau had a modest home in a working-class district of Berlin. In the family dwelling house he installed an iron foundry which he and his partner stoked and tended. Edison once spoke to me of Emil Rathenau's great ability and the prophetic insight he had into the development of modern technique. He bought the patent rights of the incandescent burner from the American inventor. Some time later Edison himself came to Berlin and visited the Rathenaus. During the conversation he had a discussion with Walther's mother on the art of physiognomy. Madame Rathenau showed the American wizard a portrait of her son, who was then sixteen years old. When he had studied it for some time Edison gave the following verdict: *This chap will one day accomplish more and know more than we all. This is a marvellous person.* In his boyhood Walther heard no other home talk and saw nothing other than technical inventions and plans for their expansion. The father was the first to bring the banking system into alliance with industry and he founded the first German company for the production and distribution of electricity. This company—the A. E. G.—has remained for half a

century the greatest of all German undertakings in the electrical
and allied industries.

Young Walther Rathenau showed an unusual gift for music
and painting and it was only natural that the boy looked forward to choosing an artistic career. But filial obedience is the
first rule in a German home and so young Rathenau studied
physical science and chemistry at the university. When he was
twenty-five years old he invented a process for producing chlo-
rine and alkalis by means of electrolysis. He thereupon took
over the management of an electro-chemical works at Bitterfeld,
between Berlin and Leipzig, and remained at that post for seven
years. In the meantime the father had become wealthy; but the
son insisted on sticking to his own post and earning his own
living amid the uninviting surroundings of Bitterfeld, until he
had achieved a position of independence in which he was able
to choose for himself.

This passionate urge to be self-supporting has a rather significant background. As a student Walther Rathenau wrote a
drama after the style of Alfred de Musset and had it printed at
his own expense. He was clearly under the influence of the æs-
thetic tradition which had come down from the grandparents;
but a sense of responsibility towards his father held him back.
From the age of twenty-four onwards he refused to accept money
from home. Even afterwards when the father grew suddenly rich
and the son took up posts in the various banks and companies
directed by Emil Rathenau he always supported himself on the
salary he earned. The reason for this extraordinary determination to be independent and self-supporting is not to be sought
in his ancestry. It was a part of his own individual nature.

As a Jew he had an acute sense of belonging to an inferior social caste. Therefore he wished to distinguish himself by his own
personal effort and thus compensate for what he felt to be a
racial handicap. This self-consciousness of too much intellect and

too much race, as he said himself, became a kind of monomania
with him. It led him logically to an undue admiration for the
physical prowess of the so-called blond races and especially for
the Prussian military aristocracy. During his whole life he was
unable to overcome his weakness for this class. He bought himself a royal country seat and at one time thought of marrying
a daughter of one of the Prussian nobility. He went in for all
kinds of sports and athletic games and did his military service
in one of the guard regiments. He even went the length of chal-
lenging his friend, Maximilian Harden, to a duel, which the
latter turned into a joke. Driven hither and thither by the inner
conflict between this inherent sense of inferiority and an overpowering ambition to tolerate nobody above him, he was forced
to withdraw into himself. During his whole life Rathenau was
without a friend and only on a rare occasion did a woman's
influence touch him.

If he were not a Jew, or if he were a Jew and had been born
in England, his life and death would have been quite otherwise.
In Germany this proud man had to be constantly on the defensive of what was considered in that country to be a birth stigma
or brand of inferiority or at least a sufficient ground for barring
a person against entry into the best social circles. Rathenau
strove to enter those circles. In his writings he criticized the Jews.
At the same time that he made efforts to be received allround in
society he criticized his own race and held them up to ignoble
comparison with the Germans, with the result that into every
salon which he entered he carried the shield of his own ancestry
with him showing the dents and fractures that he himself had
made in it. When he took his place in a salon among these high-
born Prussian Junkers in figure and manner he was quite their
compeer. It was only when he spoke that he belittled himself.
The Junkers saw it at once and guffawed. Only a few people of
this class, which he held in far too high a regard, ever had an

inkling of the interior worth of the man himself. I never asked
him what he thought about Disraeli; but I feel confident that
he had taken the British Jew as his model. He made a great
mistake in assuming that the Prussians would have tolerated
even a Disraeli.

He struggled to free himself from the bonds of his sub-
serviency to this caste, from ambition and from money. But in
vain. "I decided," he writes, "to quit the industrial life and take
up literary work. The A. E. G. (*Allgemeine Elektrizitaets Ge-
sellschaft,* General Electrical Company) invited me to join the
board of directors and take over the management of the department for the construction of central stations. I carried on that
work for three years." He constructed electrical power stations
throughout Europe and South America. And when he had
brought this work to a close he did not even then retire to the
intellectual solitude after which he had yearned. He entered a
bank. There he remained for another three years. And then he
became a member of the board of directors in upwards of a
hundred different joint stock companies. Although in those years
he wrote a great deal, yet when he had reached the age of forty
his mind was still in the experimental stage. The co-operation
between industry and the banks, which was the work of his
father, held him in its vortex. It linked him to a class of society
and a kind of work against which his higher thoughts and feelings were in constant rebellion. He paid tribute to the Berlin
court and did homage to Prussian royalty in order to gratify his
own pride. He used to spend long hours in conversation with
the Kaiser. Yet in those days when he spoke with me he criticized the Kaiser mercilessly, his bracelets and rings, his theatri-
cality and cocksureness, just as he wrote openly about Wilhelm
II at a later period.

While he delighted to move about within the social purlieus
of Prussian nobility he was at the same time a member of the

Opposition circles and made friends with those leading German artists and poets who were rebels against royalty in all its shapes and forms and against all the social sets. He was a mental freebooter who did not feel ill at ease in either of these two opposing worlds. He simply wanted to win each of them by personal conquest. Everywhere he gave himself out as a dilettante and few knew that he was a man of first-class learning and culture. "As a Jew I am a second-class citizen," he wrote. "If I had changed my religious faith I might have removed the prejudice; but I believed that by so doing my action would thereby be a vindication of the unjust attitude of the ruling caste towards the Jews."

His predilection for the Germans was not a consequence but rather a cause of the dualism in his character. He resembled Gobineau who worshipped the so-called blond race of the North; but he himself could live only in the South. In Gobineau as well as in Rathenau this contradiction was not due to a sense of inferiority but rather to a fundamental urge towards the opposite, just as happens so frequently in the case of sexual love. To this circumstance we must add Rathenau's opinions on the philosophy of history: "An epitome of world history and of the history of mankind is to be found in the drama of the Aryan race. A marvellous blond people wakes up in the North. Its super-abounding fertility sends out wave upon wave into the southern world. Each migration becomes a conquest." In view of this he claims that the Jews must lay aside those characteristics that are disliked by the nation in the midst of which they live. "The goal of the process should be not imitation Germans but Jews bred and brought up as Germans."

Thus he wrote in his youth. He abandoned the race theory afterwards and, like every other man of keen insight, saw that there is an inner bond of temperament which is more important than the external community of blood. "I am a German of Jewish stock," he wrote. "My nation is the German nation. My country is Germany. My faith is the German faith, which stands above all denominations. Yet Nature has so intermingled the two streams of that ancient blood in me that they are in foaming opposition, the one striving towards concrete reality and the other towards the abstract. . . . The only qualifications that I recognize for membership of a people and a nation are those of heart, mind, character and soul. From this standpoint I see the Jews somewhere between Saxons and the Swabians. They are more foreign to me than Brandenburgers or Holsteiners and perhaps somewhat more akin than Silesians or Lorrainers."

The land of Rathenau's heart's choice, therefore, remains the same Germany which Aryan Germans have abandoned for the Mediterranean. The Jewish Rathenau was a more perfervid German patriot than the Christian Hölderlin, Jean Paul or Nietzsche. In that way he escaped being marked definitely with one brand or another and held himself free to wander into whatever pasture his taste led him. The only woman that he loved was a typical specimen of the refined and cultured Jewess.

Nevertheless, in Rathenau's case these characteristics remained always in the shade. Throughout his life something like a glass partition stood between him and what he yearned for. Through this partition he could see and even hear the things that were the object of his heart's desire, but he could not possess them. A certain hardness or coldness prevented him from wholly surrendering himself to anything. Probably he never acknowledged this except once in his life when he wrote to his woman friend: "My one merit is that I love you and that you are sure of my love. I feel that I have never suffered through you or could suffer through you, but only through my own heart and its narrowness. But by your dear words it has been awakened and set throbbing and your beautiful image hovers before me; so that

after a long time I have again been able to feel warmth, light
and peace. But early tomorrow morning I will tear up your letter
and go into the country." Here we have delineated the utter-
most limits of his capacity for love, even to the very detail of the
accent. It is no wonder that Stefan George was the only contemporary poet whom he honoured.

Yet he was sensitive to the charms of women. I remember
seeing him obviously touched by the beauty of a lady who happened to be one of a party in his bachelor home. One summer
day when I happened to be a visitor at his country house he
brought us some fresh figs from his hothouse and seemed as
pleased with himself over the gift as if he were a little boy.
There was one woman in his life, the woman friend to whom he
wrote the letter I have quoted above. One evening at the theatre
he sketched her features five times and wrote beneath the
sketches on the little white sheets of paper the words: *The White
Cloak*.

He was widely read and widely informed and was in the habit
of giving detailed references to the sources of his information
briefly and without any intention of showing off. He quoted
from the foreign originals only when necessary, because he never
liked to parade his learning. In this he was like a wealthy lady
who refrains from displaying her best jewellery in her own
house. The impression he made at the opening of a conversation
was only slight in comparison with that which developed as the
discussion progressed. He generally wanted to get an insight into
his hearer's attitude before he launched into the midst of an
argument. Sometimes when a burning question of the day was
on the tapis he would make some quotation at the threshold
of the discussion and thus move the whole theme to a more
spacious plane. Once when I had returned from the Turkish
war front and spoke to him of the victory I thought was soon to

come he looked at me skeptically and quoted from Goethe's
Westöstlichen Diwan:

"Aber frag einmal den Kaiser
ob er dir die Städte gibt"

(But first ask the Emperor if he will surrender the cities).

These bright interludes, however, were remarkably rare and
short-lived for a man who had not yet reached the meridian of his
years. His innate pride and fundamental sense of insecurity made
his general attitude one of resignation. The letters to his woman
friend disclose this:

"What compels even those who love me most to fear me and
to hate me? The first cause is that I cannot belong entirely to
anyone. I am under the control of forces that have my life in
their hands. Whether they lead me to good or evil, whether they
are in jest or earnest, they decide my fate. It seems as if I could
do nothing of my own free will, as if I am always being led,
kindly when I comply and roughly when I resist. The second
cause is that my temperament is polyphonic. The melody rises
like a treble above the other sounds, but it is very seldom unac-
companied. The pure flute notes of more simple natures seem to
me monotonous, charming and somewhat dull. Therefore people
are mistaken about me, because sometimes they look in vain for
the melody among the mass of sounds. But I recognize one clear
strain and I know that it is there and that it controls all the
rest.

"This proves that although everything else be an illusion
life does not deceive us. Look at my life. Do you know of another life that is more earnest or more full of renunciation? No
matter how I probe into my inner thoughts I have never found
any worldly desires there. I will what I must, nothing else. That
this my life is an oblation, offered cheerfully and willingly to
the powers above it, not for reward or in hope—this I may say

and you yourself know that it is true. I know that I forfeit the love of my fellowmen in this way and I feel it sorely."

3

I came to know Rathenau before the war, when I was still a young man. He was then in the middle forties. At that time his thought was of just the same clear-cut character and his language of the same studied accuracy as it was ten years later, when I visited him just before his death. His diction and the form and richness of the language he used made an overwhelming impression on me. I went to see him to get a letter of introduction from him as I was about to pay a visit abroad. I had counted on a visit that would last for a quarter of an hour; but I had to remain for four full hours with him. He liked to win the hearts of ambitious young men, like myself. But his manner was not in the least seductive. His worldly wisdom seemed to come to the fore at least in those Platonic moments. His beautiful voice and the richness of his thought made the impression of a great cellist, as people often said of Briand. Cultured people in France used to say that Briand spoke a dialect rather than pure French and that he even made grammatical errors. But Rathenau spoke the most beautiful German I have ever heard. It was comparable, I think, only with the French of Paul Valéry or the Italian of d'Annunzio.

Like so many other great minds, Rathenau showed his powers best in dialogue. When he spoke in public his hearers felt that he had prepared his oration textually and on that account they remained unmoved. When he mixed in social conversation it was never with the intent or aim of showing off and it was only when the conversation developed that his companions began to appreciate his extraordinary mental qualities. Yet his manner was quite artless. One felt as if he were soliloquizing or just giving unconscious expression to daydreams. His habitual reserve regulated the tempo of his speech, his bodily movements and even his manner of eating. The same reserve has shown itself in the incomplete character of his writings. The perfect speaker almost never shows his powers at their full in the written work. And it is interesting in this connection also to note that the extraordinarily clear handwriting, which is striking even in his love letters, was a result of his dominating self-control.

In the same stoic earnestness with which he solved some puzzle in the shape of a chemical formula he would play a piece of music by Bach and play it well. He brought the same earnest enthusiasm to the work of constructing his own house, for which he made all the plans, sketched the doors and windows and even arranged the colour scheme of the rooms and hall. It was a kind of religion with him to organize his energies and give them outlet, and because he did so with that religious flair he was successful in so many varied undertakings.

During the middle years of his life he was generally occupied during the whole daytime with meetings and interviews and correspondence. It was only in the evening that he gave himself to his literary work. When I asked him why he did not give up his business engagements and turn himself wholly to literature, he said:

"When I have passed the whole day working in the A. E. G. and elsewhere, then I find that I can write better and more easily in the evening."

It must be remembered that from the time he was forty Rathenau was continually engaged in politics and that he regularly published press articles on the various political problems of the day. These articles were famous from the very beginning.

This versatility never lessened the quality of his work. What he did in one sphere seemed to help his faculty for working in another, and vice versa. I do not know of anyone in Germany who had such wide and varied experience in so many spheres of practical work and culture before taking over the direction of the affairs of state.

He looked upon all his work as if it were a religious mission. Here he was quite different from Masaryk, just as a peasant differs from a city man in his attitude towards nature. With the peasant it is an inborn instinct, with the city man it is something that is acquired. Unlike Masaryk, whose mind is thoroughly analytic, Rathenau was profoundly Faustian and, as a whole-hearted disciple of Goethe, his mental nature became irrevocably dualistic. "For good or for bad you will not find my like again," he wrote to his friend. "This is because God has made an experiment of me, which, even though it be a failure—and I think this is more likely than the opposite—still is interesting. The best is that I have accepted the situation seriously and honestly and follow the path marked out for me through all its windings, indifferent as to whether it will lead me to good or evil. I have no right to choose a life which is lived wholly in the imagination and contemplative spirit and thus escape mental struggles and hardship. I do not have to ask why. This winter I have come to see more clearly than ever before that a man's life has no significance unless all the forces of his mind are employed and his responsibilities fulfilled. To accept gifts even from nature is half unjust."

Under these cold aphorisms one senses the yearning for warmth and relaxation, just the gifts he would have liked to receive from the hands of nature. And precisely because he yearned to leave that twilight valley of the spirit and come out into the warm sunshine of the heart he complained of general "soullessness" as the cause of all Europe's troubles. With the searchlight of a great personality he projected the image of his own inner fate on his century, to see the reflection of himself in the epoch he was born into. He once wrote: "A man ought to be strong enough to forge his own kind of perfection from the elements of his imperfection."

4

Rathenau's lifework was that of a thinker and is clearly understandable when his personality is taken into consideration. That personality was not simple and clear but was partly clouded and partly illuminated, like the time in which he lived. It was like a projectile shot into the distance. If I except Bernard Shaw, because his brilliancy of mind outshines the educational value of his criticism, we shall find no other personality to equal Walther Rathenau as a social educator in our epoch and a prophet of the future. All the solutions of social problems which are being tried out today were put forward by him and some of them abandoned later. Anyone acquainted with the great kitchens of Rome and Moscow knows that the recipes studied there can be found in Rathenau's handwriting between 1910 and 1920.

He, of course, did not invent them. A prize was once offered by a certain periodical to anyone who could bring to light a new thought in Rathenau's writings. Rathenau, who seldom showed much of a sense of humour, increased the value of the prize and wrote a public letter to that effect. I am not competent to judge how much of his thought is taken from Marx and Sorel, Kropotkin, the English guild-socialists and others. And I could not form a judgment as to how far he was right when he once told me that he had superseded Marx. The enormous success of his principal books—his longest sold more than seventy thousand copies in one year in Germany and was translated into twenty foreign languages—and the striking impression they made on the European mind can be explained only by the actuality of his teaching and the extraordinarily versatile way in which it was presented, together with the suggestive appeal of his style.

The accusation that, though a rich man, he preached against wealth is not at all to the point. It is as if one tried to discredit Schopenhauer as a misogynist by pointing to some of his love adventures. Both men learned life's lesson by experience. Though Rathenau became very wealthy, he neither enjoyed amassing money nor spending it. He experienced how boring can be the attempt to get enjoyment out of money. He was a bachelor without any passionate desires. So the only enjoyment he took from his money was to build himself a house of artistic style and to provide himself with beautiful books. Though he was somewhat of a connoisseur of wines and good food, I am sure that except perhaps in his young days he never opened a bottle of rare wine either for his personal enjoyment or to add zest to a social conversation. He had enemies among those who pretended to be his friends. When they asked why he did not socialize his own private fortune they simply showed that they did not understand the purpose of his lifework. Rathenau had nothing in common with Tolstoi. He was not a born philanthropist. He was a political philosopher. He gave far more than he received. The cold flame of his example and teaching was not intended to illumine his immediate surroundings. It was like a lighthouse that leaves the foreground in darkness and illuminates the distance.

Therefore, there was little paradox in giving the title *Mechanism of the Spirit* to a book in which he describes the Birth of the Soul. Here we find the spiritual principles of the new social order which he had conceived in his mind, and of the new economy which he presented in his subsequent books: *The Criticism of the Age, In Days To Come* and *The New State*. Overpopulation leads to mechanization, to organization and industrial technique. And these represent a danger to the mental life and the life of the soul. On this point I may quote the following as an example of his vivid powers of description:

"There was a time in which a German was proud to call himself a Christian, a liegeman, a citizen, father of a family or member of a guild. But today he is subject and object of innumerable social organizations. He is citizen of the Reich, of the state or the city, inhabitant of the district or province and member of the parish. He is soldier, voter, taxpayer, the holder of certain honours. He is colleague, employer, tenant or landowner, customer or merchant. He is an insurance agent, a member of certain professional or social clubs, a customer of the bank, a shareholder, creditor of the state. He is a savings depositor, a mortgagee or mortgagor. He is a member of a political party, subscriber to a newspaper or the telephone or has a post office banking account. He is a subscriber to an information bureau or a season ticket holder on the tramway. He is a partner in a firm and has oral or written obligations. He is a sportsman, art collector, amateur artist, dilettante, traveller, reader of books, pupil, academician, holder of testimonials, licentiates, diplomas and titles. He is a correspondent, a firm, a reference, an address, a competitor. He is an expert, a trustee, an arbitrator, witness or juror. He is heir, testator, husband, relative, friend. These relations mean the ramification of nerve fibres on the structure of our mechanized economic system."

And yet Rathenau's disgust for such mechanization did not lead him to any romantic outburst or protest against industrial and commercial technique. He tried to make the best of a state of things that was actually there at hand and in doing so his ideas and plans led him within a few years to the plan of a socialized state, even to the frontier of the communist state. This was before these ideas had been attempted in practice. He demanded the nationalization of certain of the means of production, the abolition of the classes but not of property. He proves that in a state organized according to Platonic ideas, or in the social organization of the bees, slaves are not necessary. This new society which he forecast could be brought into being only on a vast constructional plan which would render a proletariat impossible and also an hereditary caste of the upper classes: "Property, consumption and demand are not private matters. In days to come people will find it difficult to understand that the will of a dead man could bind the living, that any individual was enabled to fence off for his own gratification several square miles of land, that without requiring any special authorization from the state he could allow fertile land to remain untilled, that he could demolish buildings or erect them and ruin beautiful landscapes, that he held himself justified in certain business methods to bring whatever portion he could hold of the public property under his own private management and that he could use this property as he pleased provided he paid a certain tax, that he could take any number of men into his service and put them to whatever work he liked so long as his contracts with them did not violate definite provisions of the law, and that he was justified in living at a rate of expenditure that was ruinous to the wealth of the community."

And so he demands that all private wealth be progressively taxed out of existence as a "recognition of the fact that a person who acquires means beyond what is necessary for the ordinary amenities of civilized life is only the hypothetical owner of what he acquires and the state is free to take the surplus in whatever measure it may think fit." All this is in harmony with his demand for the equalization of education so that it may reach all classes and bring all classes its benefits.

He gives a masterly picture of the life of the proletarian as that of a veritable slave, although nominally boasting of certain rights under the law. "The proletarian's life, however he may arrange it within the bounds of his sham liberty, will follow on from generation to generation with the same dreary uniformity. If we once realize that this life never ceases, that on his deathbed the workman sees the long sequence of his children and grandchildren doomed to the same fate, then we shall hear the voice of conscience telling us that this is a great crime. In our time people cry out for state intervention if a cab horse be ill treated. But the same class of persons find it quite natural that one section of the people should go on slaving for centuries for the aggrandizement of another class who are its brothers and fellow countrymen. And there is indignation abroad when people refuse to vote for the continuance of this state of things. . . . Entry into the upper classes is not possible. The magic circle is closed and money is its seal. To him that hath shall be given. What he has is increased; but first he must possess. Thus there are glass walls on every side, transparent but insurmountable, and beyond them is liberty, self-determination, comfort and power. The keys of the forbidden land are knowledge and property. And both are hereditary. To claim freedom for the mind of man and the opportunities for his soul to unfold its powers is incompatible with the practice whereby one half of mankind condemns to everlasting drudgery that other half which has the same features and is endowed with the same natural gifts."

He disposes brilliantly of the traditional objections. The consequences of socialization would not be that we all should become poor but that the productive power of the masses would increase. The evil influences of industrialism on the human spirit can be overcome only by the development of the mechanization process. An economic system can be constructed according to a rational plan only on the presupposition of a reasonable distribution of raw materials, etc. It is a common objection that the zest of competition would be destroyed if the possibility of making important profits were taken away. Against this Rathenau contends that the real pioneers were always urged on by a passionate will to power and not for the sake of money and material gains. In showing at how much cost labour is wasted every year he displays a magnificent mastery of details over the whole economic field. As example of this he proves that half the coal actually used in Germany would be quite sufficient for the needs of the nation if only the production and distribution were rationally organized. He devotes four chapters to demonstrating the chief faults of the present organization:

"The years of labour that are necessary for the finishing of a delicate piece of needlework, to take an example, or a piece of woven tapestry, signify a definite wastage of time and labour which might be employed to make clothing for the poor. The lawns of a great park which are shorn with the grass mower eight or ten times per year would have grown corn if far less human effort had been expended on them for another purpose. The pleasure steam yacht, including captain and crew, coal and food, is an irreparable loss to world transport. Looked at from the economic point of view, the world, and even more so the nations, signify a creative community. Whoever wastes labour, time of labour and means of labour, robs society of something."

In broad outline he sketches a plan of important reforms which would render the economic system more productive as a whole. Thus the vested interest of each citizen would be increased. The majority of co-operative societies and manufacturing associations would be nationalized or be formed into syndicates under the supervision of the state. These syndicates would enjoy certain state rights and would almost be departments of state. They would be the nerve centres of the new economics, to use Rathenau's own words. As a matter of fact, such syndicates, or corporations, are today the nerve centres of the Fascist organization in Rome and are just now being copied in Berlin. The Third Reich has taken its fundamental ideas of social organization from the murdered Jew, Walther Rathenau, without being able, however, to put them into practice.

The idea of "The People's State" (Volksstaat), the leadership of which is not drawn from the aristocracy or the bourgeoisie, nor from rich or poor as such, but through an autonomous selection of talent arising from the people, also originated with Rathenau. Even before Lenin he advanced the idea of the soviet, the local county or provincial council, which was widely canvassed long ago in both England and the United States of America. Men ought to be organized in groups according to their common occupations or professions and these groups built up into a sort of pyramidal structure which would form one of the main portions of the statal edifice.

Rathenau was not content with theoretical formulations for the new kind of society that is developing today. He also put forward the idea of the League of Nations and the principle of limitation of armaments. As far back as 1907, even before Norman Angell's book appeared, Rathenau showed how it is that in our time wars are so seldom decisive or even decided. In 1911 he called for an international control board which would proportionalize the cost of armaments with the other branches of national expenditure and lay down the maximum of man power in the various armies in relation to the population. Even during the war he had the courage to write as follows: "The concept of the state as strictly national and competitive with other states must be set aside. An international community of right, of economics, of administration, of education and of religion, which will not be under state control, must be established in order to make possible the abolition of that economic competition which always must lead to conflicts and wars, even under the most peaceful of national governments. But this goal is a distant one."

5

Such an insight into the conditions that had arisen from the social problem and the class problem must needs have foreseen the coming war. In spite of his leading position as an industrial magnate he had no influential political connections and had to rely on the information given out by the press as to what was forthcoming. Yet Rathenau often gave warning of the impending conflict. In 1913 he was very emphatic about it. He attributed the causes of the war, however, too exclusively to the pressure of the economic situation. At least that is my own opinion. But at the same time he recognized that German politics in the hands of the Junkers and the military caste, with its overbearing pride and disregard of public opinion, was a factor that inexorably forced on the war.

He saw danger in the fact that in "the most efficient industrial nation in the world, the nation that is best educated and has the greatest capacity for organization, the people are not allowed a voice in the control of their own destiny . . . When the inner forces of a country are balked, where formulas, morals and ideas have outlasted their period of vitality, then a solution will inevitably come from outside. When the hour of fate arrives obsolete rights and privileges will be wiped out at the same time as our over-pampered industrial system will collapse. One single hour will witness the downfall of what was believed capable of enduring for centuries."

This prophecy was published five years before the German debacle. What gives it psychological significance is the position which the author held. He did not write amid poverty-stricken surroundings. Nor did he write in the vengeful wrath of a destitute Marxian socialist. He was surrounded with the world's goods and blessings. He wrote at eventide, after he had spent the day supervising company affairs that were bringing in ever-increasing dividends, and in his mind were still the outlines of mammoth plans for the expansion of the industrial undertakings in which he was interested. The desk at which he sat was itself a refinement of luxury. I have seen him sitting there and watched him pick up the notes and sheets of paper on which he had written, fold them and carefully place them in the drawer. Money and commerce, which he still continued to manage, meant so little to him from the standpoint of personal desires that they never for a moment cast a cloud over his clear mental insight into abstract principles. His industrialist colleagues laughed at him and considered him a literary snob. But he continued calmly to commit his concrete plans to paper and to publish them. It did not trouble him how much his colleagues laughed at the visionary plans he put forth. Only a few months before the war he had the courage to publish his predictions on Europe's future, while the other captains of industry pooh-poohed the possibility of war. But if it were to come, they were ready to welcome it because they believed it would give them economic mastery of the world.

"There is one possibility left: an industrial customs union," he wrote, "of which, sooner or later, for better or for worse, the states of western Europe will become members. . . . The aim would be to create an industrial union which would equal and perhaps surpass that of America, and within this union there would no longer be any backward or unproductive regions. At the same time the most potent cause of international hostility would be removed . . . What prevents the nations from trusting one another, mutually supporting each other, is an economical question at the core. Forge the industries of Europe into one, and that will happen sooner than we think, and political interests will fuse accordingly."

About that time I saw two well-known leaders of German industry in a club showing each other the latest of Rathenau's articles. They were sunk in their deep armchairs and had to use both arms to lift their heavy corporations when they wished to point out with their fat fingers one passage after another that had struck them as particularly ridiculous. One of them laughed until his cigar nearly choked him. He was too lazy to remove it and have a good guffaw. A few months later opportunity knocked at the doors of both. The war broke out and they were at once able to expand their industrial undertakings. Five years later one was already dead and the other was peddling toys with a tray on the sidewalk in one of the main streets of the city. He was broken and destitute and embittered. But at the same time Rathenau's ideas began to make headway in Europe.

Even at the last moment when the shadow and cry of the great Beast of Prey had terrified all Europe Rathenau endeavoured to slay him at the very beginning of his flight. On July 31st, on the very day and almost at the same time that Jaurès raised his lion-throated voice above the tumult, Rathenau wrote as follows: "The Government and people of Germany have the right to know what Russia has demanded and what Austria has rejected. Such a question as the participation of Austrian representatives in an investigation of the Serbian plot is no reason for an international war." He had put his finger exactly on the spot which was the excuse for rejecting the Serbian reply. While the whole of Berlin went wild with enthusiasm on the first day of the war, he sought out the home of an old friend, Frau von Hindenburg, and sat there in tears. The strong man whom no one ever before had seen weeping had broken down. He had neither brothers nor sons who were bound to go to war and he himself was nearly fifty. His friends were of a contemporary age and the institutions of state and society which were imperilled by the onset of war were exactly those he had always attacked. Moreover, the war would clear the ground for that social reconstruction he had dreamed of and planned and yearned for. It was only his profound love for the country itself that made him weep now as he clearly foresaw its impending doom.

"We must win," he wrote, "we must. And yet we have no clear or absolute right. A Serbian ultimatum and a rush of confused, precipitate telegrams. I wish I had never been behind the scenes of this stage. It should not have happened as it did." For that reason Rathenau was one of the few who had the courage to refuse his signature to the famous pronunciamento of the ninety-seven German intellectuals.

Then when the first victories fanned the flame of German self-confidence and correspondingly raised the claims that Germany put forth, even Rathenau's friends called him a pessimist. At that time he said in my hearing to an enthusiastic German poet: "And you with your fine ear, can you not detect the false note?"

"But we have forced our way deep into Poland and France and Serbia!" the other exclaimed.

Rathenau remained unmoved in his chair. He looked fixedly before him and said: "And if we were even on the Pyrenees, what then? We shall be victorious unto death. That is a frail bladder which soon collapses. We are encircled. The muster roll of our enemies grows. And we have neither strategists nor statesmen."

In Kovno he made the acquaintance of Hindenburg and Ludendorff, the outstanding army leaders of the time. He spoke
with me about Ludendorff and said that he had hopes in him.
In October 1914 he wrote to a friend at army headquarters and
explained the reasons why he considered that the time was then
ripe "for a declaration of a reassuring nature about the future of
Belgium. I believe that this would help to make the eventual
peace negotiations more easy. . . . I should look upon it as the
greatest stroke of luck if we could manage to make such a peace
with France as would transform her from an enemy into an
ally and by the building up of a central European economic system we should thus secure an internal success which would far
surpass all external achievements."

At the same juncture other leaders in the iron and steel industries flocked to headquarters demanding that Belgium should be
annexed to Germany, together with the coal and iron regions of
Northern France. Even three years later, at the end of 1917, the
industrialist leaders in general pointed to Rathenau as a dreamer
and a defeatist.

Refusing to be turned aside from his path by the cries of his
colleagues around him, he appealed to Ludendorff, who was now
the real master of Germany. On account of the censorship at
headquarters it was to myself that the letters were first sent,
through a fictitious address: Lud Pless and Co. Rathenau was
the only person who had the courage and insight to show the
Supreme Command how false the Kaiser's views were about
the effectiveness of the submarine campaign. He pointed out to
Ludendorff statistics which told against the theory that the submarine war would reduce the Allied tonnage to such a degree
that it would finally be helpless. At this interview Ludendorff
admitted the truth of Rathenau's statistics but he said that it
would be "against his feelings" to admit the failure of the sub-

marine war. Rathenau then left him and gave him up as hopeless.

6

Rathenau was not merely a prophet who preached in vain to the leaders of Germany during the war. He did much more than that. He initiated and carried to completion a series of mammoth plans for the organization of Germany's raw materials. And this work more than anything else helped the German armies to stand out so long against a world of enemies. For that alone he is entitled to the eternal gratitude of his countrymen.

Three days after England had declared war against Germany, Rathenau went to the Minister of War and explained to him that the blockade which had just begun would make it impossible for the German army to count on the supply of indispensable war materials for more than a few months. The Great General Staff had never thought of that. For forty years they had been preparing, building guns of big calibre and perfecting the organization of the armies. But it was a civilian who showed them at the eleventh hour that they had not reckoned with the necessity of assuring the supply of those basic materials without which no modern army can be effective. The War Minister was quick to understand the import of Rathenau's message and he had the courage to appoint a civilian and a Jew, who was said to be a dreamer and a socialist, to an important position in the War Ministry for the purpose of providing the German army with the indispensable raw materials. It was the first time in the history of Prussia that such an appointment was made. Rathenau told afterwards how he organized the Raw Materials Department with the aid of a few assistants. They were only five people in all and they had to spend several hours a day in addressing letters. It was thus that the rationalization of German industries began, under the direction of Rathenau.

He found himself faced with the task of providing, or getting substitutes for, metal, cotton, leather, skins, flax, linen and chemicals. In the autumn of 1914 he founded about a dozen war companies. It needed tact and energy, initiative and courage. Germany was a beleaguered fortress. The problem was to get into the fortress everything necessary for a prolonged resistance. If these provisions could not be procured at home he had to procure them from the neutral countries or from those that had been occupied by the advance of the armies. He had to curb luxury and waste at home and to think out new methods of production. And all this had to be done under the eyes of military officers who distrusted him. He was the only man in the War Ministry who wore no uniform. He was a sort of pariah to the military officials. "If this man Rathenau *has* helped us, then it is a scandal and a disgrace," one of the officers declared openly. Rathenau heard the words and has recorded them. But he kept at his work in the small room allotted to him and thought to himself: "Where can I procure supplies of nitrate, as there will be no saltpetre left for explosives within a few weeks?" Nitrate had hitherto been principally an imported commodity and he had now to organize the production of it at home.

Such questions were coming before him every hour of the day. His feelings were wrenched and torn and he could see no hope as he gazed into the future. Yet his task was to organize the means whereby the war could be prolonged. He looked on the whole tragedy as a piece of unreasoning folly. One day he said to a member of the Reichstag: "Do you know what we are fighting for? I do not. And I should be glad if you could tell me." The increasing greed for territorial aggrandizement which was loudly expressed by the military leaders, and indeed by the rank and file of the people, dismayed him. His colleagues in the industrial world intrigued against him or openly attacked him. He was attacked at the same time by big business and the farmers, because these came under the iron regulations of his various war companies. The big industrialists kept sending secret reports in increasing numbers to the military and political authorities. They accused Rathenau of exploiting his position for the purpose of putting his pet theories into practice, the founding of syndicates, organization of state economics and finally of state socialism.

After nine months he was replaced by military officials. All they could do was to continue his work, for not one of them was capable of similar initiative. The founder of the War Materials Department had grown so unpopular for having saved the country in its hour of need that the publisher of his books refused to bring out a short account of Rathenau's work which I drew up at that time. Rathenau wrote to me and said: "That I a civilian and a Jew have rendered the state a service of my own accord is something that neither of the two parties concerned can forgive. I believe this attitude will continue to the end of my days. I can understand how it is repugnant to your courageous attitude to allow things to remain as they are. But the publishers will keep their doors closed to me. I shall always remember that you took pains to make my work known at a time when my country disowned it."

Rathenau stood quite alone and isolated in his Cassandra robe during those dark and bitter days when his own fate and that of his country was gradually sinking into an ever-deepening gloom. He fell ill. It was a nervous breakdown, from which he really never fully recovered. After convalescence it was a long time before he could trust his nerves sufficiently to call on his old friends. He would not enter the hotel where some of them were staying. "Even as I enter the atmosphere of the foyer overcomes me. In Berlin I can endure only my office and my daily drive. I hardly ever walk in the streets or enter any houses." Thus he wrote me at that time.

But he found relief in his intellectual pursuits, to which he gave up a good deal of time during the latter part of the war. He had failed to prevent or shorten the duration of the tragedy itself. The campaign of his colleagues against him took away any influence he had formerly possessed. So he gave his mind now entirely to thinking out problems connected with the new statal forms which he conceived as destined to emerge from the wreck of the post-war world. During the last year of the war he seems clearly to have foreseen the defeat, at least as a very strong possibility. And he did not hesitate to give warning of it. He repeated what he had said during the early days of the war, namely, that "the day will never come when the Kaiser will enter through the Brandenburger Gate as a conquering hero astride a white charger. If that event occurs then the history of the world will have lost all its meaning." Towards the close of the war the profound significance of this truth was recognized by the best minds in Germany. Its necessary implication could only be that a complete reformation of the German state and the German political system must be undertaken. The Reich could not continue to live if it still clung to the old leadership. Ludendorff declared later that all this was the outcome of Rathenau's diabolic wish to see Germany defeated. This interpretation became widespread. It was steadfastly insisted upon and propagandized by Rathenau's enemies when he became Foreign Minister. And it finally brought about his murder.

Though suffering and misery surrounded him, he looked into the future and always into the future of Europe. "The forthcoming peace will only be a short armistice," he wrote, "and innumerable wars will follow. The greatest nations will sink into decay and the world into misery, unless this peace will secure the realization of these ideals." The ideals he refers to are, to use his own words, "A League of Industry, not the abolition of national industry, or free trade or tariff agreements but the distribution and common administration of international raw materials, the distribution of international products and international finance. If these arrangements are not made Leagues of Nations and arbitration courts will merely lead to judicial extermination of the weaker by the recognized instrument of competition. . . . The raw materials of international trade will be controlled by an interstate syndicate. These materials will be put at the disposal of each nation on the same original conditions and at the beginning in proportion to the ratio of consumption for the time being. Later on the economic development of each nation will be taken into account. The same interstate authority will regulate exports on a corresponding scale. Each state can ask that the export quota accorded to it shall be retracted. This quota will be reduced in the proportion as the state in question fails to accept the imports due to it. . . . In proportion to its export quota each state may claim a share in the international finance for the purpose of securing deliveries."

Though Rathenau had foreseen it all and though he had to endure persecution for having foretold what was bound to happen, yet when the hour of collapse came he took up a much stronger attitude than those who had nursed their illusions up to the final moment. When Ludendorff lost his nerve and suddenly asked for an armistice, within twenty-four hours Rathenau opposed him. Four years earlier he had forewarned the military chiefs. But now, on October 18, 1918, he called for a *levée en masse*. He opposed the evacuation of the occupied territories, which was demanded by Wilson. He opposed the idea of unconditional surrender. It was the discredited civilian, the Jew, who raised the cry for the organization of the nation's final defence. When the generals deserted he stood in the gap. The country rose up against him because of the article he published in the *Vossische Zeitung* wherein he demanded the *levée en masse* and the establishment of a Government of Defense. When he was asked afterwards what he meant by this, he said: "I wanted Germany to offer terms to her creditors and not declare herself bankrupt forthwith."

His last stand in favour of a *levée en masse* made him quite unpopular among the social-democrats, and, though he would have been the ideal leader of the new socialist government, entry into its councils was now barred to him. His fellow members in the German Democratic Party failed to have his name placed on the electoral list except in such a position (under the proportional representation system) that he had not the faintest chance of being elected. When the National Assembly met at Weimar a telegram was handed in nominating Walther Rathenau as first President of the Reich. It was simply laughed at. About this time he wrote to Colonel House: "For myself I have nothing more to hope or fear. My country has no further need of me and I do not believe that I shall long outlive its downfall." And to a friend he wrote: "I am merely a stranger who is becoming exhausted by giving of himself and I shall continue to live only so long as I still have something to give."

And yet he continued in the struggle to help the nation. He published pamphlets and press articles, some of which put forward valuable suggestions in regard to what the country's attitude ought to be towards the peace conditions that were being formulated at Versailles. The most striking and original of the suggestions he advanced was that, if the terms of the treaty could not be altered for the better, the German representatives ought to withdraw from Versailles, the German National Assembly ought to dissolve, the President of the Reich and the ministers ought to resign and "the Governments that have formed a united front against us should be invited without delay to take over the sovereign rights of the German Reich and the whole machinery of government. Thus the responsibility for the peace, for the administration and for all German activities would rest with the enemy. Before the world, before history and before their own people they would have to take on their shoulders the care of sixty millions of human beings." In that way it would be clearly shown to the world that it was utterly impossible for Germany to fulfil the conditions inflicted upon her by the treaty.

The French press demanded that Rathenau's name should be included among the war criminals to be delivered to the Allies, although Rathenau as a matter of fact had left the German War Office eighteen months before the alleged crimes were supposed to have been committed. He wrote to a friend: "The nation must not surrender the proscribed. Yet these cannot be allowed to bring disaster on their country. Therefore, they must either give themselves up or seek refuge in flight. They ought not to walk about here ostentatiously. I had all preparations made to give myself up. But I should not demand this of others. Every effort must be made to assist those who wish to flee, but there must be no staying here. In Greece, if a man were an innocent or unwitting victim in cases like these he left the country."

While the German Chief of Staff (Ludendorff) sneaked away to Sweden under a false name and the Kaiser absconded to Holland, the Jew, Rathenau, decided to give himself up. The court was wholly illegal because in no court of law can the same person be at one and the same time a party in the case and a judge. This was one of the reasons why Rathenau wished to represent and defend his comrades. But when the list finally appeared his name was not on it. The enemy did not demand his surrender.

7

The man who finally recognized Rathenau's great qualities and decided to employ them officially in the service of the nation was Joseph Wirth, a stalwart Catholic from South Germany. Wirth became Finance Minister of the German Republic in 1920 and Chancellor in 1921. Though the opposite of Rathenau by temperament and education, he personally trusted the much misunderstood Jew. He took the risk of inviting Rathenau to the first conference of experts, though he knew that this would offend the other industrialists and also the socialists. Rathenau held that the reconstruction of France was a necessary condition for the prosperity of German national industry. He declared that this would mend relations with France, that it would ameliorate the conditions of the peace treaty, alter and mitigate the burden of the indemnities, influence the interior situation in Germany and help to regain Germany's moral prestige abroad. This recognition showed his moral and cosmopolitan outlook and was a good example of his insight as a banker and a good European. But at the Spa Conference Rathenau's policy was violently opposed by Hugo Stinnes, who represented the industrialists on the German delegation. Stinnes insisted that the demands of the Allies should be rejected and thought that thus they would have to risk the carrying out of sanctions by invading Germany. Against this policy Rathenau spoke strongly at a meeting of the German delegation. He held that negotiations might slowly lead to an alteration in the terms of the Versailles Treaty. The ability which Rathenau showed in demonstrating his case had the effect of bringing most of the other delegates to his side and thus began what afterwards became known as the "fulfilment policy." But Rathenau was foresighted enough to demand that at the same time negotiations should be carried on with Russia.

As a result of his attitude at Spa, Stinnes spread the rumour that Rathenau was aiming at the foundations of a mammoth electrical combine in collaboration with Loucheur and that he understood nothing of Germany's distress because he had "the soul of an alien race." Thus a commercial pirate and an adventurer without any serious social ideas who demanded during the war that all occupied territory should be permanently annexed, simply so that he might have more ground whereon to spread his own tentacles, a Cagliostro who made an immense fortune out of the misery of his country and was one of those who engineered the inflation policy and made enormous profits out of it, a man who disposed of his immense fortune in such a way before his death that he cheated the impoverished state of the inheritance tax—this was the man who had the effrontery to attack Rathenau, the idealist, who sought no personal advantage whatsoever in giving his services to the country. Rathenau wrote at this time:

"Man after man will have to jump into the ditch before it can be crossed. But it will never be crossed unless somebody takes the plunge first. . . . I consider that task is to smooth the way for my successors. The first two or three people can only mark the path, the fourth will straighten it out and lay it. A start must be made somewhere or other."

Wirth appointed him Minister of Reconstruction. In those days of what he called "grave decisions and breathless pause in face of the unknown," he wrote me thus. "I have cut myself away from what has been my lifework for thirty years. And I am now in the position I was in 1914, but more than seven years older."

From that moment Rathenau's path was steep and difficult. It was the last year of his life and he felt it.

His first achievement in his new position was to come to an agreement with Loucheur about making deliveries in kind to France in lieu of the gold payments which ruined the value of the mark. It was arranged that these deliveries should be supervised by a corporation set up especially for that purpose. I met him the same evening that he returned from the Wiesbaden Conference, where the agreement had been signed. He was in high spirits. He felt and said that after losing two years, in which nothing had been done, Germany was now coming into touch once again with the outside world. He demonstrated to us very clearly how the struggle against the treaty could be started at this point. Soon afterwards, however, both French and German industrialists revolted. The French industrialists felt that German deliveries in kind would mean competition against their own interests and the Germans did not relish the idea of being paid in marks for the goods they exported. They preferred to hoard the more stable French franc. If Rathenau's plan could have been carried out the invasion of the Ruhr would not have taken place, the mark would not have collapsed and the French franc would not have been eventually inflated.

A short time afterwards, in the autumn of 1921, Rathenau came to London to negotiate with Lloyd George and the London financiers about Germany's inability to make payments in gold instalments. But he was allotted to a bad hotel and treated as a prisoner there. Yet he succeeded in bringing Lloyd George to agree to a reduction of the German payments for the following year. He influenced the English ministers to look favourably on the policy of rebuilding Russia in collaboration with the other European nations, and also to conclude a pact in regard to the Rhine with Belgium and France and perhaps also with Germany. During those few days that he spent in London Rathenau brought into being a new orientation of European policy towards Russia and he mapped out the first stages of the road to Locarno.

His prestige was so great at this time that he was made Foreign Minister in spite of the protests of his financial colleagues and the socialists, and of course, the intrigues of the Wilhelmstrasse. That was about five months before his death. He foresaw the danger of his position when he said: "Any reasonable foreign policy in Germany today must run counter to popular feeling." He knew the risk he was running and he was ready to pay the price. Of course, in such moments ambition is a driving power in the case of every man of action, but in Rathenau's case it was not a decisive motive. For a time I myself thought his ambition was driving him on at this juncture, because I saw little or nothing of him during that winter; but afterwards when I read his intimate letters I realized how mistaken I had been. Those letters show that he was simply sacrificing himself to the country's good. On the evening of his appointment as Foreign Minister he wrote to his friend: "With a heavy heart I am thinking of you, Lili, late at night. You will have heard from Felix of the decision I had to make this evening. I stand before this task in deep earnest and doubt. What can one individual do in the face of a decadent world, with enemies at his back and conscious of his own limitations and failings? I shall work with a good will and do the best I can. If I do not succeed then I know that you at least will not forsake me like the others."

He was himself a Prussian and he now furnished his rooms at the Ministry in the reserved and modest manner that characterized the old times of Prussian thrift. In the previous summer I had sent him a sprig of thorn I had found in his garden and a laurel from my own. He replied with the following lines:

"Die wir den Geboten lauschen
Gegenschöpfender Dæmonen,

Mögen wir aus ihren Händen
Delphische und Zionsspenden,
Sprossen der Verheissung tauschen:
Dorn und Lorbeer flechten Kronen."

(May not we who obey the commandments of conflicting powers
send to each other from their hands those gifts of Delphi and
Zion which are buds of promise: Thorn and laurel embellish
crowns.)

When he sought renown his thoughts were so much on the
thorns that he wrote the following to his friend on the evening
before he left for the Genoa Conference, which was the last time
he represented Germany: "This is the most difficult juncture of
my life. It is nothing more than a farewell. I know that what I
am undertaking, whether it will turn out successful or not, will
mean the breaking of my life. If I come back home I shall be attacked on all sides." His thoughts were so much directed towards
death that this phrase alone, "if I come back home," shows that
he had counted on the possibility of an attempt on his life during the course of the Genoa Conference.

On that occasion, in the Easter of 1922, Lloyd George, as
arbiter of the world's affairs, tried to play a many-sided game
at Genoa. It was the first time the Russians had appeared at
a European conference. They were looked upon as if they
were wild beasts. And Lloyd George tried to trap them. Day
after day was spent discussing Russia's war debts and her
counter-claims arising out of the Denikin adventure. Within
twenty-four hours Rathenau decided to forestall the rest and
on Easter Sunday signed a treaty with Russia whereby Russia
and the defeated Germany were brought together. When
the news of the treaty was published next day the effect was
catastrophic; so much so indeed that I, who attended the
Conference as press correspondent, found myself drawn away

by the general feeling. I wrote then in defence of the treaty itself but said that the time for the signing of it was inopportune. Rathenau asked me to come and see him. He received me after midnight. He was in high spirits and elegantly dressed, as he had just returned from a political dinner. His features seemed rejuvenated. His mood was militant and active and he was entirely certain of what he was doing. When I answered his questions and told him I thought his treaty ran the danger of breaking up the Conference, he laughed and said:

"This Conference won't break up. I could not have negotiated the treaty with the Russians before the Conference met; if I had done so the Conference would not have been called at all. If I had allowed the matter to stand over to a later date, then the treaty could not have been made, because the Russians were already about to conclude negotiations with the other side." To a counter-question of mine, he replied: "That is not my fault. I took over the country in the condition it had been left by Ludendorff."

His conviction of having done the right thing banished all my doubts and when I left him I was filled with admiration for the grit and quickness he showed in acting as he did. That was only a few weeks before his death. I never saw him again. But he was the only delegate to the Genoa Conference who brought something home to show his people. And not merely the Russian Treaty, but also positive proof that he had put Germany on the right track to regain the confidence of the world at large. That was the result of his own personal influence. He was able to balk Poincaré's intention of invading the Rhineland, though the text of the Versailles Treaty gave the French the right to do so. This was the second time Rathenau saved Germany from invasion.

When he came back from Genoa those who had at first acclaimed the Russian Treaty now began to attack the author of

it. Helfferich tried to bring about his downfall in Parliament
and heap obloquy on him throughout the country. Stinnes' taunt
about Rathenau having the soul of an alien race and Ludendorff's defamation of him were made the watch-words of an anti-
Rathenau agitation among the populace. One of the semi-mili-
tary organizations in Upper Silesia used to sing a song as they
paraded the roads, the refrain of which was:

"Knallt ab den Walther Rathenau,
Die Gottverdammte Judensau."

(Shoot down Walther Rathenau, the God-damned Jewish sow.)

That was the mood of a nation which could not accept defeat
and could not bring itself to negotiate a compromise with the
victor. Though entirely powerless, the Germans still clung des-
perately to their belief in brute force. They seemed determined
to have the blood of every German who had a European outlook,
especially if he happened to be of Jewish origin. Many of the associations among the younger men committed to memory and
quoted passages from speeches made by the Junkers and their
leaders, songs of the ultra-patriotic soldiers and libels circulated
by the former military leaders of Germany. It was in these
circles of the younger generation that the decision was taken
to murder Rathenau as an enemy of the Fatherland. The seven-
teen-year-old son of one of the generals, a young naval officer,
a neurasthenic student, a few hooligans—all of whom were only
boys and had never read a word that Rathenau wrote—came together and told one another, probably sincerely, that he was a
Bolshevist, had married his sister to Radek and had made an
agreement with the Entente for the appointment of Jews to government positions in the various European countries. They had
not read a word of the patriotic speech he had made a few days
before in defence of the population of the Saar. But they read

avidly what Helfferich had said in Parliament. Helfferich declared that Rathenau had driven countless people to destitution and suicide by his policy. At the trial of the murderers which was held after Rathenau's death they confessed that these were the motives of their action.

In those dark days a Catholic priest came to the Chancellor in a very serious mood and declared that a young man had confided to him that he had been chosen to murder Rathenau. During those weeks of June, Rathenau worked hard in detailed routine fashion to bring to concrete realization the negotiations which had been concluded at Genoa. He accepted the protection of police detectives only for a short while and then refused it. He believed in his fate. He had already written of this profound belief. But he seems not only to have foreseen his own death. He also seems to have willed it as a martyr for the country. His sensitive temperament, which was so often mistaken and sneered at by public men in Germany, probably yearned for this end too as a kind of glorified consummation of all his suffering.

"What a wretched life that is which follows its even course undisturbed!" he wrote to his friend just before his death. "The wonderful thing is that all real suffering has its beauty. Only what is stupidly abnormal or arbitrarily perverted is vulgar. Will an arbitrary decision now intervene? My life has run too far along its predestined course to allow of such interference. . . . Certainly there is not much more left for me to do. My flame of life is burning low."

His murderers lay in wait for him as hunters conceal themselves behind cover to shoot some noble beast of the forest. They shot him to death in his open car. But the moment the news spread that he was dead the nation realized at least for a moment the meaning of what had happened. They recognized their loss. Over a million came together for a mass demonstration in Berlin. Germany had never given a private citizen such a funeral.

The German Republic buried him as the Romans buried their dead Emperors.

A few weeks afterwards the clouds gathered anew over the German Fatherland, and darker now than before. With the death of Rathenau as founder and representative of the fulfilment policy the nationalist spirit in Germany was free to express itself raucously again. Its cry became even louder than before, although Stresemann found that nothing was possible but to carry on Rathenau's policy in the Foreign Office. This he did, though he had been opposed to Rathenau previously. It was a moment when the atmosphere was clear for favourable negotiations with Germany's ex-enemies, but the nationalist arrogance and selfishness balked every attempt at a reasonable overture from the German side. This new outbreak of strident nationalism made the occupation of the Ruhr possible. The stab-in-the-back legend was invented. Rathenau and Stresemann were accused of high treason. The League of Nations was derided. The history of the events that led up to the war was coloured to suit the ultra-nationalist temperament. The youth was taught to believe that Germany's hands were absolutely clear of any war guilt and that Germany had not lost the war. Instead of learning from the mistakes of the Williamite era, there was an impulsive rehabilitation of its arrogance and therewith a damping down of the confidence which Rathenau's policy had enkindled abroad.

Ten years after his death the memorial sign which had been put up at the spot where the murder took place was removed by permission of the political authorities. At a mass meeting of jurists a high government official of the Third Reich declared amidst loud applause that those who had hitherto been looked upon as murderers would henceforth have their names inscribed as heroes in the Fatherland's roll of honour; their graves have been officially decorated.

MOTTA

THE SWISS EUROPEAN

MOTTA

THE SWISS EUROPEAN

THE old village is perched high on the hillside. Here the declivity is steep and rugged. Æons ago a huge mass of mountain broke away from the Gotthard peak and tumbled downwards. It took a multiform and jagged appearance, which recalls fantastically the image of a mighty monarch scorning his high throne and renouncing it precipitously to come down and live among his fellow men. At least that is the impression which the St. Gotthard has always made on me. There is a world significance in the fact that it is not merely the central feature of one country, but that it also stands in the middle of the European continent. Two of Europe's great rivers spring from the loins of this mighty monarch of the Alps, and some smaller streams. These bring the power and wealth of their source to distant lands and are the symbols of an energy that was stored up countless ages ago. For me there is a definite historical significance in the fact that the Swiss nation was born under the protection of the St. Gotthard.

Let us now turn our backs to this mighty gesture of nature and gaze southwards where the hills gradually descend and the meadows unfold their green carpet along the valleys. There is a small river that springs out exultingly from the mountainside like a torrent. As we gaze on the scene it is natural to see in it a fit background for the personality and career of a Swiss statesman whose firmness reminds one of the rock from which he has sprung, while at the same time he has that innate sense of personal humility that a man must feel who has been born and reared amid such natural grandeur.

In former days, before men bored their tunnel through this venerable mountain, before the locomotive pulled the railway train through the fissure in its body, before the motor car sped over its shoulder or the aeroplane flew above its head—before these things came to pass those who lived on its precipices looked with awe on that exalted custodian whose head was generally shrouded in cloud and storm. He stood between the North and the South. It needed long hours and days of toil for man and horse and mule before men from the North surmounted this gigantic barrier and looked into the smiling faces of the Mediterranean folk as if they were mysterious beings dwelling in some enchanted land.

In the village of Airolo, which clings to the hillside at the southern exit of the St. Gotthard Pass, there was the old post-house where horses were changed before or after surmounting the pass itself and where man and beast found shelter and food. In the early seventies the mountain still inspired a sense of awe in the soul of the traveller or trader. At that time the Mottas owned the post-house and the stage-coaches from Faido to the St. Gotthard Pass. They are one of the oldest families in the Canton of Ticino, tracing their lineage back to the fourteenth century; but unfortunately the village records were destroyed in a fire some time ago. A young fellow with an alert mind and anxious to learn from experience must have found this an interesting place in his boyhood. The trade between North and South passed to and fro. Saddlers and carpenters and wheelwrights and blacksmiths and farriers were employed by the post-house to attend to the needs of the travellers. The village natives had mostly to win their livelihood by hard toil at a height of four thousand feet, tending their cattle and sheep on the tiny uplands amid the rocks and carefully nursing every rood of soil that would grow crops for food. The life here must have been utterly different from the silent and secluded existence of the peasants in the lower valleys and different too from that lived in the towns.

It was here at Airolo that young Motta gained his first impressions of life—from mixing with men of various countries, watching their beasts of burden and hearing the opinions and notions which they aired by the post-house fire or in the smithy. In his own family the mother tongues were different; for one of his grandmothers hailed from Uri on the northern side of the mountain range, which was German-speaking, and another from Oberwallis. Six married couples represented the heads of the family group when Giuseppe Motta was a boy. They and their children possessed the Motta estates. Even the family itself was a sort of cosmopolitan republic, made up of parents and grandparents, uncles and granduncles, brothers and sisters and cousins. They were all brought up in the old Catholic tradition. If the reader tries to picture the milieu for himself, he can easily imagine the constant whirl of activity, mental and physical, that was going on, and how easy it must have been in such circumstances for a gifted youngster to develop either a revolutionary flair or a balanced outlook, and how liable a good-hearted young fellow would be in such circumstances of intimate acquaintance with all kinds of men to cultivate a liking for his kind. The latter is what happened in the case of Giuseppe Motta. The path he has followed has consistently been that of loyalty and helpfulness to his fellow men, first as the repre-

sentative of his own little village and later in the League of
Nations.

2

The little town of Ascona, amid whose sylvan surroundings I am
writing these pages, has a long history. When the nine-year-old
boy came down here from Airolo to begin his studies, the Col-
lege of Ascona was already three hundred years old. St. Charles
Borromeo built it where it stands today, a few hundred paces
from the lake and at the edge of the delta which has been formed
within our own era by the wayward river Maggia. The youth
of the Ticino studied here until they were sixteen years of age.
Their surroundings were tranquil and retired and little disturbed
by strangers. The people of this district are easy-going and not
very enterprising but much happier in their way than the
Ticino folk of the upper mountain valleys, where there is little
soil and life is hard. Here in this southern corner of Switzerland
the humble needs of the peasants and fishermen fall into their
hands almost of their own accord—at least all they needed fifty
years ago.

Amid these surroundings a boy could read the tangled history
of his country in pillars and frescoes, castle walls and ruins. If
he felt inclined, he could thus trace the story of the good and
the evil that had come to it from Milan and from its northern
confederates through half a thousand years. Though he stood
on Swiss ground here—just as much a part of Switzerland as the
ancient Swiss canton of his grandmother—yet the south wind,
the *inverna*, brought strange knowledge to him. In boats and
carts it bore hitherto unknown fruits and the woven cloths that

were made in the South. Morning after morning he could look
out over the Italian frontier. He could see the customs official
and the shovel-hatted Italian priest. Every artisan and peasant
about him was a creature of the South. In their dress, in their
ways, in their language, in the decorations of their houses, they
were the heirs of the Latin civilization. Instead of adopting a
haughty and disdainful attitude towards the neighbouring country, as often happens with frontier youth, this boy conceived a
high regard for Italy, which was at one time indeed lord and
master of his own country.

During the long holidays there was much to do and much to
see at home. But everything changed suddenly when he was
twelve years old. Childhood and boyhood came to an end all at
once: his father died and the Gotthard Railway was opened.
Almost at the same time as the family lost their breadwinner
they also lost their chief source of livelihood, which was the post-
house. The mother was left with six children. She transformed
the business to an inn. "She was a very clever woman. I owe my
self-control to her," said Motta to me when speaking about his
childhood.

And so the happy days of childhood were over. Death and
scientific progress had struck a heavy blow against the little
home. Instead of waking in the morning to hear the cracking of
the whip and the stamping of four stalwart horses and the wind-
ing of the postman's horn, the inhabitants now heard a shrill
cry and saw a black snake push its way snorting into the high
mountain. When it had disappeared a grey smoke eddied outwards, as if it were the angry hiss of the mountain spirit against
the cunning of his conqueror. The once busy junction of the
post-house became a wayside halt and soon the express trains
roared through without stopping. They showed no token of respect towards that spot from which so many thousands of men

had set out to surmount the mountain barrier during so many thousands of years.

Giuseppe Motta's father had been burgomaster and the uncles were in the parish council. At the age of twenty-one the young man took part in the village deliberations and showed himself a balancing factor even at that early age. He made his major studies first at Fribourg in Switzerland and then in Germany. At the age of twenty-four he took his Doctorate of Laws *summa cum laude* at Heidelberg. Forthwith he became a barrister and was appointed deputy to the local parliament. Although he had to travel to Bellinzona for the sessions and although his legal practice summoned him to many towns and villages of the South, he still continued to live high up on the side of the mountain and travelled by rail or carriage to his duties. He had only the week-ends by his own fireside. But he considered that a full recompense for living at Airolo; for, as he said, "I am an out-and-out mountaineer."

In both spheres of his activity, in law and in politics, young Motta always endeavoured to secure his ends through amicable agreement. The people of the Ticino loved litigation, so much so that they are said to enjoy their legal battles more than the actual winning of the case. Yet Motta won ninety per cent of his cases through friendly settlement outside the courts. He acted in the same way at the meetings of the canton parliament. He stuck steadfastly to his own party and for that reason people trusted him. Though there was a good deal of rather bitter party strife in the canton during those days, Motta always stood for tolerance and mutual understanding and compromise. Later on when all the parties were looking for someone to represent the canton of Ticino as a whole in the Federal Parliament, Motta was chosen.

He was twenty-eight years old when he was elected a member of the Federal Parliament at Berne as Senator. At that time the sessions were held in a small hall with rather low ceiling. Its size and its furniture were expressive of a simplicity and modesty that are characteristic of Swiss public life. Each provincial council chamber in Prussia was much more grandiose than this Swiss capitol. Beside it was a vacant space where the market gardeners spread out their wares twice a week.

At the beginning of the present century a new building took the place of the old federal hall. But the modern edifice is distinguished from the parliaments of almost all the other governments in the world by its strict adherence to the traditional Swiss simplicity. The vegetable market still remains. Three or four yards from the main steps of the government palace, cabbages and turnips are sold. Here are housed all the government offices of a nation of four millions of people. And on the balustrades of the approach to the main entrance, where other governments post sentries and implant cannons which they have conquered from their foes, fresh flowers are blooming and market women are weighing out the cheeses which they have brought down from the mountain in the grey dawn. It does not in the least detract from the dignity of the place, because such familiarity between public life and the private interests of the humblest of its citizens is a dominent feature of Switzerland. I have seen nothing like this in any other European democracy. It would be impossible in Athens or Stockholm or Lisbon.

And yet these are the things that give the keynote to the chief virtues of the Swiss people—solidity rather than show, simplicity rather than ceremony, mutual trust rather than the urge of competition, and silence rather than talkativeness. The men who sit in those offices that tower above the vegetable market have not been attracted to public life by the promise of gain or honour. The salary of a deputy is three thousand Swiss francs, or about six hundred dollars at normal exchange. On that salary they have to live in Berne during the sessions. They have no

titles. Nobody is called "honourable" or "Excellency" or Sir
This or Sir That. And there is no official residence, not even for
the President of the Republic, whose salary is only three thousand francs more than that of the other councillors. There are
no government motor cars and no such thing as an honours
list. I have never seen simpler stair carpets in any public building,
even those laid during the session. Yet everything inside is of
sound and solid quality, valuable wood from the Swiss forests,
dark green leather on the chairs. The office of each Secretary
of State has a little oval china disc on the door indicating the
department. In these offices and in the council chamber not the
slightest attempt has been made at luxurious furnishing. The
only pretentious thing that I saw throughout the whole building
was a colossal porcelain clock surmounted by a trumpeting genie.
It was the gift of Kaiser Wilhelm II.

But in the garden that fronts the building there is a huge
block of quartz, a symbol of the treasures that are held in the
heart of the Swiss mountains.

3

For fifty years the Canton of Ticino sent no representative to the
Federal Council. From 1864 this Ticino, the Italian-speaking section of Switzerland, had no voice in the government of the
federal Bund. Officials used to claim that it was because of internal political strife among the Swiss-Italians. But that was
merely a convenient answer for the gentlemen in Berne. I myself, a domiciled resident in the Ticino by personal choice, have
often wondered at the loyalty displayed by these neighbours
around me in clinging to the Swiss Federation in spite of all the
wrongs that they have suffered from the German-Swiss in past

times and the disabilities under which they have laboured until recently by reason of their exclusion from the Federal Council. When I put a question to Motta on this point, he replied: "The most profound reason is the passion for liberty which exists in the Ticino. Even party strife goes down before it. For the Ticinesi Switzerland is the symbol of freedom. And that is why the slogan *Liberi e Svizzeri* [Free and Swiss] rang in every market place and café one hundred and fifty years ago, during the fight of the Ticinesi for union with Switzerland."

During a span of ten years the stately figure of Francini represented the Ticino in the Berne Government. When he died, Pioda took his place. And after that nothing, or rather ceaseless party strife, as in days of the Guelfs and the Ghibellines, who waged their faction fights even up into the gorges and castles of the Ticino. Motta espoused the cause of the Ticino as if it were a religious mission. He lauded the little country and called it the favourite child of Helvetia, although the child in reality has been the recipient of few favours. "The language and love of artistic form are its characteristics, a special kind of union between nature and art. Therefore it is more than a duty, I had almost said a command from God, that the people of the Ticino should preserve their native tongue. Nature has endowed our respective races with their respective qualities. To the Germans she has given their characteristic sense of order and faculty for organization. To the French she has given a genius and passion for liberty and for the rights of the individual. To the Ticinesi she has given a warm expansiveness of soul and an inherent perception and love of Beauty, whose spirit hovers over our lakes and our valleys and our rivers. We must allow these respective virtues of our respective races in Switzerland to interact in mutual harmony, so that each may learn from the other."

Love of home is a centripetal force. Hence it is sounder and stronger at the centre than at the periphery. I can love my native village more than my canton and my canton more warmly than the country in general. If a country grows in size, so as to include forty or fifty millions of people, or even more, then the love of one's homeland is dispersed into a misty feeling to which we have given the hideous name of patriotism. Just as we are more affected by the death of a cat that has lived in our own company than by the destruction of three thousand Chinese in a typhoon, so the allegiance of a statesman is specially strong towards his native place. Sometimes, of course, it may lead him into mistakes and towards the championship of a policy somewhat unjust to the country as a whole. Motta once said that the happiest day of his life was in 1911 when the whole of the Ticino voted for him as their representative in the Federal Parliament. When he was forty years old he was elected by the almost unanimous will of the Swiss people as one of the seven members of the Federal Council and was four times chosen to fill the presidential chair. All this was due not merely to his great abilities but primarily to his faculty for spreading conciliation on all sides, with the result that he has never made enemies.

Motta is by nature supremely qualified to be a non-party leader. To reach his final position in the public life of Switzerland he had only to widen his concentric circles, from the parish council at Airolo to the canton legislature at Bellinzona, thence to the Federal Parliament at Berne and finally to the Federal Council of the Federation. This steadily developing expansion saved him from particularism. "If Switzerland were not a federation," he once said to me, "she would not exist. We can solve the various problems of diverse languages and diverse civilizations and the problem of democratic government only because we are federalistic. This conviction has grown stronger and stronger with me as the years have passed." His political philosophy is therefore opposed to fascism of every kind, which tends to force everything whether external or internal under one inexorable rule.

Having entered the Government so young, Motta has now the

longest public service record in Switzerland. He has made for
himself a kind of tradition and may be called the doyen of the
Federal Council. But he is still only in the middle sixties. The
office of Foreign Minister has only recently been established as a
permanent secretaryship of state. Hitherto the President, who is
changed every year, held this office in rotation. Since 1920 Motta
has been Minister of Foreign Affairs; so that he has held the
position longer than anyone else in the history of the country.

He has no liking for political controversy. The din and noise
amid which modern politics are conducted in other nations are
entirely alien to Motta's temperament. In fact some of the
younger Swiss generation think that somehow or other something is lacking in him simply because his work is carried on
so quietly. In Parliament he once said: "So far as concerns the
politics of the honourable gentleman who has just spoken and
banged the table so often during his speech, I cede all the honours to him and also the responsibility." And on another occasion, during a debate, he said: "I am not a lawyer pleading a
case. I cannot put an argument in such a dazzling light that all
the other arguments must retreat into the shade. Still less am I
a judge, raised above all emotion on some cold and serene level.
I am a politician who recognizes his responsibility and endeavours
to do his share towards weaving a few threads into the fabric
of our country's history." That, I believe, is the farthest this typical Swiss has ever gone in displaying his inner attitude before the
public.

4

The problem to which he has given most thought and spoken
most about is that of Switzerland itself. And not, as with other

ministers, as a mere ground for the exercise of his own political thought but as a concrete example of something which has been achieved in this country exclusively during a thousand years of European history. The form and figure of this international state which is Switzerland is constantly the object of Motta's study and admiration. Inspired by its example, he asks himself whether it may not be possible for the various nations of Europe to unite one day on terms of a similar quality and common political administration and forget the wars which they have fought during so many centuries. But he does not look upon Switzerland as merely resting on the guaranties of the international politicians who have declared that the preservation of her independence "is in the true interests of European politics," nor does he quote the repetition of this declaration at Versailles. As I am one of those who hope that one day we may see the example of Switzerland copied by the whole of Europe I have often spoken with Motta on the point. He looks forward much more confidently and definitely than others to the consummation of what we are hoping for. On one occasion he said:

"We inhabit a beautiful country. But it is a poor one. And this latter is one of the main factors that has helped the Swiss in the consolidation of their own unity. Democracy is the political expression of this solidarity. If the people are to have the final voice in the management of public affairs, then each citizen must feel it his duty to safeguard the interests of all the others. The fact that there are only a few millions of us, and not many, has helped towards Swiss unity. Shall I make a comparison with the rest of Europe? We have three great civilizations. If we had only one great civilization and two minor ones, could we have achieved the same harmony? In Belgium there is the strife between French and Flemish. If the strife were between the French and German forms of civilization things would be less difficult. Moreover, we are definitely influenced by the highest average of each civilization. Naturally there are outstanding individuals among us; but in general we are a nation of average people.

"The English democracy grew up in a different way. It cannot put its principles into practice beyond its own national boundaries. There are immense territorial possessions and a manifold ramification of industries to be protected. How could England submit such complicated interests to a referendum of the whole empire? Therefore the mission of English democracy seems to be a sort of moral and cultural one, as exemplified in its championship of an international court of arbitration. Only the small state can really be founded on liberty, for it alone has for its object the development of the individual, while in large states the power of the state itself is the principal object of care and development. The citizen ought to think: "Here [in Switzerland], I am happy because I can exercise and develop my own capacities. And the way to this end is by practical self-rule."

I have not such a high degree of confidence in the opinion of an Alpine shepherd on present-day problems as this theory would lead us logically to have. Therefore I questioned Motta on the working of this kind of popular referendum in Switzerland. In the year 1913 the French part of Switzerland became perturbed about the Gotthard agreement which the state had made with Italy and Germany. There was a movement for the establishment of a means of popular control over state treaties. Before the war the Federal Council was opposed to this movement, but it withdrew its opposition later on. And it was Motta, as spokesman for his colleagues in the Federal Council, who advocated the establishment of the State Commission, though as Foreign Minister he was fully aware of the disadvantages of this kind of popular referendum. "And yet," he said, "the Swiss people proved its worth at the first trial; for they rejected the zone agreement with France and finally found their stand ratified by the verdict of The Hague. This was perhaps the first case of its kind in which one of the great powers had to submit to the counter-decision of a small nation."

While we were talking about the limits up to which democracy may be practicable, I noticed that the twin ideals of liberty and unity seemed to be constantly before his mind and I was curious to know whether his attitude had always been the same. His speeches would certainly point to this conclusion. The fact that he is able to speak publicly in three languages gives him an advantage over other Swiss leaders. In the complete collection of his speeches we find that for a whole generation he has been constantly insisting on these two principles. In one of his speeches, he says, for instance:

"Swiss democracy holds a unique position in history. It cannot be compared to any ancient or modern republic. No nation has ever governed itself so completely according to the collective will of the people. Ancient governments were in the hands of a small élite class who ruled over a multitude of slaves. The great states around us seek their ideals in a uniformity of race and language. That is not our ideal. We abhor discussions on race and language. From this point of view the ideal of our state is supernational. And because of this specific characteristic of our country we can be a practical factor for the establishment of peace. Switzerland is today the country that has the most stable government. It is the only modern state wherein the sovereignty of the people can be felt as an everyday reality. There is no political community where the standard of public education is higher, where labour is more respected, where public affairs are more honestly administered or where the control of the people over public affairs is more steady and watchful."

In the trying time of the war and the post-war period it has always seemed to me that Switzerland remained the pivotal centre of unity and democracy. Motta once declared: "Unity is a necessary thing for every nation. For us it is a question of life or death. Our nation is almost unique in the world inasmuch as it embraces three major types of civilization: The Italian civilization, with its love for the beautiful and the human; the French, with its clarity and brilliancy, its chivalry and its readiness in debate; the German, hard-working, methodical and orderly. I am so proud of my country and I have such a high opinion of it that I believe if Switzerland should haul down the democratic flag, democracy would suffer a fatal blow not only in our own country but also elsewhere."

Probably owing to his peasant origin and also to his upbringing as a conservative, Motta is inclined to be critical of socialist innovations. "If we wish to hold firmly to our system of direct democratic government," he said during a speech delivered in 1925, "that is to say, to the system of government of the people by the people, then we must be resigned to a certain tardiness in social progress. For this delay we shall find moral compensation in the profound conviction of each citizen that he is cooperating by his active sanction and by his work in the progress that is made." These ideas sounded rather strange to me and I reminded him of the fundamental progress that resulted in Switzerland from the last two great revolutions. He did not admit the validity of the argument, because it compared Switzerland with the neighbouring nations. He attacked the principle of class struggle and accepted only the socialist idea of the masses having a common share in all property. "I have even advocated," he said, "that they [the Socialists] should be allowed to enter the Federal Council, but only on condition that they accept the Constitution and the principle of national defence, also that they should renounce the championship of physical force to carry out their aims. These conditions they refused to accept."

Motta belongs to that older class of statesmen who would save democracy even by maintaining an unequal distribution of the world's goods. They believe that internal peace can be secured by external peace, even though there are other forces working for its destruction.

5

To such a mind, whose bent is always towards conciliation, the League of Nations must appear the best means for the forwarding of that ideal. To a man who speaks so many languages and is so able an orator Geneva must seem an ideal rostrum. Hence the delegates from all parts of the world to Geneva have come to know Motta in quite a different light from that in which he is known throughout his own country. His national and international work has been carried on in the same country and in centres which are only a few hours' distant from one another. For that reason he was more effective than Briand in having the Geneva and Berne conventions brought to a successful conclusion, though Briand had the same conciliatory qualities as Motta.

Motta had also a further advantage which may be described as follows: The home policy of any Swiss government runs in harmony with its foreign policy more easily than the home and foreign policies of a French government. France is the strongest military power in Europe and at the same time has more to fear from its neighbours than Switzerland. Yet Switzerland, though it represents only one-tenth the population of France, is of almost equal importance as an international influence. Even if we entirely set aside the historical tradition of Geneva and Switzerland's central position in Europe, Switzerland would still have a predominating claim to a seat in the League of Nations, simply on the grounds of its long and fruitful struggle for international right. The objective of state government in Switzer-

land is the objective of the League. Switzerland itself is a prototype in miniature of the League of Nations, because here we
have a brilliant and successful example of different races living
harmoniously together as a European political unit.

At this point we come face to face with the Swiss sense of
realism. Motta was a dominating factor in bringing his country into the League of Nations. But in Motta's speeches you will
find practically no humanitarian phrases. There is only hard-and-
fast logic. About half the Swiss population was opposed to the
idea of their country taking a part in world politics. They wanted
a sort of Monroe Doctrine to be set up as a permanent policy.
Yet the more enlightened leaders saw that this policy was out
of date. In the modern world the interests of the various nations
are too closely intermingled. Permanent neutrality was the traditional policy of Switzerland, based also on international guaranties. Motta pointed out to his countrymen that the objective of
the League of Nations was nothing less than the neutralization,
or "Swissification," of all the other nations. He did not look
upon this new international institution as a combination of
powers that had been victorious in the war and wished to use it
as an instrument to further their own policy. If ever that were
the hope nourished by some of the founders they were disappointed, for they soon saw the League raised far above the level
of a mere puppet show in their hands. Nor did Motta look upon
the League as a seminary for the teaching of humanitarianism.
He looked upon it rather as a means of preparing the way for
the establishment of a permanent Court of Arbitration. In one of
his speeches on this point, he said: "People imagine that the
League has some magic power to change the nature of men and
nations. That is an exaggeration of mass suggestion, which sometimes expresses itself in hymns of praise for the League."

But Motta never belittled the value of the League as an instrument for preventing wars. In 1931 he declared openly that were

it not for the League of Nations further international disturbances would have followed in the wake of the World War. From the moral angle he looked on the League more seriously than did many others of the Geneva delegates. And for that reason he was profoundly angered in 1932 by certain members who threatened to withdraw from the League if this or that or the other claim were not immediately granted. "No government in the world," he said, "can act with a clear conscience in such a manner as would tend to bring about the downfall of this great hope. That is my opinion. For the smaller states it would mean the renunciation of all influence in international affairs. For the great powers it would mean a return to the system of alliances and rivalries. No matter how hampered and inefficient it may be, the League of Nations is still a means of maintaining peace and it is one of the practical signs of human progress."

A Swiss minister who champions such ideas can permit himself to laud the Swiss army; for if any army can be truly called an army of defense, the Swiss army's claim to that title is sounder than the claim of any other. Motta called the Swiss army the pillar of Swiss independence. "It alone gives practical value to the pledges made by the surrounding powers," he declared. Seldom has a statesman expressed his distrust of the great powers in a more delicate way. It amounts to a delightful slap in the face for the spirit of 1933. What he says in another place is very true also: "The Swiss soldier never forgets that he is a citizen and the citizen never forgets that he is a soldier." Hence the Swiss army, which constitutes ten per cent of the population, was mobilized on the frontiers quicker than any other army in August 1914. Motta assures us retrospectively that even if the German army had not entered Belgium the Swiss army would have been mobilized just the same once international hostilities had arisen. "A time will come," he said during the early days of the war, "when all the belligerent nations will thank Switzerland, which was so small and yet so great, for remaining neutral during the war and devoting itself to works of love for our neighbours."

In the midst of the war, Motta, who was then Finance Minister, made a pronouncement that stirred all of Europe. It was a personal gesture in the grand style. "We were at a banquet in Geneva in 1916," he said to me. "The breach between German and French sympathies was wide indeed. It was important to find some formula to which both of these hostile races in Switzerland would subscribe. No matter how keenly the German portion of Switzerland sympathized with German interests, they saw the warning hand of fate in the Belgian affair. It was important to prove to Belgium that Switzerland, as a neutral nation and to an extent the sister nation of Belgium, unanimously sympathized with Belgium in the fate that had befallen her. I did not wish to embarrass my colleague, Hoffmann, by discussing the question beforehand. As Federal Councillors we enjoyed a certain amount of free initiative. Therefore at the banquet I publicly demanded, before the whole of the world and therefore before Germany also, that Belgium should be re-established and that her complete freedom and independence should be restored. I was the only neutral statesman to take such a stand during the war."

Motta has, I think, an impartial and objective mind, in so far as any human being made up of blood and nerves can be impartial. In that banquet speech he expressed the mind of the whole Swiss nation, though it was divided into two camps and speeches and public utterances were being daily made for and against the Germans.

In the conflict between China and Japan, which shook the League to its foundations in 1932, Motta grasped the situation and saved it. As representative of a small Power at the League of Nations, he proclaimed: "If we are forced to give up our faith in the treaty, then we shall have to seek other means of security." After this warning, which was followed by others of a graver nature, the Commission ordered the Japanese to evacuate Shanghai. But the Japanese plenipotentiary delivered a speech in which he questioned the decision. It was a tense moment. A judgment delivered by the nations of the world was rejected by the nation to whom it had been addressed. Everybody at the meeting of the Commission felt that the force and unanimity necessary to put the verdict into effect would never be forthcoming. A deadlock had been reached. The chairman asked if any delegate wished to make a suggestion. "For a moment or so there was silence," Motta told me; "then I said that I desired to speak. And I declared: 'We unanimously demand that the evacuation must be carried out within the stipulated time-limit. I ask the honourable delegate for Japan not to bring up the question again.' I spoke in quite a conciliatory tone. The applause of the meeting showed that they were all on my side. And the Japanese delegate withdrew his objection. It did not need very much courage to make that speech. The difficult matter was to break the silence and begin."

6

When one says that Motta is a faithful Catholic the statement is true also in a political sense. In 1921 he said: "A Catholic is quite naturally both a patriot and a citizen of the world. Just as our religion harmonizes the antithesis of authority and liberty in a higher synthesis, so the concepts of Fatherland, of Mankind and of the Universal Church complete and perfect one another in a supreme unity." On another occasion he said: "I am an

idealist because I believe in God, in Mankind and in my
Country."

These outspoken confessions, such as I have heard from no
other statesman of our time, induced me to ask him why he once
said in a speech that Switzerland could not exist without belief
in God. He replied: "Only a positive faith can supply the foundation for that moral sense of duty which is the essential quality
that makes a democracy. Therefore a people who have no faith
cannot be a real democracy. In Switzerland the founders of our
country ordained it so. In our Constitution the name of God is
honoured. Our religious struggles were the only wars we have
had in recent centuries. These struggles taught the people tolerance. A sense of duty is an essential quality of a citizen; but a
mere man-made law cannot create so fundamental a thing in
the human soul."

Gazing at him while he speaks, one is forcibly impressed by
the type of his features. They are often found in Roman Catholic
priests of the first rank. In Cardinal Gasparri, who was also the
son of a peasant, the same impressive nose and brow are noticeable as in Motta. In both men the eyes are much less striking.
And that is rather curious in the case of Motta, because he is a
forceful orator. Perhaps it is due to his education by priests in
Ascona and also in Fribourg. It may have given him the habit
of turning the eyes upwards, a habit which is less pronounced in
him than in the average priest but much more pronounced than
in the average statesman. He will not brook any criticism of the
Vatican. He looks with favour on the settlement which the
Vatican made with Italy and also on the recent concordat with
the new Germany. He thinks the latter more favourable to the
Vatican than the concordat with Napoleon. In my travels
throughout the world I have observed that the power of the
Catholic Church is rapidly waning and therefore on this point
I do not agree with Motta.

I asked him about the Jews, whose cause he espoused in the summer of 1932, when he made the following public declaration: "Those who despise their fellow citizens on the score of religion or speech or race or social status take up a position which is opposed to the spirit of democracy. The attempts which have recently been made here and there to arouse an anti-Jewish feeling are quite contrary to the Swiss spirit."

But Switzerland does not receive all the expelled Jews with open arms, nor does she allow them to sojourn there indefinitely. This is explained by Motta as a policy which is in the interests of the Jews themselves: "At a time of persecution we offer sanctuary to everyone. A real Christian country cannot look indifferently on religious persecution. But there are Jews and Jews, just as there are Christians and Christians. We do not like to allow the quota to increase indefinitely lest we may create a Jewish question ourselves. This, thank God, we have never had yet. In our country Jews have been always respected but have seldom held office. Switzerland is against all persecutions and in favour of the persecuted. As a true democracy she is also against all arbitrary government. A Swiss dictatorship, about which some people are talking today, would be alien to our spirit. It would belie our history and our tradition and would deprive us of the very air we breathe. If Switzerland were to renounce the ideal of liberty, about which there is now so much discussion in other countries, Switzerland would cease to be Switzerland."

7

In his manner of speech and in his attitude towards life Motta is typically Latin. His speeches are constructed on the Ciceronian model. Both in his public orations and in his ordinary conversations he has the habit of putting his own questions and then answering them. In summing up pros and cons he reveals an exactitude that is up to the French tradition at its best. The epitaphs which he wrote for the tombs of his mother and sister are perfectly Latin in their style and tone. That he possesses literary powers to a higher degree than most politicians is shown in his description of the Battle of Morgarten, which he wrote for a centennial publication. Dante is the author in whose writings he revels, and this has probably enriched his religious nature. On the occasion of Switzerland's entry into the League of Nations, Motta quoted Dante in the Federal Council. The quotation evoked an ironic smile from the professional politicians, who think, more so today perhaps than ever before, that poetry is only a decoration for festive occasions and that a statesman ought to keep his cultured taste to himself as being a private affair of his own.

To judge Motta by his public utterances would not be more unjust than it might be in the case of any other democratic statesman whose real work for the interests of his country is recorded only in fragments in the official records. Only with the passing of time is it possible to make a summary of these records and present the man's lifework as a whole. But only in rare cases will that be worth the historian's time and trouble; for only few leaders of our epoch can count on the history of their deeds being of interest to the reading public a hundred years hence. In our day so many events and personalities succeed and replace one another so swiftly that only a man who has epitomized some immortal episode in his own career, or invented some extraordinary legend for himself, may reckon on being of biographical interest to posterity.

In the government office at Berne where Giuseppe Motta works day after day there are numerous tomes bound in red

which contain the records of his political achievements. But his
heart is not in these. By the tone of his voice and the wistful
mood in which he turns to the window to look out on the Alpine
landscape one readily concludes that his thoughts are elsewhere.

When he closes his portfolio and sets out for his ancestral
home on the slope of the mighty Gotthard a marvellous panorama unfolds itself in endless variety before his eyes. The first
stage of the journey is along the undulating country towards Biel
and Lucerne, the rivers becoming narrower and more turbulent
as the journey proceeds. Then the high mountains block the
view. The Lake of Lucerne takes on a deeper hue as the train
ascends and the traveller looks down from the dizzy heights.
The surface of the water becomes smaller and more tranquil and
from the upper hills it looks mysterious—reflecting something
of the spell, one thinks, under which Switzerland first arose.
Climbing rapidly in serpentine fashion, zigzagging to and fro
across the rushing river Reuss, the railway finally approaches the
historic opening in the mountain. The engine rushes inwards.
It is no longer driven by steam. It is an electric locomotive
driven by the same hydraulic power which is borne on the waters
that spring from the very rocks through which the railway tunnel has been bored.

When he sits in the railway carriage and looks out at the
little farmsteads and hamlets and villages that pass beneath his
gaze, when he looks on the green valleys and the carefully cultivated hill slopes, Motta must feel a certain fatherly pride in
this happy, hard-working and prosperous little country. For he
has done so much to make it what it is. And he must see clearly
how much better a thing it is to be a citizen of a small country
than of a big one. In these days of fantastic numbers and still
more fantastic tempo only small countries can cultivate the
homely virtues and the homely ideals of the romantic age. Switzerland is broken up by the mountain chains into numerous

valleys where a retired existence keeps men more alone and makes them more silent than elsewhere. But at the same time it safeguards them from the haste of our century and allows them to conserve the old customs almost timelessly.

When this venerable ruler of Switzerland passes through those valleys on the way to his home he must often think that, though his fellow citizens have certain woes of their own to complain of, they are on the whole happier than the inhabitants of the great countries of the globe. In the rapidly changing world of today he may foresee and dread upheavals that he cannot fit in with his scheme of human things. But at least he can have the assurance that the towering mountains which watch over his country will beat back the first violence that accompanies such upheavals and that if they are to come at all they will come here gradually and peacefully and will not affect the lives of the people so drastically as they will the lives of those who live on plain or seacoast.

He is in the midst of the Gotthard tunnel. The axles are creaking and whining as if the spirit of the mountain were in pain. This mountain was conquered by the modern technique when Motta was a boy and helped to change the post-horses at Airolo. And now he hears a slight squeak of the brake. A tiny light appears. It grows bigger. The noise of the tunnel ceases and one is suddenly plunged into a flood of bright blue light. Another second and the train stops. This active old man walks to the home that he has not seen, perhaps, for over a year. He climbs the rough road to the pass. Only a few turns and he finds himself once more where he used to stand fifty years ago and turn his gaze to the south.

The river Ticino flows at his feet. It gives its name to his canton. As the river falls from one level to another the valleys take on softer and brighter colours, until they disappear into the blue of the heavens. But he knows that down below they sink into the everlasting lakes beside which he was educated as a boy. The cares and problems of the world seem to dissolve and pass away and he thinks to himself: "Let Europe decide as it will. This, after all, is the fairest of fatherlands."

PART TWO

RULERS OF THE PEOPLE

Nature has given us no fault that could not become a virtue, no virtue that could not become a fault. And really these virtues are far the most dangerous.

GOETHE

L L O Y D   G E O R G E

THE BRITISH ODYSSEUS

Before a small farmstead on the outskirts of a country
village a woman and her children stood and watched their household effects sold by auction on the green in front of the house.
Beside the woman was a little boy who showed that he realised
what was going on, though he was only two years old. When
he saw his cot and a little cupboard and some cooking utensils
taken away by strange hands he made an effort to resist. Perhaps the landlord's daughter may have ridden by slowly and
patted the glistening shoulder of her steed as she gazed on the
scene. Perhaps the groom accompanied her on another horse.
What is certain is that the impression which this scene made on
the mind of the little boy overshadowed his whole childhood and
helped to give his ideas a definite turn at a very early age.
While still a child he naturally came to think of the difference
between the children of the rich and his own lot as the child
of poor parents and the foster-child of an uncle who was also
poor. For his father had died just a little before this scene took
place; and the little family was taken into the home of the
mother's brother, who was a village shoemaker. There the child
learned of other such family tragedies taking place in the neighbourhood. If we realise that the uncle was also lay preacher at

the local nonconformist chapel, and that all this took place in Wales during the sixties of the last century, then we can readily understand the chief elements in Lloyd George's early upbringing.

His earliest experiences impressed upon him the contrast between the way in which the children of the propertied classes were cared for and given educational facilities and the way in which the children of the poor were treated. This is why he began his public career by agitating against hereditary rights, hereditary privileges and hereditary power. He was Celtic and not English. Therefore he never worshipped tradition, which is the corner stone of the English character. In order to give the boy an education the uncle had to work for long hours and practise the severest economy. That fact impressed upon the mind of David Lloyd George the injustice of the way in which property and wealth were divided between the members of the community and the injustice of class distinction in admission to legislative power and educational advantages. He determined to devote his life to the righting of these wrongs. But that passionate determination was not directed towards the cause of the working classes as such. He championed rather the hardworking peasants against the idle landowners. And he had no grievance against the industrial employers who were energetic in directing their own enterprises. That perhaps is the reason why this social champion never became a socialist. Until his fiftieth year—that is to say, until the outbreak of the Great War—his ideals were mainly those of a social reformer. And during that period the curve of his genius ran steadily upward.

Why did he weaken later on? Why did the energizing force of his ideals fall off, and why did he fail to sustain the urge of his lifework as one of the leading personalities in the general humanitarian history of our time? The cause must be looked for in the unconscious depths of the man's character. By reason of its innate force and the manner in which its energy was developed and trained, that character was fashioned to command and might have ventured everything at one decisive hour on behalf of the truth to the upholding of which it had been sworn. But his long use of parliamentary means as an instrument for the furtherance of his ideals had divided his allegiance to these ideals for their own sake. He had so often pursued the policy of expediency rather than principle that he became too pliant. And when the decisive moment arrived his character failed him.

Seeing that Lloyd George made his great mistake only after he was long past middle age, it may be that the immense achievements which already stood to his credit had somewhat exhausted his genius and rendered it stale by the custom of parliamentary procedure. At any rate his failure makes it impossible to put him on a footing with Lincoln. When he came to the Versailles Peace Conference he had twenty years of magnificent achievement to his credit. During those twenty years he had fought for certain leading principles of liberty and justice in England and had succeeded in establishing them there, not merely for the good of England but for the good of other nations also. If Lloyd George had been assassinated in December 1918, he would have gone down in history as one of the greatest men of our time. He and Venizelos are only two instances of men who were born more than a generation too soon. They allowed themselves to be carried along with the democratic current of the times, whereas they had in their own inner character sufficient driving power to be independent of any external movement. Had they begun their careers in the post-war period they could have thrown over the democratic movement, as other men of the same strong type of character have done.

Throughout history there have been tyrants, in the classic sense of the term, who were such great philanthropists that one is sometimes almost inclined to have misgivings about the principles of democratic government and to ask whether one strong will may not be more efficient in public affairs than the system of having to wait until many wills have first to be brought into conformity before a decision can be made. In speaking of a dictator one is always conscious of the danger contingent on the fact that there is no regular means of controlling his personal prejudices or correcting his mistakes. And there is the further difficulty of finding a successor when the dictator is gone. Yet no sound political philosopher, in view of modern facts, would dare to say that the rule of one strong personality is not as good a form of state administration as that of five hundred deputies seated in parliament. The fact is that democracy has not yet achieved a statal form adequately expressive of its principles.

Besides his inexhaustible energy, his profound sense of justice and his obstinate antagonism to hereditary privileges, Lloyd George has two characteristic qualities which have contributed very largely to his success as a democratic statesman. The first of these is imagination, which is a Celtic rather than an English quality. The second is his extraordinary faculty for intuitively understanding the other characters around him and the immediate circumstances with which he has to deal. Like so many Celts, he has a musical nature rather than musical talents. With so little general culture and learning and so much imagination, men of his type are quick and sure in making decisions and for that reason will always be a step or two ahead of problematical thinkers like Balfour, though the latter are of a much higher mental quality. Lloyd George's concentrated and yet open expression, the square head and the sharp though friendly eyes, and his general appearance, which is a mixture of determination and kindness, indicate this character. His cunning is often spoken of and that he certainly has, yet he is not crafty in the vulgar sense of the term. In physical build he is rather small and stocky and generally looks up at his interlocutor with the eyebrows drawn together. While his interlocutor is speaking he now and again replies ironically sotto voce. But when he gives the final answer he does it enthusiastically and always puts forward friendly arguments in its defence. He shows imagination and sagacity while he is listening, for he always wants to learn. He never takes up the attitude of being better informed or superior to those around him; but he assimilates everything he hears and makes it his own, changing it chemically without affecting its volume.

If I were asked to state what is the general feature of Lloyd George's character, I should answer—such answers of course being always risky and misleading—that though he is the cleverest and most adroit and adaptable of all his colleagues, yet he is fundamentally naïve. Only a man whose conscience is so simple and clear to himself could have played so many parts in good faith without betraying himself and others. That is why he is irresistible, just as Briand was, who had the same kind of innate naïveté. It is interesting to compare them with men like Masaryk and Nansen, whose moral principles are clearly thought out and logically followed and who have nothing of that sort of cynical ingenuousness characteristic of men like Briand and Lloyd George.

This type of character is so un-English that to the English people Lloyd George often seemed to be some strange animal from a foreign clime. And he influenced them as such, just as did Disraeli, whose foreign racial characteristics impressed the English people in the same way. Yet this highly developed nation recognized the abilities of both these men with unstinted admiration. The more primitive feeling and cruder political mentality of other nations make it impossible for one of foreign racial character to be accepted in public life among them with the same whole-heartedness.

2

In 1890 Lloyd George entered Parliament for the first time. Two important circumstances were in his favour when he delivered his maiden speech in the House of Commons. Like Venizelos, he had come from a country that was not an organic part of the nation in whose Parliament he sat. Besides his right to sit and speak in Parliament, he had the advantage of not belonging to the country itself but of representing his own country and therefore being free to defend its claims. This gave him a more independent position than the average English member had. About this time he wrote of fidelity to one's own nation: "We must remain true to our own nation because we cannot be good people without being good Welshmen. We must admire England with all our heart, but we will not imitate it. Our chief aim must always be to remain faithful to our own country and to our own people. Therefore Home Rule for Wales." Lloyd George did not fail to take advantage of his position as a non-English member. In a political sense he had two passports and he could present the one that suited best as occasion demanded.

He was under the disadvantage of not having been educated in one of the great English universities which have generally been the training-ground for the orators who have made their mark in the House of Commons. But he profited by this disadvantage. He got through his legal studies as quickly as possible, with the aid of the money that his uncle was able to spare for him, and he started as a lawyer when he was still very young. At the age of eighteen he began to write for the newspapers under the pen-name of *Brutus*. But even at an earlier age he was officiating as a pulpit orator. In the rather strict Nonconformist sect to which he belonged, and which had definite leanings towards Calvinism, the pulpit was a kind of public platform, not merely for the propounding of religious doctrines but for social questions of the day. Many great orators have been trained in the pulpits of Wales and their example was a shining light to the ambitious young reformer.

From his childhood he had been memorizing the Bible and living in circles where it was being constantly quoted. Religion used to be discussed openly in his uncle's shoe shop. In listening to these discussions the boy's wits became sharpened and his mind filled with ideas which were generally of a radical nature and opposed to the conservative English tradition. With his knowledge of the Bible he had an advantage over the classical orators from Oxford. And he can still fascinate an English crowd, which is much more familiar with the context of quotations from the Old Testament than of those from the Greek and Latin classics. It is even more familiar with the history of the Jews as pictured in the Old Testament than it is with English history. This gave Lloyd George an enormous advantage over the more highly educated university men when it came to a question of appealing to a popular English audience.

The problem most frequently discussed at those Welsh debates in which Lloyd George took part during his boyhood days was that of the rich and the poor. He had seen landlords turn farmers out of their homes because the latter had voted Liberal. Every week he took a shilling for his uncle to the headquarters of the Liberal Association. At the age of twenty-six he was elected County Councillor for Carnarvon and was usually called "the boy alderman." At that time he fell in love with a girl whose father belonged to the well-to-do classes, which led to friction and trouble between her and her parents. But he finally won her. And when the wedding took place he was already so well known in the locality that the people lit bonfires for him and he delivered a speech. Not long afterwards he handed the management of his law office over to his brother and he himself went around the country making speeches and electioneering. In 1890 he was elected to Parliament with the astonishing majority of 18 votes.

It is interesting now to note that, in this first electioneering fight of his, he made a confession which has explained much of his later life: "First of all," he said, "I am a Welsh Nationalist, and then a Liberal." That statement, made in a small nation which was not then actually fighting for self-government, was a presentment of the conflict which Lloyd George had to face thirty years later when he had to choose between National and Liberal principles. In this latter fight he lost.

The first battles that he fought for the Liberal cause were magnificent encounters. When the Boer War broke out he was at the end of his thirtieth year. It was not his greatest, but it was his noblest period. His speeches at this time recall something of Cromwell and his pacifism was by no means in contrast with the general character of the Puritan warrior. Lloyd George proclaimed his pacifism with religious enthusiasm and great personal courage; for we must remember that the English majority was in favour of the war, even in the Liberal ranks.

"Why am I against war?" he shouted. "It is because I know nothing that arrests progress like war. I have come to the conclusion that I would be a recreant before God and man if at this opportunity I did not enter a protest against what I consider to be an infamy. . . . Is every politician who opposes a war during its progress of necessity a traitor? If so, then Chatham was a traitor, and Burke and Fox especially, and in later times

Cobden and Bright and even Mr. Chamberlain—all these were traitors. While England and Scotland are drunk with blood, the brain of Wales remains clear, and she advances with steady steps on the road of progress and liberty. . . . The Union Jack is the property of our common country, and no man who really loves it could do anything but dissent from its being converted into Mr. Chamberlain's pocket-handkerchief."

The struggle went on for two years. Lloyd George made himself the most unpopular man in England. But he always felt that the turn of events might easily make him the most popular. The driving motive behind his whole action in the anti-war campaign sprang from his sense of indignation against the policy of a mighty state that suddenly made war on a smaller one in order to rob it of its territory. The jingo feeling in England ran so high that his personal safety was threatened. Demonstrations were made in front of his house. His wife was manhandled in the street. The pulpit where he preached in Wales was smashed. And when he came to speak in Birmingham, Chamberlain's native constituency, stones were flung through the window. On that occasion the police had to take him in charge and, for the sake of his personal safety, they smuggled him from the back of the hall disguised in the uniform of a policeman.

The change in public opinion began in less than a year after the Boer War had been brought to a victorious conclusion. Millions of Englishmen now saw that Chamberlain's fiscal policy and the sacrifices which it entailed for the British consumer were necessary only as long as England remained a highly armed country. The result of this change of feeling was that the popular agitator who had spoken against cruisers and in favour of schools soon regained the confidence of the masses. The first great step which he made in re-establishing his popularity with the Eng-

lish public was on the occasion of the Conservative Educational
Bill which was designed to strengthen the position of the Church
of England, to the detriment of the Nonconformists, especially
in Wales. He protested against the proselytizing tendencies of
the bill, saying that it was as if a shepherd were to try to attract
the sheep of another flock to mingle with his own by showing
them better pasture. "This sort of strife and squabbling," he
declared, "would go on with the facilities given for what may
be called lamb-stealing, one sect crossing the boundary and taking sheep from the flock of the other." When the bill finally
was passed and Lloyd George attempted to prevent its application to Wales by organizing a policy of obstruction, the whole
of England became divided in its attitude towards him. One
part was definitely friendly; the other hostile. He had become
a popular leader in the cause of religious freedom and in the
cause of peace. And just here began the danger for a character
not yet completely fixed; unfortunately the greatest public leaders are seldom immune to the seduction of the masses. Because
the public gaze was turned towards him he began to watch and
follow the changes in that public gaze more definitely than he
had ever done before. Even King Edward invited this strange
enemy of his Conservative friends to his palace in order to have
a look at him.

He did not become a Labour leader. Now in his fortieth
year, when the revolutionary leader often develops into a statesman, Lloyd George negotiated for the first time between the
government and the proletariat when a great strike threatened.
He succeeded in quelling the unrest and discontent because he
still had the confidence of the working classes and the Liberal
Government had now come into power with the landslide of
1905. His party had to give him a Cabinet position as President
of the Board of Trade and here he surprised everybody by the
evidence he gave of his organizing abilities. For a long time

he remained silent in Parliament. He did not take part in any public controversies but devoted his whole time to studying the subjects he had to deal with and drawing up detailed plans of reform. The result was that in a short while he succeeded in entirely reorganizing the Board of Trade and this led to his being made Chancellor of the Exchequer in 1908. The man who appointed him was the new Liberal Premier, Herbert Asquith.

3

Asquith was ten years older than Lloyd George. In the beginning of their political work together as colleagues in the Cabinet, he was a sort of mentor who held a restraining hand over his enthusiastic protégé. Indeed Asquith had almost forced Lloyd George on his own colleagues. After the war I came to know these two men for the first time and in the same week. I felt the greater admiration for Asquith and was more drawn towards him, though he had nothing of the personal magnetism of Lloyd George. Asquith struck me as a classic example of the English tradition at its best.

I have always been attracted by the study of physiognomy and here I could not help comparing the two heads. Asquith had the high type of head and the face was beardless. He looked like a Roman of the classical period, with sensitive thin lips and high forehead. He had the serious meditative look of a man who thinks first and then acts. Lloyd George's head is broad rather than high and his glance is definitely fixed on something outside. The eyes are bright and attractive. Everything about him speaks of an active rather than a meditative character.

When Asquith took action on some question or other it

seemed as if he were descending from the tranquil realms of thought into the world of deed, while Lloyd George seemed to step upwards on an inclined plane, endeavouring to conquer the next step or at least make it easier. The classical education of the older statesman was in strong contrast to the practical experience of the younger. Asquith's taciturnity contrasted with Lloyd George's loquacity. The difference of their characters became manifest only because they used different means to gain their ends, for both followed the same ideals in the administration of the state. But Asquith was by far the nobler character. He never would have participated in transactions on the Stock Exchange as Lloyd George did, with results that were disturbing to his political career. Asquith would never have forsaken a political friend. Asquith, of course, had energy just as Lloyd George had character; but these were mixed so differently in each that only the sense of humour united them, and even that was of a different kind in each case. Asquith was a typical gentleman, Lloyd George a tribune of the people. Therefore it is no wonder that eventually they parted company politically. But it is surprising that, in spite of so many opposite qualities in their characters, they worked together in harmony for ten years. The whole merit of this seemed to belong to Asquith.

Lloyd George began his activity as Chancellor of the Exchequer in 1909 with an innovation that was historical. In bringing in what was called his "war budget," though it was in the midst of peace, Lloyd George gave a sign to the feudal lords of Europe either to get their abdication papers ready or to prepare for a terrific fight. The whole world listened when the insignificant little attorney from Wales, the shoemaker's ward, turned on the mighty lords in their century-old castles, under the banner of justice and humanity. He envisaged three forms of insurance whereby the state should take care of the poor. This he had studied in Germany a year previous. For this policy he needed fourteen million pounds and he determined to get it by taxing the land of the rich. The English public and the outside world was not so much surprised by the amount as by the fact that Lloyd George was determined to get it from such a source.

He introduced his budget into the House of Commons and defended it in a speech that lasted four hours. He descended to no popular style of appeal but maintained throughout a high and solemn earnestness of tone so that the House could not deny him its admiration. The English public recognized the next day, and the whole world recognized soon afterwards, that these were the first blows of a woodsman's axe on the roots of the old feudal tree. At the end of his speech, he said:

"Why should I put burdens on the people? I am one of the children of the people. I was brought up amongst them, I know their trials, and God forbid I should add one grain of trouble to the anxieties which they bear with such patience and fortitude. When the Prime Minister did me the honour of inviting me to take charge of the National Exchequer at a time of great difficulty, I made up my mind that in framing my Budget, no cupboard should be barer, no lot should be harder to bear. . . . I cannot help hoping and believing that before this generation has passed away we shall have advanced a great step towards that good time when poverty, and the wretchedness and human degradation which always follow in its camp, will be as remote to the people of this country as the wolves which once infested the forests. . . . They are forcing a revolution and they will get it. The Lords may decree a revolution but the people will direct it. If they begin, issues will be raised that they little dream of. Questions will be asked that are now whispered in humble voices and answers will be demanded then with authority. The question will be whether five hundred men, ordinary men drawn accidentally from the unemployed, shall override the judgment of millions of people who are engaged in the industry which makes the wealth of the country. That is one question. Another will be: Who ordained that a few should have the land of Britain as a perquisite? Who made ten thousand people owners of the soil and the rest of us trespassers in the land of our birth?"

The Lords vetoed the budget, thus for the first time in centuries opposing the exclusive right of the House of Commons to deal with the public purse. The result was that the Liberal Government dissolved Parliament and appealed to the country, in a new General Election.

The landed proprietors rallied enthusiastically to the defence of the House of Lords and they were backed up by all the Conservative elements throughout the country. Lloyd George was now for the first time in his real element. If the Lords had passed the budget without a question, their action would have been a grave disappointment for him. In his campaign against the South African War he had been forced to remain in a merely negative position all the time, for he could not hope to stop the war. But his opponents were now forced into the defensive position and the initiative of the attack was in his hands. It was a plain and simple issue. Here was a great social reformer leading what he claimed to be a constitutional fight against the vested interests of wealth, power and privilege.

Behind him was the moral driving force of the masses from whom he had sprung, and their age-long grievance against the propertied classes. "Do you want to be the cause of a revolution?" he cried out. "Well, you may have it. The Lords may start it, but the people will finish it. The consequences will be gigantic. Questions will be put that up to now were only modestly whispered . . ."

The Lords declared that since the days of Cleon there never had been so mean a demagogue and charlatan as this Chan-

cellor of the Exchequer. One of the peers declared that he
would like to set his hunting pack of forty hounds on the agitator from Wales and have him torn to pieces. Another promised
his people that he would have a whole ox roasted at a public
banquet in his park to celebrate the downfall of the Chancellor.
His lordship did not realize how much he justified the attack
of his enemy by this proclamation of feudal rights. All these
proclamations were out of date. Those who made them had forgotten that the twentieth century had dawned some years before.
The Liberals were victorious in the election and the House of
Lords had to accept the budget. When Asquith made a speech
during one of the opening sessions of the new Parliament and
highly commended Lloyd George for the stand he had taken,
the latter looked with pride to the Visitors' Gallery where his
uncle was seated. The old shoemaker had been invited to come,
so as to have practical evidence of the worth of all the sacrifices
he had made.

One blow followed another. Having succeeded in taxing the
Lords, the Chancellor was now determined to deprive them of
their legislative supremacy. He attacked the whole principle of
the right of veto and brought in a bill depriving the House of
Lords of that right. This led to another General Election, which
was a test election on the Veto Bill. The Chancellor was again
victorious and the supremacy of the House of Lords was gone
for ever. Thus he had succeeded in abolishing one of the chief
articles of the English Constitution. This whole campaign was
not carried on as if it were a political game. Lloyd George
fought with the profound enthusiasm of a revolutionary against
hereditary rights, because he himself and his people had suffered
so much under them. Speaking of the Lords, he said: "They
are born within that magic circle of the Cherubim with flaming
swords in that Garden of Paradise where plenty is obtained
without labour. They know nothing of the daily worries of a

trader's existence, the care and thought spent, the knowledge and experience gathered, the skill acquired in the million ways of earning a living—that is no possession of theirs. The manna is strewn plenteously on their path through life and others gather it for them from the cradle to the grave. All is provided for them. As Mr. Chamberlain once said, 'They toil not, neither do they spin'—except those who indulge in the caprices of a lonely furrow and even that furrow is never driven straight. And they do not sow, they do not reap, they do not mill the golden grain, they do not convert it into bread, they meet it first where it is daintily spread on their tables. I will only say this of them— the sunshine of their lives blinds them to the squalor around them."

The victory which the little magician from Wales gained over the Lords was the greatest of his life. It was far more important and more enduring in its consequences than the victory gained ten years later when he returned to London after the conclusion of the Peace Treaty and rode in the same carriage with the King, and was pointed out by the monarch to the people, as the saviour of his country.

4

Lloyd George has often been called merely a politician and denied the title of statesman. Where can the line be drawn between these two terms? Critics sometimes hold that a successful politician whose career is a gradual ascent is not to be looked upon as a statesman, just as they think there is a difference between the author who has started as a mere journalist and the author who was born, as it were, into his job. If it be granted that the statesman is a man of constructive mind, then how is it possible to deny that title to a man whose genius opened a new epoch in the life of Europe, to the detriment of an infinitesimal minority and the benefit of millions? All the social progress that has taken place since Lloyd George's famous budget in 1909 proves the clarity of his foresight. In bringing about these great changes his mind was carried onwards by the momentum of a profound moral conviction.

He failed to foresee developments in Europe as acutely as he foresaw them in England. For a long time he could not decide between the cause of pacifism and his sense of responsibility for the safety of his own country. When England had to increase her armaments at sea in order to meet the increasing strength of the German navy, Lloyd George—and with him Churchill— opposed the demands of the British Admiralty. He did not see that the reasons he had put forward against the aggressive war in South Africa were not to the point when it came to the question of a defensive armament.

Only in the last few years before the war did he recognize the German danger. In 1911 he delivered a warning speech on his own initiative, for which the Cabinet was not responsible. This was a historic proclamation. Count Wolff-Metternich, at that time German ambassador in London, told me later that in a conversation with Lloyd George the latter demanded a ratio of 3 to 2 in the naval strength of England as compared with Germany. When he made that claim he was neither Premier nor First Lord of the Admiralty and he did not know that the German diplomat with whom he was speaking had tried to put through the same formula in Berlin. It is not true that Metternich asked for the resignation of Lloyd George after he made his threatening speech. That experiment had been successfully tried in Paris with Delcassé. Winston Churchill has stated that Lloyd George realized fully then that there was imminent danger of war and with sure insight saw the course which England should take. His position was that Germany ought to be told straightforwardly that in case of a conflict she would have England against her. But early in 1914 he spoke again of the necessity of disarmament in order to lower taxation and obtain certain benefits for the poorer classes. He asserted that this was the most favourable moment for disarmament that had come within the past twenty years, that both countries would have nothing to gain in a war, but had much to lose. Even as late as July 23, 1914, he said in the House of Commons: "Our international relations are better. We do not hiss at each other any more. We are beginning to understand one another in order to work in common for the common good." That statement shows that he entirely misunderstood the situation.

It was in June 1914 that I met him for the first time. There was a gala performance at the opera in honour of some king or other, where more crowns and jewellery were displayed than will ever be seen again in our time. The ministers sat in a box on the left of the King, together with their brilliantly dressed feminine entourage. To the right of the royal box was the still more brilliant assembly of the foreign diplomatic body. During the performance I watched the head of the Chancellor of the Exchequer in a corner of the left-hand box.

He had just then carried through a measure for a better arrangement of the hours during which public houses, restaurants and bars might remain open throughout England and especially in London. The little man sat in his corner, looking quite bored and annoyed. He seemed to be thinking of the taxes he had levied on these bejewelled do-nothings beside him, and during the interval he disappeared.

Next day I read in the newspapers that the House of Commons, which was still sitting at 11 p.m., had greeted him with a jeer and shouted "Opera" when he returned. But later on he made a brilliant speech. When the National Anthem was being played at the Opera House and the carriages were drawn into line to take home the rulers and the peers and all their jewellery, the adopted son of the shoemaker declared to his adversaries from the Treasury Bench in the House of Commons: "The times have gone by when the poor accepted their fate as a necessity which had been decreed by God. The revolution is on the march not only in Ulster. Democracy is stronger than ever before. Be careful."

The conflict between his dual outlook, that of a Britisher and that of a European, was not singular in the case of Lloyd George. He clearly realized what socialists throughout Europe generally felt at that moment, when they had to decide whether they should fight for their country or oppose the whole war movement for the sake of humanity. Even Jaurès wavered and was in doubt a few hours before his death, as his last published article shows.

To understand how the conflict of the two principles expressed itself in the mind of Lloyd George, we must realize the fact that a split had been threatening in the Liberal Party ever since the time of the Boer War. The fact was that the imperialist element of the party did not trust the pacifist element. The result of this was that Asquith and Grey and Haldane did not discuss frankly with their colleagues what was taking place. Later on I asked each of these three what their feeling and attitude was during those last days of July 1914. I felt that Haldane was telling me the truth when he said, "The alliance between our fleet and the French was neither a military convention nor a diplomatic pact." And yet Churchill was right in calling this naval understanding "an extraordinarily strong alliance." And I am quite convinced that Grey was entirely sincere when he told me that two months earlier he did not believe in the possibility of war.

Of the whole Cabinet, Lloyd George was probably the most surprised. This was because of his optimism, his naïveté and his pacificism. He told me afterwards that when the financiers of the City, including the Governor of the Bank of England, came to him, as Chancellor of the Exchequer, and urged that peace should be preserved, he decided to resign rather than share responsibility for the war. At that time he said to me: "Morley and Burns and myself decided to resign if we should not succeed in winning over the other side of the Cabinet. But on Sunday both of these resigned from the Cabinet and I remained because I hoped to be able to alter its policy."

The deeper reasons which explain the change of front made by Lloyd George on August 3, and by Count Tisza in the middle of July 1914, must be looked for in the sphere of domestic politics rather than in the moral sphere. One of his enemies, who was at the centre of things at that time and who had never taken part in any action against Lloyd George, told me that the situation developed as follows:

Early in 1914 Lloyd George had already recognized that the Liberal régime had become somewhat stale and worn through its long years of government and that if he himself were to retain power it could only be by the founding of a new party. His idea was to collaborate with Ramsay MacDonald in the founding of a party that might correspond to that of the French Radical-Socialists. As a friend of peace he was not in favour of adopting a threatening attitude towards Germany, though this was the policy recommended by Chamberlain and Asquith, Grey and Haldane. Lloyd George's idea was that if the English Government put Germany in the position of having to reject its demands, then England would inevitably be drawn into the war. Today, after twenty years, everyone who knows what the position then was, and has any knowledge of the German character, is quite convinced that an open declaration on the part of England, stating that she would march on the side of France, would have forced Germany to retreat. It would have prevented the outbreak of the war. I have already pointed out this fact in my book entitled *July 14th*. At that time Lloyd George seems to have influenced the pacifist members of the Cabinet and to be largely responsible for the fact that Grey did not come out sooner with a decisive declaration. Lloyd George had in his head the idea that in a neutral England he might found his new party and win victory at the polls on a "No-War" slogan. Asquith and Grey could not risk the resignation of their most popular minister. Else they would have had to resign too and appeal to the country; so that at the critical moment the English Government would not have been in a position to make a decision. This explanation accounts for Grey's procrastination and Lloyd George's sudden change of front.*

Then came the German invasion of Belgium. With his acute sense of popular psychology Lloyd George promptly realized that the British Nonconformist conscience would rise up in revolt against this violation of an international treaty. On August 2 he changed his attitude towards the war. He did not notify any of his friends and thus left Ramsay MacDonald wholly uninformed in regard to this sudden volte-face. On August 3 he threw in his lot with the war policy of the Cabinet.

The motives which induced Lloyd George to change his policy so quickly were by no means simple. He decided perhaps that entry into the war would be the best way of safeguarding British

---

* In a volume of his memoirs published since the above was written, Mr. Lloyd George criticizes Lord Grey adversely for not having warned the German Government before the invasion of Belgium and thus prevented the war. In the first place, such a course was formally impossible; for how could he have threatened war on a nation with which his Government still remained on friendly terms? Had he done so he would have been accused of having precipitated the crisis. Moreover, if this solution of the difficulty was in the mind of Lloyd George, it is strange that he makes no mention of having suggested it himself either privately or at a Cabinet Meeting.

He accuses me of having given a dangerous and misleading impression in my book *July 14th* because I stated there that the masses in London were in favour of peace. Everywhere they gave proof of being so. And Lloyd George's own attitude up to August 1st corroborates my estimate of the situation. His statement that "all wars are popular on the day of their declaration" is contradicted a hundred times by the events of modern history. Lloyd George was impressed particularly by the demonstrations he saw in Whitehall. In this he gave another tragic example of the truth that ruling Ministers hear only the voices of a few hundred people demonstrating beneath their windows but do not hear the angry outcry of the millions when the latter read in the newspapers that they are to be sacrificed as cannon fodder on the morrow, because the neutrality of some country or other, of which they know nothing, has been violated.

interests. Most of the leading minds in English public life at that time were convinced that England was the principal and final objective of Germany's war plans. If England had remained neutral Germany would undoubtedly have gained a swift victory. Against this victorious Germany England would have found it difficult to hold her own, except with the aid of America. In the circumstances, however, America's attitude was very doubtful. Six years earlier Lloyd George had made a tour of Germany for the purpose of studying the German system of National Insurance, which had been in operation since 1893. Harold Spender accompanied him on the tour. One evening in Stuttgart, as they sat at table, the conversation turned on the possibilities of a war between England and Germany. The parallel of Rome and Carthage came to the mind of Lloyd George. For a few moments he was lost in thought and then said: "I wonder if we shall be as unprepared as Carthage." This was quite in keeping with the declaration he had made at the age of twenty-six during the county council elections, when he said: "I am first a Nationalist, and then a Liberal."

He was now fifty-two years old, a leading man in the British Empire, feared as a social reformer, recognized for his tireless energy, to which a fertile imagination was always supplying fresh fuel. Carthage's hour had struck. He was against war as a hindrance to progress. But there was the question of this treaty which guaranteed the inviolability of Belgium. And there was such a thing as a European conscience which defended the treaty as sacrosanct. He now saw one of the great European nations in the prime of its youthful strength, as Rome did in another age, tear the treaty to pieces and hurl its gigantic military force against a small nation. To make this power atone for its crime was a moral command.

But at the same time Lloyd George saw before him a magnificent arena for the display of his individual talents. And this arena was his own country. Here was a man of fiery temperament who felt that the decisive hour had come to settle matters with his country's most powerful rival. He must have felt sure that he had the energy and the talent to stir up the nation and hold it at fighting pitch better than any other public leader. And he must have realized that he knew how to electrify the public better than did the other leaders. Under such circumstances it would have been out of the question for such a man to drop away into the background during his country's struggle and accept a position as Red Cross organizer or director of hospitals.

It is interesting to note that after all he had a good deal in common with his old war opponent, Joseph Chamberlain. In the inner recesses of their characters they were somewhat akin, much more so than their expressed policies would have led one to believe. Lloyd George was a born fighter. In the early days of his public career he had objected only to that kind of fighting which is called war. Now at last came the opportunity to call upon the immense fund of fighting energy which he naturally possessed and employ it in a cause which seemed to him much more gigantic than any he had yet fought for. The stored-up emotion that had been accumulating from his long devotion to the ideals of equality and democracy and peace, and even his inborn urge towards dictatorship, now burst forth. He plunged headlong into the war campaign and struck out with such mighty energy that he soon became looked upon as England's chosen protagonist.

5

Lloyd George made the shells. As Chancellor of the Exchequer he already had spoken of the "silver bullets," by which he meant the popular contribution to the financial war chest. Though the term did not enhance his reputation very much abroad, it worked very well at home. The time came for him to leave the Chancellorship of the Exchequer and make the real bullets—the munitions—that would finally decide the contest. He was the driving force behind the organization of a Coalition Government, which was a necessity at this critical juncture. One of the chief features of the coalition policy was the immediate creation of a new Department of State, called the Ministry of Munitions, with Lloyd George at its head. He toured the country and in some of the very same halls where fifteen years previously he had vociferated against war he now scattered the fury of Mars. His speeches were at once published in the press of all England's allies and in the neutral countries. Not only did he stand out as the spokesman of the British Empire but even as the spokesman of the whole Entente. He toured the factory towns and within three months he had mustered 800,000 hands at the lathes and benches and furnaces, making guns and shells for their brothers at the front. At that time he did for England what Rathenau was doing for Germany—not quite the same, of course, but with the same kind of foresight and push he organized the home resources that were necessary to supply munitions steadily to the fighting front.

England had long been accustomed to individualism and taking life easy. Only slowly and gradually was it possible to unite these people and train them to sink their individual interests in a common sacrifice in the face of dire necessity. What was already a fixed tradition with the Germans had to be created in England—the tradition of the individual giving up everything in the service of the state the moment that public need demanded it. For the first time in fifteen years of public life, Lloyd George blew the war trumpet that summoned the sons of the nation to arms. Even his own son he did not spare. Though he might easily have found a position for him at home, he sent him to the trenches in France, where he met his death. The phalanx of steel which the Germans had drawn across France and Belgium seemed impenetrable. Attack after attack broke against it. But as one followed the other the aggressive spirit of the Celtic warrior was only whetted the more. The spirit of the match, of the battle, was all over England. But Vengeance and Victory and Hatred, which do not appeal very much to the English character, fired Lloyd George's mind. With the flame of his own passion he was able to enkindle much the same kind of emotion even in the phlegmatic English character. It was only natural that as the fight went on this chief of the national protagonists should gradually overshadow his Conservative colleagues in the coalition, while he himself moved more and more to the right. Just because his previous career was a standing proof that he did not wish for war for its own sake, he was able to wake a peace-loving nation and urge it to war much more efficiently than a Conservative leader could have done.

In the summer of 1916 Lord Kitchener was drowned. Thus the office of War Minister became vacant. This key position seemed of itself to call for the kind of energy which only Lloyd George could bring to it. A dramatist might find an interesting theme in the mixed feelings with which Lloyd George received the news of Kitchener's death; for Kitchener had once spoken disparagingly of him as "the peppery little Welshman" and had stood for two years in his way. The new War Minister immediately took some of the more important branches of military policy out of the hands of the generals and, confident in his own powers, began to formulate strategic plans of his own. In the spring of 1916, when Kitchener was still at the War Office, Lloyd George had advised that military support be given to Roumania; but his advice was ignored, just as it was ignored when he had urged that the Entente forces should be sent to Serbia's defence. On both occasions his advice was based on the belief that the war could be decided on the Balkan front rather than in France. Hence he always stood out in favour of the Salonika front.

When he was taunted with being a mere dilettante, he answered: "I know political strategy." That was admitted on all hands; but Lloyd George now proved that political strategy is much more an integral part of military strategy than the mere tactical control of fighting forces in battle. The truth is that the war was won for the Allies by Clemenceau and Lloyd George, rather than by Haig and Joffre and Foch. When Field Marshal Haig once said, "Tomorrow I shall conquer Passchendaele," Lloyd George replied, "You reduced a hamlet to ruins and we lost Serbia. You reduced another hamlet to ruins and we lost Roumania. We have enough of that."

That was now his attitude towards everybody with whom he had to collaborate. After Kitchener's death Lloyd George's elemental energy triumphed over everything else in the Cabinet. He was ready for the dictatorship. The prolongation of the war on all sides called for dictators whose energy and force of character could win through to victory. Lloyd George was the first of the dictators in Europe. Fully convinced that he and no other could lead the nation to the achievement of its final purpose, he determined to allow no obstacle to stand in his way.

The most un-English feature of this move was that he, as a Liberal, accepted the help of the Conservative leaders to overthrow his Liberal colleague, who was at the same time his chief and had been his political sponsor. Bonar Law could have taken over the premiership at that time; but, as he himself declared to some of his friends, he felt that as a Conservative Imperialist he could not have carried with him the pacifist elements of the country in pursuing the war to the bitter end.

No matter how one looks at it, Lloyd George's treatment of Asquith is indefensible. Three days before Asquith's fall a family friend warned Mrs. Asquith of the intrigues that were afoot. She told her informant that he was mistaken, because only the day before Lloyd George had taken her hand after dinner and asked her not to believe what was being said about these intrigues. He assured her that he would never betray the man who had done so much for him. In saying this he undoubtedly referred to the financial scandal on the occasion when Asquith had defended Lloyd George's conduct in the House of Commons. It is undoubtedly true that at that moment Lloyd George was not an active party in organizing the intrigue against Asquith; but he must have known Northcliffe's plan and the men whom Northcliffe intended to put forward. And he knew that in this plan he himself was meant to take Asquith's place.

It is impossible to tell the full and true story of Lloyd George's conflict with Asquith, because the documents in the case give only the outline and bare facts. It is known that, with the aid of Bonar Law and Northcliffe, he made three attempts to overthrow his own Prime Minister in December 1916, by the proposal to form a smaller War Council from which Asquith, as Prime Minister, would be excluded.

A short time before Asquith's death I discussed the incident with him and found that he did not complain so much about being ousted from power and that even the personal betrayal did not affect him profoundly. What he felt most keenly of all was the betrayal of the party which he had taken over from Rosebery and Gladstone as a political patrimony. Naturally my sympathies were with Asquith and I felt that no explanation could excuse the action of the opponent who had triumphed over him.*

* The Memoirs which have appeared since this was written give me no grounds whatsoever, either by reason of the documents published or by Mr. Lloyd George's own construction of the case, why I should alter my opinion. It is amusing to notice how both ministers changed their form of addressing one another within four days. Of course we believe Mr. Lloyd George when he says that the famous article published in the *Times* of December 4th, 1916 was unknown to him beforehand.

But Mr. Lloyd George makes one statement which he should not have made before the bar of history. When he had overthrown Asquith he was sent for by the King next day to form a government himself. On relating this fact in his memoirs he says: "I neither sought nor desired the premiership." If that statement is only a mere formality it is quite as unworthy of Mr. Lloyd George as a similar statement made by Bismarck when he wrote to his wife of the "misfortune" that had befallen him, the truth being that he had struggled with might and main to bring about the "misfortune"—namely, to secure for himself the Prussian chancellorship.

In the whole history of this conflict the chief excuse to be made for Lloyd George is that he won the war. Asquith had been Prime Minister for ten years. Some of his closest friends assured me that his political energy was already exhausted, and it is certain that two years after Lloyd George seized power the British public was convinced that he, and he alone, could have led the Entente to victory. In 1916, after the collapse of Roumania, the outlook for the Entente was certainly dark. With his inborn sense of leadership Lloyd George then realized that he was faced with the question of sacrificing everything to save his country. At the opening of the war he turned his back on everything he had hitherto believed in and proclaimed; now he turned his back on the party in whose ranks he had worked and for whose principles he had fought. In both cases the will-to-power seems to have overshadowed every other thought. Here, as in many other such instances, an overpowering egoism was hidden behind the altruistic motives.

Within a few weeks after he had assumed the premiership he succeeded in taking over the full control of affairs and concentrating it in an inner council of only three men. The promises he made to the dominions were the beginning of a fundamental reconstruction of the British Empire. He ruled as another Cromwell. As an individualist and an opponent of power in high places, he assumed full sovereign power himself and transformed the most independent people in the world into an army of serfs for the duration of the war. The Foreign Office had to listen to him, and even Balfour, who was the direct opposite of Lloyd George in almost every conceivable feature, unwillingly bowed

---

Personally I hope that this is not the real truth. If it is, then Lloyd George takes upon his shoulders the full historical responsibility for the attack against his friend and predecessor in the office of Prime Minister. Only on one ground will the judgment of history excuse his action. That ground is as follows: if he wished to have power in his own hands because he thought that only his own extraordinary energy could push the war through and snatch an already half-won victory from the enemy, if in his heart and soul he was convinced that he and no other was then called to lead England and save her from disaster, his action might be pardoned by the judgment of history.

before this uncultured colleague. Lloyd George gave his own secretaries so much authority that they were able to override the Cabinet Ministers. And on one occasion, while taking a holiday in Inverness, he held a Cabinet session there, though it was twenty-four hours' journey from London.

He had become a human dynamo. The British Empire became too small for him and he now began to take a decisive part in guiding the war policy of the whole Entente. Russia had fallen out of the war just as Lloyd George became Premier. To make up for this loss he now determined to secure the co-operation of America, a plan which was already in his mind at the very beginning of the war. He described the result of his efforts thus: "I shall never forget the morning when I sent a cable to President Wilson, telling him what the facts were and how it was essential that we should get American help at the speediest possible rate, inviting him to send 120,000 infantry-men and machine-gunners per month to Europe and if he did that, we would do our best to help to carry them. . . . The following day came a telegram from President Wilson: *Send your ships across and we will send the 120,000 men.* Then I invited the Shipping Controller to 10, Downing Street and said: *Send every ship you can.* They were all engaged in essential trades, because we were cut down to the bone. There was nothing that was not essential. We said: *This is the time for taking risks. We run risks with our food; we ran risks with essential raw materials.* We said: *The thing to do is to get these men across at all hazards.* America sent 1,900,000 men and out of that number 1,100,000 were carried by The British Mercantile Marine."

At the same time he worked energetically for the unification of the supreme command. Here his outlook was quite European. After the Italian defeat at Caporetto he openly attacked the military generals in Paris for their professional jealousy and said to them: "The Italian front is quite as important for France and England as it is for Germany. The Germans realized this at the right moment and unfortunately we did not. National traditions and petty prejudices, prestige and mistrust, have prevented us from making proper decisions. This sectarianism has prolonged the war. Only solidarity can expedite it." In March 1918 Ludendorff's last offensive seemed at first to be crowned with success. Lloyd George then broke through all opposition and during the actual battle he had a French commander, Ferdinand Foch, appointed as Generalissimo over the Allied Armies. He declared afterwards that if the British Cabinet had attempted two weeks earlier to force the army leaders to take orders under a foreign general the Cabinet would have fallen.

As Mr. Winston Churchill, from the fullness of his intimate knowledge, has testified in a just tribute to Lloyd George's remarkable record of achievement during the struggle: "He possessed two characteristics, which were in harmony with the period of convulsion. First, a power of living in the present, without taking short views. Every day for him was filled with the hope and the impulse of a fresh beginning. He surveyed the problems of each morning with an eye unobstructed by preconceived notions, past utterances, or previous disappointments and defeats. . . . His intuition fitted the crisis better than the logical reasoning of more rigid minds. . . . Mr. Lloyd George in this period seemed to have a peculiar power of drawing from misfortune itself the means of future success. From the U-boat depredations he obtained the convoy-system. Out of the disaster of Caporetto he extracted the supreme War Council: from the catastrophe of the 21st of March he drew the Unified Command and the immense American reinforcement. . . . He lived solely for his work and was never oppressed by it. He gave every decision when it was required. He scarcely ever seemed to bend under the burden."

When the ninth of November came, and with it the end of the war, Lloyd George and Churchill sat down together and thought over what was next to be done. I afterwards asked Lloyd

George why he did not immediately send a couple of food ships to Germany to relieve the famine caused by the blockade. Such a gesture would have made a profound moral impression and would have firmly laid the foundations of a lasting friendship between Germany and England. "On Armistice evening," he answered, "I mentioned that very idea to Churchill. But we had to recognize the fact that the public hatred against Germany was too intense to have tolerated such a move on our part."

6

In this modern age it would be difficult to hold any individual responsible for the outbreak of a war, for the achievement of victory or for the conclusion of a disastrous peace. In the twentieth century so many elements act in collaboration that individual responsibility plays a far smaller part than it did in former times. At the same time, however, it must be remembered that in every modern situation there are central figures whose personality and position place them above all their colleagues, so that they must to a certain extent be held responsible for what happens. Count Berchtold must be held responsible in that sense for the outbreak of the war; and in the same sense Clemenceau and Lloyd George must be held responsible for winning the war and losing the peace.

"War is a ghastly thing," declared Lloyd George in one of his speeches, "but not as grim as a bad peace. There is an end to the most horrible war, but a bad peace goes on and on, staggering from one war to another. Already the Prussian war lords are talking of *the next time*. Next time! There must be no next time! . . . Let us be the generation that manfully, courageously, resolutely eliminated war from among the tragedies of human life. Let us, at any rate, make victory so complete that national liberty, whether for great nations or small nations, can never be challenged."

Yet this same man who thus spoke from the broad European angle misused the greatest victory in history, over the last of the Emperors, for the consolidation and prolongation of his own hold on political power. More hurriedly than any other political leader, he appealed to the electorate and in December 1918 he opened a campaign of inflammatory speech-making. He told the British electorate that the Kaiser would be brought to trial in London and that the Germans would have to pay for the war up to the last farthing. He did not explicitly declare that the Kaiser would be hanged, but he allowed that statement to be published over and over again. And I know on first-class au thority that he proposed to King George that the trial of the Kaiser should be held in Westminster Hall. The suggestion was immediately flouted by the King. When I asked him afterwards about these election speeches, he answered: "At a later date you yourself formulated the charge of responsibility against the Kaiser better than any other person."

"I described the man himself," I said, "who because of his position could not be made responsible. And I attacked the system which had placed so much power in his hands. I wrote directly against his activities but I never said that he ought to be impeached."

"Neither did I," answered Lloyd George laughingly. "And I spoke of Germany's guilt not from a feeling of revenge but from a feeling of righteousness. And in my election addresses I only declared that, according to principles of justice accepted universally, the loser would have to pay the cost." This was said after his fall from power. He seems to have forgotten the fact that the two leading shibboleths used at the election of 1918—about hanging the Kaiser and the Germans paying for the war up to the last penny—brought him eighty per cent of the whole vote of the English electorate, and thus laid on his shoulders a tremendous task when he entered the Peace Conference. If he had trusted to his own influence at that time and his standing with the people, and if he had told the British public in that December of 1918 what he knew very well, namely, that the Kaiser could not be brought to trial and that the Germans could not pay 25,000 million pounds for the war, the Coalition might not have been returned by such a large majority at the election, but it would have been returned with a sufficient working majority. Thus he could have gone to Paris with a mandate which he could have carried through at the Peace Conference and could have made a peace that would have corresponded to his own feeling for what was just and right and at the same time be practical. But the tragic truth is that this same Lloyd George, who had acted with such energy during the war and had clearly seen the right road also at certain critical turning-points during the peace negotiations, within two months lost his instinct for popular leadership. Instead of putting the truth of the situation before his people and encouraging them to face it as it stood, he simply bamboozled them. His great historical mistake is to be found in the electioneering campaign of December 1918. All that happened in Paris afterwards was only a consequence of this.

Of the three supreme arbiters who sat in judgment on the old world at Versailles one had the right ideas but did not have the energy to put them through; another had the energy but did not have the right ideas; the third was endowed with plenty of energy and had a mind that saw clearly and fairly but was wanting in steadfastness of character. At the most critical junctures during those negotiations he weakened and lost, not indeed everything, but some of the most important positions on which the peace of the world depended.

"What shall I do?" Lloyd George once shouted in a sort of

comical dilemma between the rôles of a pseudo Napoleon and pseudo Christ. If somebody had told him that he was a pseudo Cromwell he would have answered that the change of the centuries had made it impossible for him to play that rôle.

He was in an extraordinarily strong position when he came to the Peace Conference, and his personality gave him an immense influence. England already had what she wanted to get out of the Conference, namely, the German fleet and the German colonies. Lloyd George was much younger than Clemenceau and much more practical than Wilson. Moreover, he had certain biological qualities which were missing in the other two. J. M. Keynes, who watched him closely during those days in Paris, admired his extraordinarily acute feeling for each situation as it turned up, saying that he had the gift of telepathy with the addition of something like a sixth and a seventh sense. He was ignorant of geography and history, but so were all the other Entente leaders, except Benes and Venizelos. During a speech afterwards in the House of Commons he excused his ignorance of geography in regard to Teschen by saying that the other Members of Parliament had known nothing about that city until "they saw it in the paper yesterday." That sort of defence is quite as inadmissible as if a professor of medicine were to excuse his own ignorance of anatomy in regard to some particular bone or other by saying that his students were ignorant of it also.

The Versailles negotiations were finally carried on not by ten or even four of the plenipotentiaries, but by three. Lloyd George now stood between the idealist of tomorrow and the realist of yesterday. His past career ought to have forced him uncompromisingly to the side of Wilson. If British interests had been in jeopardy, he declared, he would have stood steadfastly by Wilson. He was responsible for the establishment of the inner council which excluded the small nations from taking part in the principal decisions affecting the Peace Treaty. And it was he himself who proposed, and had the proposal accepted, that the terms of the treaty should be kept secret from the smaller nations until twenty-four hours before they were placed before the Germans. This conduct was a denial of the very principles for the sake of which he had entered the war: the rights of small nations. And it was a denial of the principle of freedom of the press on the side of which he had always been a great Liberal protagonist.

Added to all these deficiencies there were certain personal antipathies which affected the impressionable, or what may be called the feminine, side of his character. He could scarcely give a reason for opposing the Poles and enthusiastically siding with the Czechs. The pliability of his nature and his innate naïveté made it possible for him to change his opinion from day to day without recognizing his own inconsistency or being able to think that outsiders could look upon him as acting in bad faith. He was impulsive and he rightly recognized that the condition of Europe did not permit of any delay in taking the situation in hand. He had exercised his dictatorial powers for two years and therefore he could not accustom himself to pause and consider and take counsel before coming to a decision. To get on with the business as rapidly as possible seemed to him the matter of chief importance. "When it was shown to him," writes Lansing, "that his argument was based on a false supposition, he changed the supposition but not the argument. The cleverness with which he ignored logic bluffed everybody. In the Council of Four he acted more as a Parliamentarian than as a Diplomat, he denied facts, he became sarcastic, he was better in attack because defence calls for more knowledge. He broke in with sharp questions and coughed loudly when the argument was going against him."

This conflict between his liberal principles and the habits of mind that had resulted from two years of dictatorial rule account for the inconsistency between his programme and the provisions of the Peace Treaty to which he agreed. The programme was magnificent. In a memorandum which he wrote at Fontainebleau in April 1919, after struggling for three months with the opposing forces at the Conference, he sketched the chief lines along which a reasonable treaty could be drawn up.

"Pictures of heroism and triumph allure only those who know nothing of the sufferings and horrors of the war. When nations are exhausted by wars in which they have put forth all their strength and which leave them tired, bleeding and broken, it is not difficult to patch up a peace that may last until the generation which experienced the horrors of war has passed away. What is difficult, however, is to patch up a peace which will not provoke fresh struggles when those who have had practical experience of what war means have passed away. History shows that a peace which was looked upon as a triumph of the statesman's art and even praised as moderate turned out to be shortsighted, as the German Peace of 1871. France herself has proved that those who say that Germany can be so weakened that she will never again be able to come back are entirely in the wrong. You may strip Germany of her colonies, reduce her armaments to a mere police force and her navy to that of a fifth-rate Power; it will be all the same in the end. If she feels that she has been unjustly treated in the peace of 1919, she will find means of exacting retribution from her conquerors. Our terms may be severe. They may be stern and ruthless, but at the same time they can be so just that the country on which they are imposed will feel in its heart that it has no right to complain. But injustice, arrogance, displayed in the hour of triumph will never be forgotten or forgiven.

"Europe is filled with the spirit of revolution. A profound feeling not merely of unrest but of anger and revolt dominates the working classes. From one end of Europe to the other the established social order is being called into question. In many countries, such as Germany and Russia, this unrest takes the form of open revolt and in other countries, such as France and Great Britain and Italy, it shows itself in strikes, and in general unwillingness to work. Much of this unrest is healthy. We can never bring it to a lasting peace if we try to revert to the conditions of 1914. The men who triumphed in Russia did so at a fearful cost. But they have succeeded in gaining power over the masses of Russian people and, what is still more astonishing, they have organized a great army which is manifestly well led, disciplined and for the most part ready to die for its ideas. Indeed it is the only army that still thinks there is something worth fighting for.

"If we are intelligent we shall offer Germany a peace which, because it is just, will for all reasonable men be preferable to Bolshevism. Therefore in the protocol to the peace I would state that as soon as Germany accepts our terms she will have access to the raw material and markets of the world on the same condition as ourselves and that we shall do our earthly best to help the German nation on its feet once again. We cannot make it a cripple and at the same time expect it to pay.

"From every standpoint therefore it seems to me that we ought to draw up a Peace as if we were impartial arbitrators who had forgotten the sufferings of the war. It is an essential feature of the League of Nations and in itself a necessity that its leading members should come to an understanding on disarmament. It appears to me to be a vain endeavour to attempt to force Germany to a permanent limitation of armament if we are not ready ourselves to reduce our own armed strength. If the League is to be successful in its work for the world its members must trust one another and allow of no rivalries in the matter of armament. If that cannot be obtained before the signing of the Peace then the League of Nations will be only a scandal and a mockery. I should also like to know why Germany cannot be admitted to the League of Nations when she accepts our terms, or at least why she cannot be admitted as soon as a democratic government is firmly established there. Would it not be safer to have Germany within the League of Nations than to leave her outside?"

In reading that memorandum one almost hears the voice of Wilson. Clemenceau's ironical and malicious reply proves the European worth of the document itself and modern developments have demonstrated the wisdom of its outlook. Indeed it remains a unique gesture in the whole history of the Conference and is far more convincing than Wilson's anæmic Fourteen Points. The reprehensible feature of it is that it was not written to be put into practice but rather to protect the future political career of its author, as a party leader, and show him to history as a Statesman. I afterwards discussed the document with one of Lloyd George's collaborators who was very much au fait with the conditions under which the memorandum had been drawn up and was proud of his master's work in this respect. After our conversation he wrote me as follows:

"I compared Lloyd George with Cæsar and Napoleon, not because he is equal to them in talent and achievement but because the mental attitude of Cæsar and Napoleon, at any rate in their early days, as also the mental attitude of Lloyd George, was determined by an objective investigation of the abiding political realities of their time, and because their conduct was directed accordingly. Wilson wanted to make a new world according to his own ideas. Clemenceau wanted to transform Europe in the interests of France. Lloyd George, who is no Englishman but a Welshman, first wanted to find out what the political forces in Europe are likely to be during the next twenty years and to find an arrangement which would last because it would correspond to these realities."

If all this be true, why did Lloyd George desert his own position? His agreement with Wilson, on the one hand, or with

Clemenceau, on the other, was the deciding factor in the whole situation.

7

Let us first ascertain what it was he actually achieved at the Conference. Had it not been for the stand he took up, Wilson could not have saved the Rhine for Germany, a titanic reparations account would have been fixed right away, the whole of Upper Silesia and parts of Prussia would have become Polish and probably the League of Nations would never have come into existence.

But when a statesman has risen to power through his success as a popular politician he cannot free himself all at once from his demagogic habits. When a man has kept his ear cocked during a long thirty years, eagerly listening for the slightest articulate sound whereby he might interpret the dim wishes of the mob, and when he has seldom discussed political principles and policies in open argument with individual colleagues, this long usage must necessarily have its effect. When a Liberal statesman is shouldered and chaired by a Conservative Party and by a Coalition which had lost its meaning entirely after the war, the experience must necessarily be detrimental to his inner integrity. His conduct in agreeing to a League of Nations founded by five great powers, all jealous of one another, for the sole purpose of keeping a sixth power downtrodden must also have had its evil effect. The fact that the war had to be carried on by a Coalition of Allies was in itself a drawback, which had the additional drawback of having to be carried on by a Coalition Cabinet. In the hour of danger to his country Lloyd George was able to establish a unified front and a unified command and he now found himself face to face with the problem of continuing this unity once the danger had passed.

It was a piece of malicious contriving on the part of Clemenceau to have Lloyd George's memorandum published in the Paris and London newspapers. The inference which the British public was meant to draw from it was that the Prime Minister did not intend to honour the pledges he had given at the General Election. He was now frightened at his Conservative majority, which unanimously demanded an imperialist peace. Clemenceau lay ill at home in consequence of an attempt on his life, while Lloyd George hurried hither and thither between the Council of Four in Paris and the House of Commons in London. He tried to stem the tide of suspicion rising against him on both sides. He brought Churchill to Paris, though the latter was in favour of a new war against the Bolshevists, while Lloyd George had actually proposed that Lenin should be invited to the Peace Conference.

In April he received a threatening telegram from two hundred Members of Parliament. In answer to it he returned quickly to London and defended the Conference before the House of Commons. He succeeded in appeasing the temper of the House and securing its support. But in the midst of such an immense majority his personal influence was practically negative. Both parties had lost their trust in him: the Conservatives, because he was a Liberal, and the Liberals because he had broken up the solidarity of their party. The general result was that he felt himself forced to agree to much more stringent peace terms than Wilson wanted. Yet it was he himself who had gathered together this importunate khaki majority. It is strange that the shrewdest demagogue of his time did not foresee that an infuriated majority, intoxicated with victory and elected by a nation that had been allured with a wealth of Neronic promises, should at least demand the partial fulfilment of these promises. It was a widespread taunt that Great Britain had to call upon one who was not an Englishman to pull the nation through the war. Here we have once more an example of the immoral character of war itself, because it brings into a position of leadership these problematic characters who are endowed with great energy and whom the nation finds it difficult to rid itself of once that war is over, just as it is difficult to get rid of the megalomaniac military generals. At the height of the crisis in Paris, when Wilson decided to withdraw and return home, Lloyd George decided to remain. In an effort to save the Rhine for the Germans he proposed to Clemenceau that France should make a pact with England and America whereby the two latter countries would guarantee her security against any future aggression on the part of the Germans.

The rejection of the proposal by the American Congress liberated him from that rather precarious undertaking. And then as the conflict became gradually more embittered between the Big Three in Paris, a new fear seized Lloyd George. He began to think that the Germans would not sign the Peace Treaty. With all his acute insight into the minds of the masses at home, this demagogue did not understand foreign nations. What he wrote in his memorandum of the danger of communism in Germany proves that he had entirely misunderstood the character of the German people. After the signing of that very bad Peace Treaty he returned to England and was fêted as a national hero. J. L. Garvin, one of the most influential politicians in England, wrote on this occasion: "On conditions, Lloyd George may be even greater in peace than he was in war. If he takes the right course, he may be for years the greatest man in the world. Above all he must begin to settle in his own mind the epoch-making question whether he means on the whole to move to the Right or to the Left."

During the three years that followed, and indeed up to his downfall, he could not have answered the question if anybody had asked him to which party he belonged. Gratitude is a personal virtue and does not belong to the mass. Neither Lloyd George nor Clemenceau received it from his people. When I spoke later with some of the leading people of England about Lloyd George they all agreed that he had saved the country, but they all spoke against him. Only two well-known men spoke gratefully of him. Lloyd George himself once said rightly that gratitude is like the manna; it must be eaten quickly in order to be enjoyed, for it soon loses its flavour.

When I met Lloyd George at the Genoa Conference, where he was surrounded by admirers as if he were the lord of the world, I thought he would hold the reins of government for a long time to come. He complained to me of Rathenau and said that the latter had torpedoed the Conference. But as a matter of fact there was no disloyalty whatsoever on Rathenau's side; because the English were already secretly negotiating with the Russians. It was not the failure of the General Conference that brought on Lloyd George's downfall. The occasion of it was the Chanak crisis—that is to say, the Greco-Turkish war, for which Lloyd George was responsible. But the actual cause of his downfall must be sought in the fact that the Conservatives were afraid of maintaining him in their midst, lest he might disintegrate their party as he had already disintegrated the Liberals. Before the Genoa Conference took place he tried to repeat his tactics of December 1918 and mount a new General Election, with a gigantic programme, for the purpose of liberating himself from his unwieldy Conservative majority. When Briand was told that a new election would take place in England he gave his consent to the new World Conference.

But the political platform is not like a circus or even a stage.

Tricks may safely be repeated in the circus and with a little more
risk on the stage; but it is dangerous to try the same tricks a second time in politics. The Conservatives prevented a new election. They threw over the man who had won the war, just as
Paris threw over Clemenceau. When one considers who it was
that led the attack which brought about Lloyd George's downfall one sees in it the avenging hand of Fate. His successor was
the same Bonar Law with whom he had joined hands six years
before for the overthrow of Asquith.

Lloyd George had been a Cabinet Minister uninterruptedly
for sixteen years.

8

After Lloyd George's downfall I saw him on three different
occasions. On the first of these I met him at his country house
in Churt where he was working with a staff of men and women.
They were making an effort to secure the co-operation of
Ramsay MacDonald, who was friendly to Lloyd George and
still active in the ranks of the Socialists, and also to secure the
goodwill of the Socialist Party though it was quite hostile to
Lloyd George. When I admired the wood in his dining-room
he told me that they called it the Poincaré room, because he
had purchased the wood from the money he had received from
a newspaper article he had written on Poincaré. I realized then
that I was speaking with the world's greatest living journalist.

On this occasion and later, in his London home, I spoke
with him about the Versailles Treaty. He said that Clemenceau's malice and Wilson's weakness of character were responsible for it. He spoke with feeling and I am sure he was honestly

convinced of the truth of what he said. I asked him why he did not resign immediately upon receiving the threatening telegram from the House of Commons during the Peace Conference. He paused for a considerable time and then said, "If I had taken that course a still more disastrous peace would have been made."

The third time I met him after his downfall was in the Bay of Portofino on board a small yacht. It was in the beginning of January and everybody was in good humour. He sat in the cabin quietly with his family. His wife was knitting and his daughter seemed to take no interest in the company that had assembled on the yacht. Although the Union Jack floated from the mast, I heard French being spoken on deck. When I put a question to Lloyd George, he said, "The ship is English, and the commander is French, just as in the World War."

The humour of the statement is rather poignant in view of the fact that it was he himself who placed the British army under French control. Afterwards I produced one of my plays in London, in which the character of Lloyd George was represented. But he did not come to see himself. In this respect he was entirely unlike Socrates, who took a keen delight in seeing himself satirically represented on the stage.

Despite all that he has been through and despite all the manœuvres in which he has taken part during his long political career, he still retains his straightforward look and his open-hearted way of talking; and, if I am not mistaken, in the depths of his nature he is still naïve. Honour and power have never allured him to forget his home. To celebrate his seventieth birthday he went back to the little nest in Wales from which he had set forth into the world nearly fifty years before. On the occasion of a state burial in Westminster Abbey a friend who stood beside him said that he himself would one day be laid to rest here. Lloyd George shook his grey locks and said emphatically, "I shall rest beneath the trees of my own home."

VENIZELOS

THE GREEK ODYSSEUS

The Turks cannot be wholly driven out of Europe; for no Christian power can hold Constantinople without having the mastery of the world. But the Turkish power in Europe can be considerably reduced.

GOETHE

V E N I Z E L O S

THE GREEK ODYSSEUS

O<small>N THE</small> sea journey from Venice to Alexandria a rocky promontory appears to the left soon after the ship passes Cape Matapan. It seems to offer no landing-place and to have no harbours—a gaunt mass of rock without any signs of human habitation. But it is only the narrow end of a long island. If the traveller consults his map, he will find that this is the largest of the Grecian Isles. It is longer than the Peloponnesus. On the northern coast, which our traveller does not see, the mountains slope gently towards the shore and have rich valleys opening into spacious harbours.

It is the island of Crete. And the history of the great Cretan statesman who spent half his life here can best be understood when studied within this geographical framework. In the many sudden departures and surprise returns of this seafaring islander, one can recognize the revolutionary spirit which was inherited from his ancestors and nurtured in these lonely hills. And indeed the drama of his astounding career becomes clearly outlined in its action if we take it as a representation, within the span of one human life, of the conflict which two elemental forces have waged in and about the island for thousands of years. If we think of the revolutions and upheavals in which he played a

leading part, and forget for the time being the smallness of the
territory over which they were waged, then it would be no exaggeration to say that the career of Venizelos has been the most
dramatic of any statesman of our time. Without Crete it is not
intelligible.

2

For a long three hundred years the inhabitants of that island,
which was Hellenic even before Homer's time, had yearned and
struggled to get rid of the Turkish rule. The Sultan's régime
had been persistently oppressive and harassing, showing little
or no refinement in the arbitrary methods it employed to stamp
out the native religion and culture and the native speech. The
struggle for liberty in Crete was carried on contemporaneously
with periodical revolts on the neighbouring continent. But island
insurrections have a violence and bitterness of their own; and
even when they are quelled for the time being it is difficult to
restore the established order. This was especially so in Crete,
where the primitive nature of the people, mostly shepherds and
hunters, revolted against the rule of a few lawyers and military
officials giving orders from the chief town on the shore. The Isles
of Greece have always influenced the course of Grecian history.
Exile, persecution, suppression, confiscation—all these the islanders experienced. And it was in one of these upheavals that the
forbears of Venizelos fled from the Peloponnesus to Crete after
a rebellion which took place in 1770.

The anti-Turkish tradition was handed on from generation
to generation in the family with undiminished vehemence. A
hundred years after the first Venizelos fugitives had arrived in

Crete the father of the modern statesman, a man without home
or means, became involved in a new conspiracy engineered by
Cretan patriots and had to flee to the island of Syra with his wife
and little son—the only one left him after the early deaths of
three other boys. Thus at the age of three the little boy became
acquainted with the emotions of fear and vengeance that surge
in the soul of the political refugee. Later on he had to undergo
similar experiences again and again. That first exile, which lasted
for eight years, was the beginning of his lifelong animosity
towards the Turks. During the sojourn on the little Grecian
island of Syra his father, who was born in Crete and therefore
a Turkish-born subject, became formally nationalized as a Grecian citizen, together with his son. The document attesting this
naturalization served Venizelos at an important moment in later
life. The environment in which his boyhood years were passed
was actively anti-Turkish. Even at recreation the children used
to play games in which the Turk was always the enemy. It was
not merely because they were Greeks that this opposition was
sharp and bitter, but also because they were Christians.

In the eighteen-sixties the question of liberating the Greeks of
the islands and of Asia Minor became an important problem in
European politics. In view of this it was not strange that a
French scholar, M. Perot, wrote in his diary while on the visit
to Crete: "Who knows whether at this moment there may not
be some Grecian boy about to be born whom Providence has
chosen as the Liberator of all these Greeks." In itself the sentence
was not strange; but in the light of what we now know it was
certainly a remarkable pronouncement, for it was written in the
very year Venizelos was born.

The boy knew nothing about this prophecy of the French
scholar. But at the age of fourteen, as a student at Athens, his
sharp intellect accurately assessed the meaning of the conclusions
arrived at by the Congress of Berlin. By the stipulations of the

Congress a sort of National Assembly was established on the island of Crete; but this was only a sham reform in the direction of national liberty. Venizelos once assured me that the personalities and prestige of Bismarck and Cavour played the chief part in stirring up his own ambition as a youth.

When he came to Athens as a student, a new and wider world opened to his view. Here lived the influential persons who encouraged and at the same time often hindered Crete's struggle for independence. And here in Athens the King resided. But who was this King? Was he genuinely opposed to the Turks? What did the life of a Cretan peasant mean to him? Was he acquainted with the island from which the call of destiny had brought this young man? The King, of course, was not a Greek. That was clear enough. When the young student from Crete first saw him he was forty years old. His tall figure and Nordic appearance, the fair hair and small face, must have seemed strange to the young student; for George I was a Danish prince, whom the Greeks had imported as King a few weeks after they had turned out another Nordic. That was at the time when Venizelos was born. One idea held the mind of the young student in its thrall and kept his nature throbbing with passionate emotion. This was the idea of liberating Crete. At that juncture Venizelos did not wish for any association with the royal stranger at Athens; but at the same time he did not foresee the long series of difficulties which he would have to encounter during his career in the struggle for and against the monarchy.

Soon after he returned home and had become a lawyer and at the same time a Deputy in the local National Assembly he was forced to flee a second time to Athens because of his entanglement in a patriotic revolt. The Sultan had broken the pledges given at Berlin and had once again precipitated a revolution. A year later Venizelos returned to the island. At the head of twenty-six leaders he organized against the Turks, and at the same time against the moderates in his own country, a campaign which lasted for fifteen years without interruption.

As Venizelos was now a Deputy in the small parliament of Canea and at the same time played the part of insurrectionary chief, the scene of the struggle was constantly changing. Sometimes it took place in parliamentary sessions, in offices and at newspaper headquarters and in various clubrooms on the coast. Sometimes it took the shape of armed conflicts in the mountains. At the same time negotiations were being carried on with the consuls of the great powers whose Governments were constantly interfering and sometimes directly with the admirals who were in command of the international fleet which the powers had sent to Crete. The sea was the eternal foreground of all the plottings, sham battles, retreats and outrages, speech-making, newspaper propaganda and public proclamations. The background was in the mountains, where the intricate canyons afforded refuge to those who knew them. Venizelos, who likes to speak of his young days, said to me once: "We had a revolution every three years. Then I disappeared into the mountains and remained there for months, on one occasion for fifteen months and on another for nearly two years. We had our arms and we carried on our own war against the Turks. I learned English in the mountains in order to be able to negotiate with the enemy."

There could scarcely have been a better school for the youthful training of a statesman and popular leader than this Cretan scene where courage and will power, decision, the effective use of force and the initiative of attack were exercised at the same time as debates and popular polemics were being waged. And the innumerable negotiations that had to be carried on with three or four of the great powers who had invested this little island only because its possession signified much more than appeared on the surface—all the debates and negotiations and trials of wit vis-à-vis these foreign powers were a magnificent training for the man who was to play such a big part afterwards at international conferences. In the unique and even anomalous position which he occupied, Venizelos had to be a cosmopolitan European and at the same time an insular nationalist. His name began to be mentioned in the consular reports and soon in the chancelleries of the various European powers. A famous French philhellenist, who had visited Greece and Crete for the purpose of studying the archæological remains and the excavations, said to his friends on his return to Paris: "I have been to see strange and picturesque lands, among them Crete. You will never guess, though, my most interesting discovery in the island, one more interesting by far than the splendours of the excavations. I will tell you. A young advocate, a M. Venezuélos ... Venizelos? Frankly, I cannot quite recall his name, but the whole of Europe will be speaking of him in a few years." This Frenchman was the hawk-eyed Clemenceau.

Meanwhile the princes and military officers at Athens forced the easy-going King into a war with Turkey. The result was that the Turks soon swamped Thessaly and the Greek army would have been annihilated, and the King would have lost his throne, had it not been for the intervention of the Czar and the bringing about of an armistice, in 1897. The Cretan revolutionaries had seized the opportune moment of the Turkish War to rise against their rulers in alliance with the Greeks, whereupon the great powers again intervened. They blockaded the Grecian Isles and tried to find a way out of the Greco-Turkish difficulties by guaranteeing to Crete autonomous administration under Turkish government. Venizelos was then thirty years old. He organized a defence corps in the island in order to make an impression on the representatives of the powers and to show that his fellow countrymen were not all quite as supine as had been imagined. He was determined that part at least of the Cretan claims should be granted.

"At that time," he told me, "I was the leader of the revolutionary Government. My plan was to pay out the Turks a certain sum of money in order to get rid of them; but I denounced the policy of autonomy under Turkish sovereignty. The armed bodies that I had organized held the peninsula which separates Canea from Suda Bay. There beneath us lay the European ships. Their four flags, as well as the Turkish crescent, were hoisted on a small island to the south; else they would have been torn down. During our negotiations I advised the English to arrange a feint assault for the purpose of pacifying the Turks. The plan was that I should retire to a certain line, and if the sailors overstepped this line I would shoot."

By a small majority the local parliament finally accepted constitutional autonomy under the Turks. Venizelos had spoken and voted against acceptance. An organized attack was made on him and his house was burned. Once more he sought refuge in the mountains.

3

King George I of Greece has often been accused of indifference towards the affairs of the country over which he ruled. Probably the truth is that he foresaw what was coming and was skeptical. During the fifty years of his reign he gave constant evidence of the typical Danish qualities—equanimity, level-headedness and kind-heartedness. Those statesmen who have survived that period and who have had dealings with him, whether Greek or German, have declared that though he was no hero he was a shrewd and intelligent man. Because of his marriage with a Russian Grand Duchess, he submitted in family matters to the rule of his wife, simply on the score of her claim to be of nobler blood. Two of their sons whose careers have a place in the history of our times turned out entirely different from their father and displayed the grand-ducal characteristics of the maternal line— restless, jealous, easily influenced and megalomaniac. Their father may have remarked this, for in his will he admonished his son: "Never forget that you are the ruler of a southern people whose emotions may be quickly aroused and that what they say or do at one moment may be easily forgotten in the next."

The first of the King's sons whom Venizelos came to know was the younger one, Prince George. In December 1898 he was sent as High Commissioner to Crete, at the bidding of the great powers. This position recognized, nominally at least, Turkish sovereignty over the island. The arrival of the High Commissioner was the occasion of the first attempt at collaboration between Venizelos and a member of the Greek dynasty. This conjunction of two forces, which was finally to decide the fate of each, was unfortunate from the start.

Venizelos soon recognized that Prince George's attitude towards Cretan autonomy was weak and vacillating. He preferred to play the rôle of dictator. He suppressed newspapers that criticized his actions, and imprisoned both writers and editors. Venizelos soon realized that the King of Greece was seeking to create a sort of viceregal position for his son in Crete. Thus the first struggle between the dynasty and Venizelos arose, and led to the latter's dismissal from public office within two years. How could two such men have worked harmoniously together? The Cretan patriot, who was only a modest lawyer and worked energetically for the liberation of Crete from the Turkish rule and its annexation to Greece, was enraged at the spectacle of this foreign royal family in Greece simply seeking positions for its sons without any respect whatsoever for the feelings or interests of one country or another. He saw an elegant young officer who had no knowledge of the country deporting himself royally in a position which he owed to nothing except the accident of having been born of foreign-bred parents.

Here for the first time he began to recognize the absurdity of inherited power, with only personal incompetency to recommend it. He himself knew every canyon and every family in the island and was familiar with all their mutual intrigues and differences and alliances; but he was supposed to obey this young man who only wanted to go on hunting expeditions and hold social receptions and give commands and sign decrees as if he were an operatic impersonation of Louis XIV. And so for the first time Venizelos found himself urged to take his stand against a Greek Prince. How was he to get the better of him? As a born democrat, he adopted the electoral principle as a solution.

He started a campaign of popular agitation and after a few years, in 1905, he secured a decisive electoral mandate against the policy followed by the Prince. Once again the European powers sent their ships. Once again there was armed conflict in the mountains, with guns and revolvers, and once again came defeat and coercion. But at the same time he succeeded in isolating the Prince, so that the powers had to sack their royal appointee and hand over the post of High Commissioner to a middle-class government official from Athens. Here we have a forecast of the subsequent struggle: The Prince repudiates his minister. The minister appeals to the people. These side with the minister and the Prince is turned out. And so the dynasty at Athens became Venizelos' enemy. The Prince employed the ecclesiastical powers on his side and had Venizelos excommunicated by the Archbishop of Crete. But Venizelos, as President of the Chamber, made the new Commissioner the strongest force in the island.

The Bosnian crisis of 1908 placed the Government of the

Young Turks in a precarious position. Venizelos availed himself
of this new difficulty and the absence of the High Commissioner
to proclaim the office of High Commissioner as no longer exist-
ent. The Greek flag was hoisted and the annexation of Crete
to the motherland was formally declared. The King of Greece
was now in an awkward position. He did not wish to add the
perilous lustre of this shining gem to his crown; for the Turks
threatened to declare war on Greece if even a single Deputy
from Crete dared to enter the Athenian Parliament. The King
and his ministers at Athens protested their innocence and disowned the Cretan leader. Venizelos sailed away from Crete and
travelled to Switzerland. Here again, as in the careers of so
many statesmen, especially those of first rank, we see circumstances triumphant for the time being over the personality who
tries to control and direct them. But when such statesmen have
patience and stick to their cause they eventually attain their
purpose.

In this case it was not far distant. In the eyes of the Greek
military officers the monarchy had disgraced itself in the war
with Turkey. This failure was re-echoed in Crete. The Military
League at Athens forced the retirement of Prince Constantine
and Prince George from the leadership of the army. They were
obliged to emigrate, while the new national hero was called from
Crete to Athens amidst the loud applause of the populace. Thus
the revolutionary leader and opponent of the monarchy, a man
almost unknown in the capital, was appointed head of a state in
whose cause he had worked only indirectly and never in the
country itself, for more than twenty years.

Venizelos did not act hastily. Having advised the King, he
proceeded to interview the Western powers without having
any formal mandate. His purpose was to allay the misgivings of
the Governments in Paris and London before he took over
power, as Bismarck did before him; for he knew that the Cabi-

nets of the big powers did not trust the strong man. He returned to Crete and put affairs in order there. Then he arranged for a Greek deputation to wait on him and bring him to Athens. There was a splendid send-off, like that of a favourite son leaving home.

His small steamer sailed from Suda Bay where the big war vessels of the powers had lain at anchor so often to bombard him and his flag and his little armed forces in the mountains. He was now forty-six years old, already turning grey. In this little island, which he was now leaving, one failure after another had eventually led only to a series of successes. His youth and the days of his apprenticeship were left behind; but the future success of his career could never have been achieved had he not gone through the experiences he had encountered here. In that moment his thoughts were probably directed towards the grave near the coast where the body of his wife lay; for he had always mourned this woman whom he had lost in the early years of their wedlock. And he did not marry again until thirty years after her death.

4

Venizelos sailed into the Piræus next day like a conquering hero. Those who witnessed that event, in September 1910, have admitted that at that moment he might have dismissed the King, made himself dictator and proclaimed a republic. The official statesmen must have winced when they beheld this stranger, who was half a foreigner and almost entirely unknown at Athens, now coming to direct the affairs of the country with a new tempo and a new emphasis. It is interesting to think of the mistrust with which he must have been received by the party leaders who for ages had played the old game of parliamentary poker wherein portfolios are shuffled and reshuffled and dealt out to one hand after another. What anomalous feelings must have been aroused at the royal residence when this stranger, who had turned the youngest son of the royal family out of a comfortable job, now appeared before the gates. The anti-monarchical Military League had lifted this rebel on their shields and the people received him with cheers. Would he treat the royal person of the King with consideration? In the broad Syntagma Square, close to the bare and almost unoccupied royal palace, he addressed a crowd of some thousands from the balcony of his hotel. The mob shouted for a New Constitution. He realized at once that if he was to master this changeable people he must show them the whip hand. "No," he answered, "I insist upon a Revisionist Chamber." "We want a New Constitution," thousands of voices repeated. "No," he answered, "I say Revision." The mob now felt that they were dealing with a master who was not to be trifled with. They remained silent during the remainder of his speech.

The monarch himself was not prepared for what happened. Next day the imperturbable, tall and grey-haired man of sixty from the northern seas, received the much younger man from the Mediterranean island. Instead of finding himself confronted by a mountain rebel with high boots and a brace of pistols, the King came face to face with a man who disarmed all suspicion the very moment they met. "If Your Majesty," said he, "will accept my programme I can promise Your Majesty within five years a restored Greece with new rights and increased prestige." It was almost an echo of the words Bismarck had addressed to King Wilhelm when he took over control of the Prussian Government. But Venizelos was destined to carry out his promise in three instead of five years. The King had been frightened

by what his former ministers had told him. Therefore he asked:
"But what will happen if we are all wiped out by this Military
League?" The Prime Minister answered: "The League will be
dissolved on the very day that Parliament assembles." But the
King said confidentially elsewhere: "I hope to see him dangling
from the mast of a warship within a few months."

Naturally Venizelos could not care much for these people—
the King and his sons. They were not Greeks. They had no
patriotic feelings. They had been opposed to the annexation of
Crete. Yet he took the monarchy into his calculations as an
active factor in the whole situation. The plan he had set before
himself was too big to be entrusted to the fortunes of a personal
dictatorship. His plan was nothing less than the banishment of
Turkish rule from all the Grecian lands and the uniting of all
Greeks to the motherland—not only the Greeks in Macedonia
and Thrace and Asia Minor, but also those on the islands of
the Archipelago. All these should be liberated from Turkish
dominance and brought into the mother fold. This plan was
only an amplification of his earliest yearnings. It was the dream
of his childhood.

But now on the threshold of reality. The hour had struck.
The threatening attitude of the Young Turks necessitated a
union of all the Balkan states. Only the pressing demands of the
situation made it possible to consider an alliance among some
of those rival states as within the limits of practical politics.
But that alliance could never be brought about under a discredited monarchy. The prestige of the monarchy must first be
restored. Therefore, the new Prime Minister decided to work
energetically for the restoration of confidence in the monarchy
and its consolidation in the eyes of the Greek people, though
this was against his personal feelings for this foreign dynasty.

That was why he declared himself on the side of the monarchy
during the elections, and why he openly rebuked the monarchy

at the same time. "As for the dynasty," he said, "it is rooted in the country, but I consider that the crown ought to take a more energetic part in the affairs of the state." He even went further in favour of the monarchy and, to the general surprise, restored the Crown Prince Constantine to his old position as Commander-in-Chief of the army. At the same time he rehabilitated Prince George. He collaborated with them in reorganizing the army and the navy. In this task he was assisted by France and England.

One of his first aims was to establish a Balkan League for the purpose of driving the Turk from Europe once and for all. The intensity of his hostility to the Turk did not arise from purely religious motives. I do not think that Venizelos is religious in the dogmatic sense. Indeed, I found him so tolerant of Protestants and Jews that I imagine he must have outlived any old religious prejudices he may have had. Nor was his hatred of the Turks based on racial feelings. He recognized that his own race was a mixed one. But he remembered what he had suffered in his childhood, the exiles and oppressions and humiliations and enforced backwardness which the boys and young men of his time were subjected to at the hands of a Sultan's emissaries. He was a Cretan and therefore not in the same position as the Greeks of the mainland, who had been liberated from the Turkish yoke two generations earlier. For this reason his anti-Turkish feeling was much more profound and real; and thus his life's mission has a truer historical significance.

As a political leader in Greece, it was to his disadvantage that he had always remained a Cretan. In that island he knew the whole population of 300,000, or at least all the men of influence among them. But here in Greece these three millions were strangers to him. He was not acquainted with local feeling in various cities and districts. He had not the experience of the historical party leaders; nor did he know the story of their mutual interests, frictions and intrigues. Though he was triumphant at the first elections, later on he misunderstood the popular feeling and only by his mistakes did he become acquainted with the variegated temperament of the Greek electorate. Because he insisted on democratic principles he fell foul of the electorate on two critical occasions. Thus the stranger who was originally received by the hosannas of the mob had to pay the price of his inexperience later on.

The negotiations with the Balkan states, for the purpose of organizing the League, had to be carried on with extreme caution. During some critical weeks Venizelos and Bratianu had to communicate by secret codes and keep the key to themselves; because in the background was always one of the great powers or a group of them, constantly on the alert to prevent the union of the Balkans. It was especially necessary to keep Vienna in the dark until the moment for the dénouement came. As a matter of fact, Count Berchtold, the elegant culprit who was mainly responsible for the actual outbreak of the war, confessed, as befitted a cavalier, that the Treaty of Bukarest had taken him absolutely by surprise.

The political wisdom of Venizelos is shown in what he omitted from the treaties he made. While Bulgaria and Serbia clearly defined their share of the booty in the coming war—and afterwards fought a new war between themselves on that account, Venizelos left the chief point of interest, that of Salonika, entirely unmentioned; but he was determined to seize it on the first opportunity and keep possession of it.

What was to become of Crete in this war which the Balkan League was planning? In general, the four signatories to the treaty stipulated that they would come to one another's aid the moment the Turks attacked one or the other. The Turks had threatened to march against Greece the moment the Cretan Deputies entered the Parliament at Athens. In such an eventuality the other signatories were not bound to come to Greece's aid. But the Cretans became excited at the prospect of the coming war. In the spring of 1912 they sent their Deputies to Athens, following the general elections. These demanded admission to Parliament, though they were prohibited by the Prime Minister.

For twenty years Venizelos had been looking forward to that moment. He did not wish at any price to betray his undertakings to the Balkan allies. Therefore, he placed a cordon of cavalry round the House of Parliament and ordered that nobody should pass through without a special permit. The Cretan Deputies tried to force their way through the cordon of troops and managed to get as far as the entrance of the building and hurled themselves on the military guards. A member of the Opposition drew his revolver; but in a moment peace was restored by the announcement that Venizelos would receive a deputation of the Cretans in the Prime Minister's private room. There he announced to them that Parliament would be prorogued until October 1. Thus the incident came to a close.

His plan had carried. On September 30 the Turks began to mobilize. The Balkan League now acted. An ultimatum was sent to the Turks and on the same day Venizelos proclaimed the annexation of Crete to Greece. His fellow countrymen now understood and took their places in the Athenian Parliament. The army was on the march. And the Grecian Commander-in-Chief was the Crown Prince.

5

Constantine was four years younger than Venizelos. He was a tall, strapping, brown-haired officer of the Russian type. He was not what one might call aristocratic in his mien; but he was dapper. He was quick in his movements and had a decisive way of speaking—in short, he was a man without any imposing personal qualities; but still in the nineteenth century he could command authority because he was born on the couch of a queen. About the middle of the Great War I made his acquaintance, while he was still King; and I saw him afterwards in exile. There was a certain frankness and gusto about him which I liked, because it made up for his lack of ideas. Although he was always asking questions and thus giving the impression that he was desirous of being informed, he never considered what was said in reply but brusquely asserted his own opposite view and gave no reasons for it.

I have often noticed that when one studies such characters closely one finds a fundamental sense of insecurity which they attempt to conceal by an outwardly decisive manner. Personally, however, I have not sufficient grounds for saying this of Constantine; because I have been alone with him face to face only for a couple of hours. But from what I have heard from his friends and enemies I am convinced that in this characteristic, though to a lesser degree, he resembled Kaiser Wilhelm II.

As an officer of one of the Guard regiments at Potsdam and later as brother-in-law of Wilhelm II, he must have acquired a good deal of the Prussian spirit, though he was much more likable than the average Prussian. His speech smacked of the Berlin dialect, but with a soft, foreign intonation that was rather amusing. His début as a thirty-year-old Field Marshal was most unhappy. Not only was he beaten by the Turks in the Thessalian campaign, but he abandoned the most important strategic positions in such a panic that, if he had been an ordinary general, he would have been court-martialled. Such at least is the opinion of eyewitnesses and experts, who will not accept his explanation. The anger of the Officers' League, which subsequently forced him to relinquish his command, cannot be explained by referring to blunders made by him after the war. Yet this was the man whom Venizelos reinstated to a position of high responsibility in the hour of danger. He must have had some confidence in the Prince. When I questioned Venizelos on this point later, he said:

"In reality Constantine was not the leader in that war. I had lived for a long time in the mountains and fought for years there and led my little armed bands and ambushed my enemy. That experience gives a man a practical experience for tactics. I had also studied military history a good deal. Yes, I claim to have taken a hand in formulating the strategy of the Balkan War and to have influenced it decisively. Where were the forces to be concentrated—in Albania, in Thessaly or in Thrace? That was a decision which had to be made from the political angle and I had to make it. Only a week after the opening of the campaign I encountered difficulties. Constantine sent me the following wire from Cosani: 'There are two routes only. I have decided to take the left and march along the road to Monastir. There I shall find the main body of the Turkish forces and, according to strategic rules, I ought to meet the enemy's main force and defeat it—unless my Government objects to the plan.' I replied: 'You would be right, if this war were a duel between Greeks and Turks. But as we have allies it would be a great mistake to march on Monastir and allow the Bulgarians to take Salonika. I must insist that you march to Salonika rather than have the Bulgarians take it.' The King was then at Gidda, close to the army. I called him up during the night and made his adjutant wake him and I forced him to persuade his son to carry out my command; else I could not remain responsible. And so we got into Salonika first. A few hours later the advance scouts of the Bulgarian army found it, a conquered city."

In the same city of Salonika, which symbolized the first military victory gained under his rule after having reigned for fifty years, King George was murdered soon after hostilities had ceased. So that Constantine returned not merely as conqueror, but as King. "I have made two great mistakes in my life," Venizelos once assured me. "I made the new King a war god and a national hero. I allowed him to be received in triumph and I allowed him to take all the credit in the public eye for what had been achieved. That was my first mistake."

Not satisfied with what they had gained in their first Balkan war, the Bulgarians went to war again, this time against their allies, and were completely defeated. The Greek gains were increased. They included Crete, a large portion of Macedonia, with Salonika, Western Thrace, together with Cavalla and the Tabak, Epirus and most of the islands of the Archipelago. First by military successes and later by his own personal successes at two conferences, Venizelos gained for his country much more than the other allies received.

Yet Constantine took the credit for it all. The tragic death of his father, the conquest of the provinces which had been the object of Grecian yearning for so long, and the historic symbolism of the name *Constantine*—all this contributed to make the young King look like a hero in the eyes of the nation. The result was that a feeling of conceit developed and took hold of him; and this was later turned against the man who had been the artificer of his power and fame. The traditional ingratitude of kings was reinforced by the traditional ingratitude of the Greeks. One year after the conclusion of the Balkan war came July 1914. The internal dissonance between these two personalities, hitherto concealed behind the statesmanship of Venizelos, now appeared in the light of day and influenced the course of history.

In these cases there are always political grounds for such divergencies, but here there was something else. The divergence had a more profound origin. It must be sought in the contrasts of human temperament and emotion. In such hours of fate kings and ministers are influenced definitely by inherited prejudices, upbringing and education, women, ambition, jealousy. Constantine had a sort of superstitious regard for Germany; Venizelos had something of the same kind of regard for the Entente. But these considerations do not furnish a complete explanation.

Constantine, who was a vacillating character and easily influenced by a stronger will, allowed his principles of conduct to be definitely shaped by his education and his marriage. He certainly did not look upon Kaiser Wilhelm as an idol, nor did he like him personally. He had misgivings about the Kaiser, because the latter had treated Constantine at one time kindly and at another imperiously, with the sudden change of feeling characteristic of a neurasthenic. After the Balkan war the Prussian Kaiser conferred a marshal's baton on the Grecian King. Later on he bullied Constantine, and especially now when he wished him to come in as an ally in the Great War. The Queen, who always spoke English with her husband and hated the French as the hereditary enemy, returned from Berlin in August 1914, profoundly impressed by the spectacle of military discipline and the military apotheosis of her brother which she had witnessed in Berlin. She became a frequent visitor at the German Embassy in Athens. Her conversation there was certainly not characterized by a sense of regal dignity when she mentioned France, and she is also said to have written in that tone to Berlin. I did not read the letter, though I brought it in a sealed bag across the still open frontier of the Entente from Athens to Serbia. At this moment of supreme political importance the King realized that his wife was the sister of the German Kaiser and was influenced by that consideration. Venizelos assured me that at the very beginning of the Great War the King said to him during a conversation: "I am afraid the Queen will come back [from Berlin] with other ideas."

He certainly did not wish to jeopardize the position of Greece and he feared that if she joined the enemies of Germany she would become a second Belgium. For he seriously believed that, if the war was to be won at all, it would be won by Germany. His influence still definitely outweighed that of the Queen. Within his own circle he had made use of it for years. When I visited him in February 1916, he showed me a special map he had and pointed out the progress which the Germans were making at one of the Verdun fortresses—I believe it was Douaumont. And when I spoke with him in St. Moritz, in August 1917, about the increasing distress in Austria, he was annoyed. "My doctor, who has just arrived from Vienna," he said sharply, "has assured me of the contrary." Constantine did not only see wrongly at the beginning of the war; even at the end of it he did not want to see rightly.

Personal motives of ambition and jealousy played a big part in shaping his policy. The laurels of victory which he had won in the Balkan War were still fresh. Why should he risk their being torn from him? He was like an author who has made a fortune with a single book, not by his talents but by the fact that it was produced at the opportune moment and well advertised, and who is now afraid to risk a failure by bringing out a second book. Hatred of the Turks, which was the primal motive power in the breast of his Chief Minister, could make no particular appeal to a Russian Dane. Anyhow, who was this Cretan who was urging Greece on to war on the side of the Entente? "Constantine trusted me very much," Venizelos once said to myself. "I had restored him to the head of the army and afterwards allowed him to take the laurels of victory for himself. But it annoyed him to have at his side a man whom the populace liked. He wished to see William of Prussia win the war; for that victory would bring a reflected glory on himself. He was influenced also by his German-born friend, Georges Streit [Greek Minister of Foreign Affairs]. But he did not treat me fairly. I shall tell you about it later on."

Whereas the King did not lean to any side, either nationally or politically, Venizelos was fundamentally affected by his personal hatred of the Turks. What an opportunity to turn the mortal enemy out of the Grecian parts of Asia Minor, and perhaps even out of Constantinople, in collaboration with the mighty armies of the Entente! That was his thought. For, since the two German battleships were freely allowed to enter the Dardanelles ten days after the war had commenced, Venizelos knew that the Turks would join the Germans. Thus the chief motive that moved Venizelos was not opposition to the Germans but hatred of the Turks. If the Turks had been the allies of the Entente he never would have joined it.

In addition to this personal bias, he was influenced by political considerations on a broad national basis. The geographical position of the country in relation to the sea rendered any friction with England a source of danger. And it was natural that Greece should join the three powers that had guaranteed her independence a hundred years before. Moreover, Venizelos was a democrat. He believed in the efficiency of that form of statal government and his political principles, in the wide philosophic sense, logically demanded the overthrow of all autocratic power. The treaty with Serbia which bound Greece to come to her aid in case of invasion, and which had been in force for two years, was used by Venizelos as a means of appealing to Right and Honour, whereas his own personal motives were inspired by passion and national interest.

Difference of character and in the respective positions of power

which they held headed inevitably for a break between the King
and his Prime Minister.

6

"Your Majesty, still happily in the bloom of his early manhood,
may have the chance not only to create something grand by
means of the sword but also to consolidate the political order.
And when your reign will have come to a close you will be
able to hand on to your successor a work of such greatness as
few monarchs have been privileged to bequeath. But even if
you fail you will fail with a good conscience; because we shall
have struggled for the liberation of our countrymen from the
Turks. . . . We shall have won friendship and respect from
the powers which have established the Greek nation and defended it for so long. Hellenism will never again have such an
opportunity as it has now."

The above are extracts from the long exposé in which Venizelos tried to convince his sovereign, or at least to talk him
over, during the first months of the war. At the same time he
had a well-grounded fear that his letters might find their way
to Berlin. He was not personally liked at the palace. The Queen
withdrew when he entered. In an antechamber or on the stair-
case he often encountered the German ambassador. It is not
difficult to imagine how he felt when, in February 1915, the
Allied powers bombarded Gallipoli, and Greece was not with
them. Ten years later Venizelos said to me: "If I had been
allowed in February 1915 to attack Gallipoli, the Turks would
have withdrawn, the Russians would have been able to bring
their war material through the Straits, when they were attack-

ing Przemysl in Galicia. In the spring of 1916, after the failure of the Verdun offensive, the war would have been at an end, Bulgaria would not have joined and Europe would have made peace two-and-a-half years earlier. That is the responsibility of the King before the bar of history—the extension of the war to double its duration."

About this time, when Serbia lay strangled, Sir Edward Grey asked for Grecian assistance and offered in return certain territorial concessions in Asia Minor, together with Smyrna. But the whole proposal was vague, like all the promises which the Allies made to Greece.

It was after this that the British Government decided on the Dardanelles campaign and invited Greece to participate. King Constantine seemed for a moment to be convinced. On March 5, 1915, when Venizelos had directed his attention to the precarious position of the Greeks living in Asia Minor, the King said: "Well, all right. In God's name, then." A Crown Council was called on the same day and pronounced in favour of participation, with only one dissenting vote. The King asked for one night more to consider. As a protest against the decision of the Crown Council, the pro-German Chief of Staff resigned. Venizelos, however, was so sure of his case that he had the necessary papers prepared overnight. On the following morning the King refused to sanction the decision of the Crown Council. Whereupon Venizelos resigned and forced a general election. He convinced the people that this was their sole opportunity to conquer the Turks and he won the elections. Thus he found himself face to face with a united people who wished that the two men to whom they had entrusted their leadership would act together. In the circumstances it was the duty of the King to send for Venizelos; but His Majesty pretended to be ill. At least, so Venizelos says. He allowed his minister to wait from July to September. Then Bulgaria showed signs of getting ready to enter the war on Germany's side. And the Greek monarch had to call on the tantalizing Cretan once more.

His subsequent period of office was the shortest that Venizelos ever held. It lasted only two weeks, in the autumn of 1915. It was characterized by a series of oblique manœuvres on both sides. Obviously it could not last long; for neither the King nor his Prime Minister was frank with the other. The army was mobilized. But the country did not really know for what or against whom. One of the participants in the farce said to me, quite in the Attic style: "Venizelos mobilized against Bulgaria; but the King mobilized against Venizelos."

Both men realized that the Allied powers, who wished to land their troops at Salonika for the purpose of marching on Constantinople, could be held back only by force. At a later date each accused the other of having invited the armies of the Allies into the country. The truth was that both worked more towards that end than either of them wished the country to know afterwards. If the nation thought that the Allied troops had been actually invited, they would never have pardoned the responsible party, not even if victory had resulted. From the depths of the national soul in such cases a deep distrust rises, a feeling which women have when strange men try to delve into their inner secrets. Even when the first phases of shock have already given way to love, a later moment comes in which the male predominance is resented.

Here was another case in which the King took two steps to the rear after having taken one step forward. After the first resignation of Venizelos, he opened pourparlers with the Allied powers, through the new Prime Minister, Gounaris. In reference to this move, he said: "I do this because my country sympathizes with those nations; but I am frightened lest they may accept." In the following autumn the French request became more pressing. Venizelos, once again Prime Minister, ar-

ranged for the landing of 150,000 men. The King understood this
to mean the protection of his northern frontiers against Bulgaria.
Venizelos meant it for the purpose of making Greece's intervention a necessity. Once again Venizelos had planned to take
his sovereign unawares.

In July 1870, when Bismarck wanted war and found an opportunity to exploit the blunders of his French rival so as to allow
it to appear that France was the aggressor, he changed the text
of a telegram which his King had written and published it to
the world. The purpose of this alteration was to place the
King of Prussia, who was bent on maintaining peace, in a
situation which drew him inevitably into war. The ruse that
had been employed by Bismarck in connection with the famous
Ems telegram was now adopted by Venizelos. During a weak
moment, in September 1915, the King of Greece was made to
part with his consent to the landing of 150,000 Allied troops.

"Half an hour later," Venizelos said to me, "Mercati, the
Lord Chamberlain, came to me and announced that I was not
to take any further step until I had consulted the King again,
the next morning. I looked at him and replied: 'The step has
been taken already.' When I afterwards explained my policy in
a speech delivered before Parliament the King told me angrily
that I had gone too far, that I must protest against the landing
of the Allied troops at Salonika, that this really was an act of
usurpation on the part of the Entente, that it was a breach of
International Law, the *scrap of paper* tactics again. At the same
time the King had left me in the dark about the truth of the
whole situation. When Bulgaria was about to attack Serbia the
consequence would most probably have been a violation of our
frontiers. I brought the mobilization decree to the King for his
signature, so that we could be a few days ahead of the Bulgarians. The *casus belli* was self-evident.

" 'But you know,' said the King, 'that I don't wish for a war against Bulgaria.' 'You might have said that last February,' I replied. 'In the meantime, the nation has accepted my programme. I stand here as its chosen representative, responsible, according to the Constitution, only to the King.'

" 'Your position would be correct,' said the King, 'if it were a matter of domestic policy. When great questions arise on which the life of the nation depends I am responsible only to God.'

"I recognized the doctrine propounded by Wilhelm II and replied, 'I am sorry to say, as a famous man once said, that I am not in the confidence of the Almighty. Aristotle has spoken of the religiosity of Kings when they hold certain views. So far as concerns our case I am aware of the fact that my father voted to make Your Majesty's father King over us.'

"Later on I learned from documentary evidence that the King had played me false. Five days before this conversation he had sent for the Bulgarian minister and said:

" 'I know that your sovereign is coming to the help of Germany and is going to attack the Serbians. In that case I have promised Berlin to remain neutral. I will not allow Venizelos to carry out his programme.' In such a situation there was no course left open for me except to hand in my resignation and act again on my own."

This crisis, with all its secret plottings and Venizelos' Voltairian criticism of the divine right of kings, can be understood only when we recognize his power of suggestion over the weaker-minded King Constantine. One day during the crisis the King said of him: "He has his own way of talking me over. When he is not here everything looks different. He wanted to bamboozle me." And on another occasion he said to his secretary, when the latter remarked that His Majesty was not looking well: "Of course I'm ill again. You know who has been with me just now, don't you?"

At that time the attitude of Venizelos was not always the same. Sly and able by nature, he was not at all a Mephistopheles. He had tried all sorts of legal manœuvres before he finally struck out on his revolutionary move. This *modus agendi* was familiar to him since the time of his insurrectionary activities in Crete. During the Great War all the nations kept the real motives of their actions in the background and talked loudly about national honour and the sanctity of treaties. Nevertheless, each acted according to its own instincts and interests. Venizelos was not enthusiastic for the Serbs. But he was against the Turks. The King was not so much against the French as he was in favour of the Germans. In 1916 the Allied powers blockaded the neutral ports of Greece on grounds of morality and sentiment. They cut off the imports of coal and corn and they had their political spies concealed on the islands. They opened the post-bags and were always finding new legal grounds for their high-handedness. The only public statesman who spoke the truth was Clemenceau when he said: "Nous sommes entrés en Grèce par l'argument de la force"; and Bernard Shaw who declared ironically that if it was to the military advantage of the Allies they would violate the neutrality of Paradise even if they had to admit the moral impossibility of their attitude towards Greece.

In February 1916, when the Bulgarians had already marched into Greece unchallenged, I visited the King in his villa at Athens. He tried to conceal his illness, a serious attack of pleuritis, from which he died five years later. He spoke a good deal and spoke rapidly. He hardly listened at all to what I said. All his arguments were inspired by an unquestioning faith in Germany. I put some objections rather carefully and then he replied:

"The London periodical, *Punch,* has caricatured me dressed in the costume of an ancient Greek, after the style of the old

vases. My feet are tottering and I am pulled in different directions by two ropes, one held by the Kaiser and the other by
Britannia. Must I allow the English to bombard my ports and
reduce them to ruins? I have to set my feelings aside. I can act
only as a Greek. These gentlemen will not come to me here in
Athens and will not even make an attempt to do so. With the
Bulgarians it is not quite so bad. As soon as they have driven
their enemies out of my country they will depart in peace. If
the English had more power everything would have gone better. But it is the French who are always trying to extort new
concessions from me."

When I pointed out to him the possibility of internal trouble,
he said quickly and frankly: "You mean revolution? No. No.
That does not happen in our country." I noticed that on this
point he had the same kind of optimism as Venizelos had.

He spoke of the latter without any animosity. He did not
look upon Venizelos as a rival but rather as a man who saw
differently from himself. "His foreign policy, unfortunately,"
said the King, "is often fantastic. When Grey offered him from
London a patch of the shore of Asia Minor as a reward for
Greece's entry into the war on the side of the Entente he thereupon declared in Parliament that we were to receive the whole
western part of Asia Minor as far as Anfiun and he drew a
picture of the fields and their flocks of sheep as they appeared
to his fancy."

Some weeks later I saw the two rivals in front of the Great
Golden Cross of the Athens Cathedral on the occasion of the
Greek National Festival. They were united and at the same
time separated. At one spot stood the tall figure of the King,
wearing across his uniform the blue ribbon of the Order of the
Redeemer. He was surrounded by his people. At some distance
Venizelos was standing in the midst of his own group, his
morning coat decorated with the same ribbon. This open divi-

sion in face of the members of the legations from the belligerent powers, the smile on the King's face and his obvious attempt to pretend that he did not see the other party, the subdued conversation of the hostile group, and, above all, the absence of any obvious reason for the situation—all this in the glare of a thousand candles, the reverberations of the organ and the exchanges of greetings, with pictures of Jesus and the Saints all round, emphasized for me especially on that occasion the tension between the two men, and at the same time called forth my admiration for the democratic spirit of a nation that permitted its King to take part in such a public manifestation.

7

Some months later, on a September night in 1916, a group of young people drinking in a restaurant on the Phaleron beach had their attention attracted to some gentlemen who had arrived by car from Athens. They noticed them pass through the hotel quickly and saw them embark in a little boat which brought them to a ship that stood in the distance out at sea. It was Venizelos and two friends, one of whom subsequently became President of the Grecian Republic. The man who for the past six years had been the greatest power on this shore now slunk away like a conspirator in the night. It was his third flight; but this flight had a special characteristic; for he had now definitely decided on a course which involved high treason. In case he was successful he would become a hero and the saviour of his country. If he failed he would be executed by order of his opponent. He was now fifty-two years old and he did not flee the country as he had fled from Crete before, as a child and a young man, driven out by persecution and thereby all the more determined to turn eventually on his persecutors. On the present occasion, in 1916, his flight was not from Crete but to Crete. There amid the old scenes of his revolutionary days he once more assembled volunteers to his support and refreshed his courage at its native spring. After a short time he left for Salonika, where he was awaited and received by his friends.

It was hard to believe that only four years had passed since he had entered this town in triumph by the overland route from Athens, accompanied by the King and the Crown Prince, for the purpose of formally annexing to the motherland this city of Salonika which had just been liberated from the detested rule of the Turks. On that occasion he was surrounded by Greek uniforms and banners and bands and he must have felt that the reception was a worthy recompense for the struggle he had been through.

The quay still bore the name of Venizelos, but it was not the Greek troops who were drawn up in line to receive him. He saw the French and English and Italian and Serbian troops, all alike in their grey war uniforms and caps; but their countenances and languages were strange to him. On the landing stage he was received by General Sarrail, who wore a splendid uniform and greeted him in the name of half of Europe as head of the Provisional Government of Greece. Years before, when he had approached a military representative of the great powers, it was as an idealist insurrectionary from a little island to submit to the threat of a mightier force. But now he was honored by the General as the representative of a country whose legitimate head was soon to be dismissed and banned—the same man whom Venizelos himself had placed in position and power four years earlier. At this perilous moment of his career when Venizelos, not forcibly but of his own free will and believing in his political star, left his country and sought protection at the hands of a foreign people, he must have felt more deeply than ever the absurdity of inherited rule. For his programme had been completely accepted at the last general election; but he had failed to carry it through, because of the resistance of one man who on his own account had no claim to gratitude on the part of the people.

What must have been his feelings when a small division of soldiers cried out: "Down with the King"? After careful deliberation he issued a proclamation accusing the King of a breach of the Constitution. Nevertheless, he claimed the right to govern on behalf of the King when he made the garrison of the city, which was only lukewarmly royalist, take the oath of allegiance, but not to the new Government. Everything was prepared. He established the seat of government at Salonika and remained for nine months. King Constantine sent him a confidential emissary to inquire whether he would agree to become Prime Minister in case the Greek monarchy consented to join the Allied powers. Venizelos replied: "Neither I nor any one of my friends."

In Athens he was condemned as a criminal. Immediately after his departure his house was searched, with the result that 60 guns, 49 revolvers and 15 hand grenades were confiscated. The old revolutionary from the mountains had not forgotten his traditional tactics. On Christmas Day the King's Government had a heap of stones erected in the public square and had Venizelos publicly denounced by eight bishops, in a solemn ceremonial carried out according to an old Grecian rite. This was his second excommunication, and much more solemn than the first, which took place in Crete. *"Anathema!"* (Let him be accursed!) each bishop shouted out as he threw a stone on the heap. Then from the attending crowd of fifty thousand, who had greeted him formerly as a national hero, each threw a stone at him and at the same time cried out *"Anathema!"* The King found it more difficult to excommunicate him than the people did. On one occasion, when the aged Premier Skaludis delivered His Majesty a long harangue, to which he did not listen, the King suddenly wakened up as if from a dream and asked: "Is Venizelos still here?" So strong was the magic power of this man that even his shadow frightened the unhappy monarch.

Both rivals looked to the great powers for a solution. The attitude of the powers towards the King steadily grew more stern and threatening while at the same time they increased their promises to his rebellious minister. The northern part of the country, which had been only recently acquired in the Balkan War, was entirely cut off from the older portion of Greece. The army wavered, as also did public opinion and the press. Both rivals were hopeful, but nobody could see a way out. Some great battle fought a thousand miles away might easily decide their fate and that of the country. But one fine day, in the spring of 1917, the Allied Governments sent a French emissary on a battleship to the Piræus and gave the King of Greece twenty-four hours in which either to resign the throne in favour of one of his sons or to allow a republic to be established in Athens. The King departed, but he did not formally abdicate. He left Alexander, his second son, behind as his successor. The people were strongly opposed to the King's departure. A movement was spontaneously organized to prevent his going. And this he had to overcome before he could finally leave. Two weeks later Venizelos entered Athens as master of the situation, welcomed by the same bishops who had stoned him the previous autumn.

Why did he not march upon Athens from the north with his sixty thousand Grecian troops and as Greek to Greek, as the conqueror of Macedonia in the Balkan War to his former Field Marshal, why did he not present an ultimatum to the King, forcing the latter either to agree to an alliance with the Entente or else to resign? Why did he allow foreign Governments, backed by foreign troops, to restore him to power? "Why did you not follow the other course?" I asked him. He made a long pause, which is unusual with Venizelos. Then he replied: "Yes, why not? I wanted to march on Athens and turn out the King. But the powers forbade it. Was it perhaps that they feared there was no controlling force back of my three divisions? The fact that I returned to Athens only after Constantine's abdication was not favourably received by many Greek people."

There is a report which says that in a conversation with General Sarrail he even went the length of shedding tears in the hope of bringing the General to agree to his march on Athens. I consider the story genuine, but not the tears.

When he entered Athens he was horror-stricken to find a dead city, with no Athenian on the streets and only long cordons of French soldiers guarding his way. At the end of the journey however, as he reached the King's villa, he saw the heads of the natives behind the foreigners. Poletis, who rode with him in the car, told me how both of them immediately saw the error that had been committed in organizing the return after this fashion, and that Venizelos said to him: "What a blunder the Allies have made."

Two powers awaited him in the capital, that of the old Parliament and that of the new King. In a magnificent speech which lasted eight hours, Venizelos described to the Parliament the past circumstances and the future prospects which justified his programme. He had before him the same leading thought which determined Masaryk's war policy. "We must be there with our troops and share in the mutual sacrifice if we would sit side by side at the conference table with the victor and put forward our claims." Parliament passed a vote of confidence in him with an overwhelming majority.

The new King, a handsome young fellow in the middle twenties, seemed to have made up his mind to collaborate with this dangerous minister and play practically the same rôle as

Wilhelm II did with Bismarck. For the first few weeks he felt uncomfortable, as if he were merely keeping the throne warm for somebody else; but he gradually began to like his work, especially after he had been received with royal honours in Paris. For Venizelos rushed him to Paris and London with a view to securing food and money for Greece. Venizelos remained in full power until the end of the war, and when the Bulgarians and Turks finally submitted he was able to demonstrate to the most distant Greek peasant that he had seen rightly and that the King of Greece had seen wrongly.

He placed quite a high value on the contribution Greece had made to the Allied victory.

"I do not want to exaggerate the value of our services," he said to me, "but the last attack of the Entente, in the autumn of nineteen-eighteen, would never have been successful had it not been for the collaboration of our ten divisions on the Macedonian front. The break-through here forced the Bulgarians and afterwards the Kaiser to start the peace negotiations. The result of our co-operation was, therefore, much more significant than might be implied by the mere number of Greek troops in action. I do not say that if it had not been for us the Allied powers would have lost the war. But without our collaboration it would have been prolonged, perhaps to the spring of nineteen-nineteen, and might have ended without bringing about such a decisive defeat. To say the least of it, we saved some hundreds of thousands of lives on both sides."

8

Almighty God had planted a human heart even in the breast of the Tiger. When Clemenceau, as one of the three supreme judges of the old world, sat on the golden chair in Paris he had a kindly smile for the Greek; for he remained a Philhellenist to his old age. Twenty years earlier he had met the Cretan for the first time and had immediately recognized his genius.

At the Paris Conference, Venizelos was able to place Greece in a different situation from that of the other twenty-three Allied states. In the first place, he came with no secret treaties to the provisions of which the Roumanians and Italians and others might object. In a frank speech he was able to place his case before the Conference and make his personality felt. Moreover, he had an admirable way of treating everybody individually during the negotiations. "If President Wilson says to me," he once declared, "that the people of Thrace are not Grecian I shall prove the contrary. If he should attempt to deprive us of territory on other grounds, then I shall show his action to be contradictory to the principles laid down in the Fourteen Points." Venizelos had the knack of being able to convince the great powers that all the revendications which he claimed were in their interests too, especially the annexation of Asia Minor. Nitti once said of him: "He seems to be always granting something even when his own claims are being met." Finally, he had a practical knowledge of the Near East and he had the statistics, geography and history of it at his finger's ends. Therefore, he was quite different from the mass of ignorant and half-educated people who had come as delegates to the Conference. It was no mere chance that at one time in Paris there was an idea of making Venizelos *Chancellor of the League of Nations*; but the Cretan was clever enough to avoid that entanglement.

He treated Clemenceau as much as possible from the human side, and Wilson from the dogmatical side. He needed only to be himself in order to come to an understanding with a third. Lloyd George soon became his friend, for Venizelos could accommodate himself to circumstances as easily as the Welshman could. Moreover, the latter had no special knowledge of situations as they cropped up and he was able to get a good deal of guidance from Venizelos, who has much the same kind of brain and temperament. They understood each other by a mere nod, both being democrats by principle and education and dictators by temperament. Both also were popular agitators who had developed into constructive statesmen. One day, as the Italians had left the Peace Conference and the Turks were beginning to pack up, Lloyd George called the Greek aside and said to him: "Could you land in Smyrna within three or four days?"

Venizelos had been waiting for that moment. It had to come. Was it not an important interest of the English to establish the Greeks at a place where the Turks, the Italians or the French might eventually become inconvenient? The occupation of Smyrna meant no less to him than the crowning of his lifework. For in Smyrna and the hinterland there lived at least a million Greeks under Turkish rule. He did not put forward this claim, however; he waited for the fulfilment of his dreams to be donated him by the great powers. That day one of them did so. If the reader imagines the half-bald heads of the two men, both in the middle fifties, both with pink cheeks and white hair and sharp inquisitive eyes, both quick to grasp a situation and to understand the feelings of others in a moment—then it will be easier to understand the dramatic importance of that moment and also the feeling of suspicion which made the Greek stipulate for the assent of France and Italy. The stipulation was granted in the careless and informal way that so many stipulations were granted at that Paris Conference. Venizelos hastened to Athens. Within a few days, in the middle of May 1919, his ships took possession of the harbour and his still mobilized army occupied the strategic points around Smyrna.

Did he have a guaranty from the powers? Here was one of the mistakes of his career; but it was only human. Venizelos

ought to have known and ought to have taken into consideration Lloyd George's impetuous way and his habit of not thinking out the consequences before taking action. He ought also
to have remembered that Lloyd George was at times unreliable;
and he ought to have been more circumspect in dealing with
him. But he was fascinated by the extraordinary opportunity
offered him. In a certain sense this move cost both men the loss
of their laurels. Lloyd George's ship would soon have run
aground anyhow. But Venizelos, like the heroes of the Grecian
dramas, had to suffer a heavy blow of Fate because of one
small mistake. He believed that the United States would accept
the mandate for Armenia and would keep the Turks in check.
He believed also that if he did not take Smyrna now, the Turks
would take it in a few years. His assumption in regard to the
American mandate was wrong; his assumption in regard to the
Turks was only too fatally true. Why should he seek a guaranty
from the great powers, like those who were now quarrelling for
guaranties although they had treaties already in their hands?
Had he not achieved magnificent results in the Balkan League
by remaining silent over essential points rather than defining
them? Venizelos always has been the type of statesman who is
long-headed but at the same time ready to step lightly over
difficult ground, and therefore inclined to consider an open
agreement more important than insistence upon each paragraph.
He always tried to create situations that he could exploit. This
kind of statesmanship is ingenious but fraught with peril.

A few months later Clemenceau declared the occupation of
Smyrna to be provisional. Venizelos was astounded. Not one of
the Big Three had mentioned this to him at the various discussions they had held with him; neither had they clearly pointed
out what purpose they had in mind when proposing and assent-
ing to the Greek occupation; nor had they declared whether
the occupying power should be looked upon as the possessor.

At the Armistice the British neglected to take out of Turkey itself the arms they had taken from the defeated Turks. These arms were kept in hangars over which there was no control, so that they could be easily secured by the Turks when needed. Then a strong man soon conceived the idea of discarding all the non-Turkish fringes of his country and reorganizing the purely Turkish land and Turkish people. But when Kemal Pasha concentrated his forces and the Greeks were ready to advance against them from Smyrna they were prevented from doing so by the great powers. Later on the Greeks were allowed to advance, but it was too late. They had to fall back to the base at Smyrna. Finally, they were left with quite extensive gains in Asia Minor.

A year later Venizelos succeeded in acquiring the most important of the Grecian territories in Asia Minor. This was through the treaties of Neuilly and Sèvres, signed in August 1920. The French agreed to the treaty reluctantly; but at that time they wanted to have England's consent for their own treatment of Germany. And they hoped secretly that their Parliament would not ratify it. Anyhow the treaty existed and by virtue of it Venizelos was able to hand over to Greece the territories of Eastern Thrace, Smyrna, several islands, a piece of northern Epirus, one shore of the Sea of Marmora, and the Dardanelles. His dream had been fulfilled to the letter. The following day some demobilized Greek officers tried to shoot him at a Paris railway station. "I got the first shot in my shoulder," he told me. "I understood at once. It was an attempt at assassination. There was a bench for luggage there. I threw myself on it, so that the following shots missed me." By his presence of mind he saved his own life, just as Bismarck did in 1866. When they brought him away they found in the pocket of his coat a book entitled *The History of English Democracy*.

In the meantime the Royalists at Athens and all the other

enemies which such a man naturally has, endeavoured to undermine his position. He had been away for nearly two years, negotiating on Greece's behalf, while they had remained in the capital and were able to further their own party interests. In September he ordered a general election, against the advice of Politis and his other friends. He counted on his good relations with the King for the security of his position. Alexander had fallen out with his father and brother over a love affair. Venizelos intervened in favour of Alexander all the more because the young King wanted to marry a girl of the old Grecian nobility—whom he did marry afterwards. Certainly the Prime Minister was right to prefer a Queen who was descended from a real Grecian family, rather than a foreign princess. The habit of getting princes and princesses from abroad had never turned out fortunately for the Greeks.

But the old Grecian gods seem never to have quitted their ancient home. After thousands of years they are still active, to reinforce the themes of the ancient tragedians. One King had left the country and now another was to die from the bite of a monkey. Young Alexander liked animals. One day when he was playing with his dogs in the garden a monkey whom they chased became excited and bit its master's leg. The wound grew septic and some doctors of European fame were called. They promised to save his life if allowed to amputate his leg. But the young man's handsome physique and royal appearance made his advisers hesitate, and then oppose the operation. It was hoped to save his life; but within ten days he was dead.

The tragedy supplied the Constantinists with a popular catch-cry. Was not this a sign from the gods to call back the martyr King? A romantic appeal was made to public sentiment, to restore the exiled father of the youth who had so suddenly died. Once again, and for the third time, Venizelos was faced with the dynastic problem. But this time he failed to master it. "At

that moment," he told me later, "I should not have appealed to
the country in a general election. I had the army, the administration and half the nation behind me. The Royalists promised
peace to the electors, after they had been in arms for six and a
half years. But I could not tell the women when they would
meet their sons again. When Alexander died I should have
taken George as King. I asked Take Jonescu whether we might
not again unite with the Roumanian House. (George's wife is a
Roumanian.) George was without children. Therefore he might
have ruled to the end of his life and the republic would have
followed in a natural way. I could have postponed the elections
until the end of the war and then have had the peace accepted.
At that time I was exhausted from the strain of so many years.
The attempt on my life was really a symbol. Yes, my prestige
with the Allied powers was such that I could have placed George
on the throne."

During the preceding ten years Venizelos had omitted to
keep his own party machine in working order. He depended
on his personal popularity and believed that an audience of
three thousand people who applauded his speeches in the public
square would also elect him. But he was not acquainted with
the dark corners of local rivalries. He was an optimist. He went
from one success to another, surrounded only too often by mere
flatterers. He did not realize that thousands of these belonged
to families who hated him because he had sent their friends to
the islands under strict regimental orders. He did not understand that thousands found it difficult to accustom themselves
to the vernacular form of speech he had introduced. He did not
realize that there were millions who were fascinated by the
romance of the dead King but felt a repugnance at the spectacle
of the dictator returning under French protection. Tired out as
they were from the long years of war, could he hope to impress

the people once again by preaching a crusade against the Turks? The battle-cry of his enemies was *"Constantine and Peace!"*

Thus Venizelos was beaten and disowned when he was at the pinnacle of his life's achievement. And the final cause of his undoing was the general election which he himself had arranged. He was not even re-elected in his own constituency at Athens. Still he could have carried out a coup d'état. "I did not do so; for I respected the democracy," he said. On board an English destroyer he left the Piræus for the second time, of his own accord but also as one rejected by his people. From the vessel he saw the fireworks which the rejoicing mob shot into the clouds. Perhaps at this moment he remembered the ingratitude of the ancient Greeks.

Soon after his departure the exiled King Constantine returned. He was received like a god and a redeemer.

But peace did not return. Though Constantine had vacillated a good deal during the World War, his conduct as a whole was fairly consistent with the main lines of his policy. The game he played might have been won had the Germans been victorious. He now had the reins of his own destiny in his hands once more. And he rode headlong to disaster.

What could have been more simple than to stop the war in Smyrna? Why did he not say, as he said to me in 1916, and as thousands said afterwards on the public platform and in the press?—*Venizelos is a visionary. Without any guaranties that he will receive something in return, he sends the Greeks to Asia Minor as cannon fodder, as slaves of the great powers. We cannot continue this adventurer's policy. We shall withdraw our troops and liquidate the whole business honourably. We have already pledged ourselves in this sense to the electorate.* That was the kind of peace message the nation was waiting for. If he had thus taken the interest of his own country into consideration and allowed his action to be guided exclusively by his sense of duty to it, the Entente powers could make no reasonable objection. But now he looked upon himself as a member of the Entente group, the one thing that he had refused to be throughout all the preceding years. And he thought that by joining the Allies at this stage he would get help against the Turks, who had fought against the Allies in the World War.

When he returned from his three years' exile, Christmas, 1920, he was very ill. Therefore his ministers must be held principally responsible for what happened at that time. The blunders which they made, and which the King made, can be explained on no other grounds except their common jealousy of Venizelos. Their hated rival had advanced so far in Asia Minor. In order to go him one better and rob him of his laurels, they said to themselves that they would march a few hundred kilometres into the heart of Turkey.

"How could they possibly think," exclaimed Venizelos to me when discussing this period, "of being able to accomplish all this without any help? In Constantine's return the French saw a welcome excuse for not ratifying the Treaty of Sèvres. Didn't they realize that the French would now do everything to strengthen Kemal Pasha against us? How could they possibly march another four hundred kilometres in the midst of an absolutely hostile population? I had always made them rest on Smyrna as the fulcrum of their operations. When in nineteen-nineteen they marched so far as to get out of touch with this base I wired the general in command and said: 'You must telegraph to me a confession of your mistake and promise not to repeat it; else I shall have to dismiss you.' Once Constantine had returned to Greece, then the Entente would no longer recognize the undertaking or give it financial or any other kind of support. It was criminal to continue the policy under such circumstances.

"On his restoration the King appointed Gounaris as Premier

once again. I had come to know this man during the war and looked upon him as a man of integrity. His enemies have never dared to discredit the magnificent struggle he made. One of his closest collaborators, Politis, said to me later on that Gounaris was a walking encyclopædia and that he read notes sent to him as carefully as if they were judicial verdicts. But he had no feeling for facts. A Bethmann-Hollweg, whom he resembled in outer appearance also, was more useless in Greece than in Prussia. If one could judge his mind from his outward appearance and manner, then I must say that Gounaris was full of hope when I met him at the Genoa Conference in nineteen-twenty-two. Yet this was on the eve of the catastrophe. While admitting that he intended well and honourably, the fact of his blunder remains. It led to his own ruin and the ruin of the nation."

The subsequent Greco-Turkish war lasted for more than a year and a half under Constantine's rule. At three different stages of the struggle the Allied powers offered to intervene and bring about an amicable settlement. But their offer was categorically rejected on all three occasions. Venizelos intervened even oftener. He sent letters and warnings to Athens. He negotiated personally with the Entente. When he found it impossible for him to effect anything he thought it better to sacrifice some of his dreams rather than the final reserves of man power which Greece still possessed. He sat in his hotel, a few hundred yards from the Foreign Office in London; but when Gounaris came to negotiate with the British authorities he refused to see Venizelos. Gounaris hoped that he would change the disfavourable attitude of the Allied powers towards Constantine by gaining a few new victories in Asia Minor. After they had warned him the Greek army still advanced. In view of this, the Allied powers washed their hands of the whole affair by proclaiming their neutrality. The French now actually supported Kemal Pasha.

Venizelos was certainly as fierce a hater as his enemies. In his anxiety lest his whole lifework would be wrecked he set aside all fear of consequences and wrote directly to the leader of the Liberals. This letter arrived a year before the final disaster came; therefore, there was still time to prevent it. The letter was published afterwards to the whole nation. It ran thus: "The policy of not accepting the intervention of the Allied powers, even in principle, is the greatest crime which the Government has committed against Greece. Could I ever have thought of making war alone against the Turks, without the aid of the Entente? Much less could I have thought of doing it in opposition to the Entente. Only by a compromise can the present Government bring the war to an end and save from the fruits of our policy what is still to be saved. . . . If the Turks should refuse the compromise, then England could bring official pressure to bear on them in order to see that the provisions of the Sèvres Treaty be carried out. But now, when the refusal to settle comes from us, English official opinion is beginning to take the other side. Thus the Government is leading Greece to complete disaster, for the idea of a victory so great and overwhelming as to enable us to force our terms on the enemy is preposterous in the eyes of every sensible man. As things are going, our financial resources and our military strength will be exhausted in a few months. They will collapse and then under much worse conditions we shall have to beg for the intervention which we formerly refused. That is the sad prospect which the present state of affairs brings before my eyes."

Soon after this warning the King suffered his first defeat in Asia Minor. Out of touch with their base at Smyrna, without the help of the Allied powers and uncertain what the latter might or might not do to help the Turks, the two principal

Greek generals advised the King to halt. But two of his ministers advised him to go forward. He took the advice of the latter and decided to march on Angora. What was the meaning of it? Was he still under the arrogant illusion, since the time of the Balkan War, that he was a genius at military strategy? Was it the inherited granducal megalomania? Was it jealousy of his rival, who had originally embarked on this war, or was it some sort of perverse wish to make a fiasco of the whole affair? Even when he was defeated he did not fall back on Smyrna.

The enemy waited, all the time developing his military strength and concentrating it for one drive. A year later, in August 1922, Kemal took the offensive. He split up Constantine's forces and advanced on Smyrna by rapid marches, driving the exhausted Greek army before him. The Greek troops set fire to the city. Their work of devastation was added to by the terrified inhabitants who feared that the advancing Turks would sack the place and put the Christians to the sword. Scenes were enacted which made it almost impossible to believe that we were living in the twentieth century. The Moslems attacked and slaughtered the Christians wholesale. Even the world which had experienced the horrors of the Great War and grown callous to such tidings was shocked anew at the tragedy of Smyrna. Several units of the Greek army landed at Chios and there demanded the dismissal of the Government. Constantine, who had been received as the saviour of the country eighteen months earlier, now had to resign for the second time. His son George, whom he had appointed as his successor, was forced by military officers to absent himself from Greece for a while. He and the Queen went to Roumania.

A Danish-Russian prince and a German princess had promised themselves a home, a kingdom and a people here in the Mediterranean. But in their inner hearts they had always remained strangers and they were driven out twice within five

years. A son of theirs who had been bitten by an African animal
was buried on this shore. They left behind them another son
who was soon to follow them into exile at the request of the
people's representatives. The Queen saw her mighty brother in
the North running to a foreign country for refuge, and she
saw her cousins and nephews banned from the Prussian throne.
She survived the catastrophe for ten years. But the King, who
had sought safety in Palermo, died there brokenhearted within
a few months.

Thus the Genius of Tragedy, guarding the land of Greece,
had issued its fiat against those foreigners from the North, and
doomed them as it had doomed the ancient kings.

9

But, on the other side, there was no victor. Venizelos lived to
see the results of half his lifework ruined and lost, at the same
time as his political enemies were executed. Bismarck had died
with the melancholy presentiment that the heir to the Prussian
throne would destroy his lifework. But he did not live to witness that destruction. Venizelos was fated to gaze on the ruins
with his own eyes, and all within a few years after his great
achievements. What induced him once again to resume his old
post and replace the same King who had been previously driven
out? Why did he not go into retirement and devote his leisure
to reading and writing? He was essentially a man of action,
indeed of creative action. Therefore he decided to go to Lausanne
to represent the new Government at the Peace Conference there
and save what could be saved.

In Athens the anger of a disappointed and misled and scan-

dalously beaten army was raging. They looked for a scapegoat
and they laid their hands on eight statesmen and generals whom
they deemed responsible. Among them were three ex-Premiers
and some members of famous families. The accusation against
Gounaris was that he ought to have deposed the King when the
latter marched into Asia; for he was in a position to know that
the Allied powers would not come to Greece's help. He and his
companions were sentenced to death. The prospect of this judicial bloodshed shocked Europe. In such cases foreign nations
are inclined to feel that their own level of Christian civilization
is much higher than that of a nation which clamours for the
blood of the leaders who have wronged and misled it. But
should a similar fate befall their own country they would readily
object to interference from outside.

Venizelos was the only person who took a stand entirely above
the whole complex of misfortunes and was able to assess the responsibility of the nation's leaders. He was the only one fitted to
judge the situation on moral grounds. He steadfastly respected
the principle of judicial procedure and made no attempt to influence the course of justice in a case with which he had nothing to do. He could not have taken part in the proceedings
without having a profound feeling of personal wrath against
the accused. The enemies who had destroyed his lifework stood
there in the dock. Were he a philosopher, and not a political
leader who had been buffeted in one struggle after another for
several decades past, he might have saved them by making a
human appeal to the judge.

Our natural feelings revolt against the assassination of men
who did not look for any personal gain, but who were merely
wrong in their judgments or deluded by false hopes when they
set on foot or counselled or failed to prevent a military undertaking which had been disastrously planned. But to one who had
seen private soldiers shot on the battlefield because of cowardice

in the face of death, while incapable ministers and wooden-
headed generals were allowed to go scot-free after their tragic
blunders, this decision at Athens to execute the responsible generals and political leaders did not seem so terribly inhuman. At
a later date Venizelos gave his judgment of the situation thus:
"At that time the whole nation was suffering a terrible tragedy.
Remnants of the defeated army were arriving daily. There were
countless deserters. Whole sections of the population had been
uprooted from their homes. The leaders of the revolution believed that it would be impossible to reorganize the army and
defend the northern provinces unless that drastic sentence were
carried out, which would not have been passed by any régime
under normal conditions."

He explained to me his own part in the affair: "From abroad
I advised that a civil court be appointed to try the case. They
replied that they intended to judge the accused as soldiers. In
case they were not sentenced to death they would be massacred
by the populace. I was of the opinion that the danger of murder
at the hands of the people could be avoided if one general and
one minister only were sentenced to death. They were all guilty,
of course; but that was because they were ardent Grecian patriots. The King, however, did not have a drop of Greek blood
in his veins."

Some time later Venizelos read the news of Constantine's
death. My own impression, from the talks I had with both these
men, was that Venizelos hated the King less than the King
feared Venizelos. If we suppose that the King could have ruled
without the co-operation of the Cretan, he certainly would not
have embarked on the Balkan wars, his country would not have
secured an extension of her territory, it would not have been
overrun by foreign troops during the World War and the
King would have ruled without climax or catastrophe to the end
of his natural days. Suppose, on the other hand, that Venizelos

governed without Constantine but under King George I, and
suppose the latter had not been assassinated but that he lived to
be eighty years old, then Venizelos could probably have brought
his lifework to perfect completion.

He now had to undertake a series of negotiations at the Peace
Conference, with conditions very unfavourable to him, and
against him the magnificent brain of the Turkish delegate, Is-
met. Yet the circumstances brought about a surprising settlement of the old question. "Even before the World War," he said
to me, "the Turks had exiled half a million Grecian citizens.
I had the idea of having them exchanged for the Turks in
Grecian Macedonia. For this purpose I arranged a meeting with
the Grand Vizier. On my way to Brussels, in July nineteen-
fourteen, I got news of the ultimatum to Serbia and the conse-
quent outbreak of the war. And now, eight years later, I suggested again this exchange, but this time in the grand style.
More than a million Greeks, mostly from Asia Minor, and
four hundred thousand Turks in Macedonia were to leave their
homes in order to return to their own people after an absence of
centuries. Instead of new wars arising from the problem of foreign minorities, instead of centuries of hatred, I wanted understanding and exchange."

This magnificent conception met with all kinds of obstacles.
These arose naturally from the disappointments of thousands of
uprooted families who tried to settle again; and arose partly, too,
from quarrels about the valuation of property. In an earlier case,
where the same thing was attempted, it took ten years to exchange 130,000 Greeks and Bulgarians. If a proportionate time
were taken now, people estimated that a hundred years would be
needed for the Greco-Turkish exchange. As a matter of fact,
it took only seven years. Magnificent new towns and urban districts were built and organized outside of Athens and in the
northern districts, with the help of the League of Nations act-

ing through settlement committees. This undertaking may be the sign of a new epoch which points to a better medium than war for the settlement of racial difficulties.

When Venizelos signed the Greco-Turkish convention at Lausanne he had to surrender all that he had acquired for his country as a result of the World War. All the critical experiences which he went through in his struggle with his royal opponent, the catastrophe that had befallen the dynasty, the dismemberment of the nation, the gigantic sacrifices of human life, all his hopes and yearnings and plottings and exiles—all had been in vain. The frontiers were now reduced to those of 1913, thus allowing the acquisitions of the Balkan Wars to remain.

But one paragraph of the treaty announced that the last of the Turks would have to leave Crete. The cause that inspired Venizelos to take up arms when he was thirty, the battles that he fought in the mountains and on the coast, the debates and the polemics and the speeches and the pamphlets—all these now bore their fruit, when he was sixty. At the moment when he suffered his greatest defeat he also put his signature to the document that attested his greatest victory.

10

It was during those years of voluntary exile that he carried out the wisest coup d'état of his life. When he was sixty years old he married a highly educated and good-hearted woman whose care and courage enabled him to go through the struggle which fell to his lot in that seventh decade of his life. She once came within a hair's breadth of being shot when she attempted to save him while driving in their car. Out of all the gifts life had bestowed upon him, for a long time he used only power and for decades he never tested the peace of home life. That came to him now.

In January 1924, two years after the Lausanne Conference, he returned to Athens. The King was gone and the country was about to establish a republic by a vote of the electorate. During his fourth premiership he was ill or at least believed to be ill. He could not brook opposition and he could not take part in the debates. And when he left, a few weeks afterwards, it may only have been due to his political tact, which induced him to be absent on a day when, if he had taken part in the proceedings, he would seem to have overthrown the King and the monarchical principle. Two weeks after his departure the Greek nation constitutionally set up their republic. Only four years later, when he was in the middle sixties, he returned once more to his country and took over the reins of power. The tragic experiences of the past had not broken, but rather strengthened him. He had now achieved such a balance and inner harmony of mind and soul that he was able to spend several months in Crete without taking part in any political activity whatsoever. He occupied his time in translating Thucydides into modern Greek. At almost the same time Clemenceau wrote his book on Demosthenes. The Hellenist and the Helene were reflected, somewhat ironically, in their Hellenic idols.

Then Venizelos came back to Athens and formed his fifth Cabinet. What plan had he now before his mind as he returned to the capital? He felt that no Greek except himself could make a real and abiding peace with the Turks. So he now elaborated a friendly pact with Kemal Pasha under the influence of the same enthusiasm which for so many years had urged him against the Turks. In 1930 he went to Angora to sign the pact. The festivities that greeted his arrival and sojourn there proved to the world that centuries of hatred and bad feeling had come to an

end at last. In carrying through this plan of his Venizelos showed
that he had understood the epoch-making change in public
thought that has taken place in our day.

Do the Greeks believe in the monarchical or in the republican
principle? For the past hundred years—that is to say, from the
establishment of their political independence exactly a hundred
years ago—their premiers have always been dictators, even when
they did not wish to be that. Of course, they did not proclaim
themselves dictators. Capodistria, the first Premier, was murdered. And Otto, the first King, was dethroned. This century
of Greek history is packed with the founding of new statal institutions or the reforming of old ones. There has been an un-
ending series of conflicts between lawyers and military officers.
There have been conspiracies and banishments and triumphant
returns. Everything has been just as it was in ancient Athens.
The continuance of this state of affairs for over two thousand
years proves the direct succession of the modern from the ancient
Greeks much better than any racial theory could prove it.

In this long chain of vicissitudes Venizelos is a grand and entirely typical instance. He once told me that he had organized
seven revolutions. I believe there was one other that he forgot
to count. This protagonist has always been a revolutionary when
he didn't have power in his hands. Once he held the reins of
power he became a dictator. He does not like this to be said.
And the principles which he explicitly holds are against it.

"I am in favour of the English form of democracy," he said to
me. "In France and Belgium it has worked well too, and now
also in Czechoslovakia. Despite all its drawbacks, it still remains the least objectionable form of government. In the long
run autocracy can never turn out as satisfactory as the democratic
system. I believe in the freedom of the press, as you yourself
can see from the mad attacks against myself which I have allowed to be published in the Athenian papers. Aristotle distin-

guishes between two forces of government: the one plain and clear, the other opaque. When the monarch has the common interests at heart, then the monarchy is a clear and simple form of constitution. But if the monarch thinks only of his family interests, then the monarchical principle is opaque and confused. The same is true of the oligarchical form of government."

When I referred to his own autocratic methods, he said:

"I am a man of fixed purpose. Again and again I appealed to the country in general elections, even when there was no need of doing so. But when I have been chosen by the nation I must govern. Therefore, I am against the French practice, where the ministers are turned out of office by the Chamber. And I am in favour of the American practice. A good dictator is a man who rules dictatorially when he has the country behind him. I must have the feeling that my people are behind me. Then I can draw inspiration from them for my ideas. But I cannot ignore public feeling in the hope that later on the people will come to understand me. When I know that the country is behind me I am strong. When I lose this conviction I am weak and I resign."

As he spoke the above words he was not feeling very well and was stretched on a sofa, wearing a peaked black cap. A six-year-old grandson of his stood at the foot of the sofa. Though the boy did not understand our conversation in French he realized that the old gentleman was talking on serious matters. To indicate his grasp of the situation, he gave an audible manly sigh.

This remarkable democratic dictator, who was nine times head of his country, does not look as if he had been born for tragedy. That is why he laid himself open to it in the midst of the terrible events through which he had to pass. In his older years his kindly nature led him to seek reconciliation with his enemies. For by nature Venizelos is of a kindly and bright and optimistic disposition. The open look, the shining forehead and even the transparent skin seem to indicate that, in spite of all his subtlety and cleverness, he has nothing to hide. His silver-grey head, which reminds one of Bernard Shaw's, the blue eyes and the beautifully arched nose give the impression of a character who can be clever and revengeful but never tricky.

His career has been that of a brave man. He is big-minded and warm-hearted. He has always faced life courageously and even now he is still young, still active, never tired and seldom depressed. At the beginning of the World War he was urged to take advantage of Serbia's difficulties and, under cover of friendship for Germany, to attack the Serbs. He answered in Parliament: "Greece is too small a country to perpetrate such an infamy." That expression showed that through all his party struggles he had kept his moral principles intact. Perhaps it was indicative of that inner nobility of mind and spirit which is so often a characteristic of islanders in their conflicts and party affiliations.

Yes. This seafarer and warrior from the Cretan mountains, who has always been genuinely and ingenuously revolutionary, has preserved from his own labyrinthine island the native character of a straightforward and single-minded man.

MUSSOLINI

THE ITALIAN AUTOCRAT

Dictators, friend, it must be confessed,
You'll never banish them, never,
And I like to talk to tyrants best,
They are so uncommonly clever.

GOETHE

MUSSOLINI

THE ITALIAN AUTOCRAT

A STATESMAN can be the subject of criticism more easily than an artist or a scientific inventor. These latter offer us their finished products, which we can take or leave according to our tastes and knowledge. But the statesman has assumed the right to direct our lives. He has placed himself above us. Even his personal opinions and prejudices may affect our daily existence. It is for this reason that criticism of a statesman, no matter how frivolous or foolish it may be, has a profound justification in the very nature of the relations between him and those over whom he rules. For every individual will defend his personal liberty so far as possible, and when he finds himself subjected to the will of another he will naturally turn the sting of his criticism on that other, just as the bee stings its captor.

In a democracy the statesman can to some extent defend himself against popular criticism. He can point to the fact that he has been chosen by the popular will and that he holds office subject to its sanction. He is only a sort of managing director whom the shareholders of the state can dismiss if they think he has muddled their public affairs. At one time the hereditary monarch could defend himself against the popular clamour by fostering a belief among his people that he held his position by divine right and choice. But those were days when the public was not quite so enlightened as it is now. Today the hereditary monarch is treated as a sort of decorative chairman, whose duty it is to receive distinguished visitors and, during the intervals of their business with ministers of state, to entertain them at luncheon or accompany them in his royal equipage to see a waterfall or a museum or witness a theatrical performance. The most difficult part is that which the dictator has to play. He can never dispense with Fear as his ally.

In the great circus which we call human society the elected president takes the part of the juggler who twirls six plates on the ends of two poles. In case the plates fall people merely laugh at the juggler. The king is like the fat old circus master who whips ten very tame horses round the ring, just as his father and his forefathers did before him with the same whip, making the whip crack, but never touching a hair of the animals, and applauded by the public merely because he is the chief representative of the whole menagerie. The dictator is like the lion tamer who stands in front of eight or ten growling beasts, constantly holding them in awe with scourge and revolver. They both hate him and obey him. At the tent door of the circus men stand ready with hydrants and rifles. Nevertheless, he forces the animals turn after turn to take their respective places on the wooden platform while at any moment one of them may make a single stroke with paw or tooth and stamp out the life of the tamer. It is not at all strange then that the lion tamer is rarely a favourite with the rest of the circus company. His chief admirers are the outside visitors who come to look on.

The history of the great dictators shows that when their rule had come to an end there was a general slacking off and even a relapse into a sort of coma after the extraordinary tension that had to be endured. And yet in spite of this it would be wrong to conclude that the dictatorships have done no creative work merely because a reaction follows. The case of Napoleon is in point here. After his banishment to St. Helena it was widely proclaimed in France, especially in democratic circles, that he left the country smaller in territorial extent than he had found it, that hundreds of thousands of his subjects had fallen in the wars, that the exchequer was empty and that huge numbers of Frenchmen had been banished from the country or otherwise persecuted. These are true statements so far as the facts are concerned. But in drawing conclusions from them two points must be taken into account: first, that on the soil of France itself he did constructive work of enduring value; second, that the example of personal achievement which he left to future generations of Frenchmen has been an invaluable asset to the French nation, especially as a source of inspiration for the youth. Napoleon himself would probably never have made his mark in life had it not been for the fact that as a boy his imagination was set on fire by reading Plutarch's *Lives*. Just in the same way today every ambitious young Frenchman has the great example of Napoleon to inspire him. It is too often forgotten nowadays that this ambition is a creative urge or instinct and there is no reason whatsoever why the vision of domination over one's fellow men should necessarily be its goal.

Napoleon's contemporaries could not easily recognize his greatness. They were too near him. The revolutions of a planet can be observed only from another planet, except where the observers are expert astronomers and are in a position scientifically to calculate the revolutions of the planet on which they live. In a similar manner, the task of delineating the qualities of the outstanding men of our time must fall to those who can look upon them in a detached way and judge them in their proper historical perspective according to permanent standards of value.

2

When Mussolini assumed political power in Italy every act of him was looked upon with misgiving. He was a turncoat from socialism and had repudiated all international ideals. And we all feel today that only by the spirit of internationalism can that light be enkindled which will lead us out of the present wilderness. Mussolini's parentage and the conditions under which he lived as a youth made him antagonistic to the established social order and even a professed anarchist. "My real biography is to be found in the first fifteen years of my life," he once declared. He was the son of a revolutionary blacksmith in a tiny village. He used to sit in the evenings with his father on the hob of the smithy drinking hot spiced wine in the glow of the embers and reading publications that recorded the heroic deeds and sayings of the great socialists who were then in the van of the movement. He saw his father dragged off to prison because of the wild speeches he had made in their native Romagna, a province notorious at that time as a stronghold of the anarchists. The father died comparatively young. This was probably attributable to overwork and the nervous strain which his constant political activities entailed. Five thousand fellow workmen followed his remains to the grave. People were then wondering whether the son would take after him. Would he one day hurl a bomb at King Victor Emmanuel, as another anarchist had annihilated his predecessor and father, King Humbert? Or perhaps the young

Benito would become a Member of Parliament and head a constitutional movement for the abolition of the monarchy.

But there was another side to Benito Mussolini's character.
This was the side that he inherited from his mother. She was a
school-teacher by profession. In her nature she was reserved,
thoughtful and gentle. If one makes a close study of Mussolini
today at the age of fifty it is easy to detect that side of his nature
which he inherited from his mother now coming into the foreground. He is becoming gradually less violent, less volcanic and
less extreme. And he is correspondingly more pensive, slower to
come to conclusions and far more careful about taking drastic
decisions.

Yet while we watch this side of his temperament now becoming
almost dominant we must not forget that up to his thirty-
second year he was an out-and-out revolutionary. At the age of
nineteen he threw up his job as a teacher, though it brought him
in a livelihood, and went to Switzerland. Here he worked as
bricklayer's assistant and is still proud of the fact that he knows
how to build a round-arched window. He carried his hod of
bricks up the scaffold to the second storey a hundred twenty
times a day. And he often slept under the arches of the bridges
beside the lake in Geneva. One summer evening he was suddenly
dismissed from his job and found himself without anything to
eat. He saw a rich bourgeois family sitting around a well-laden
table in their garden. The thought struck him to ask them for
food. But as he approached the table a sense of self-loathing came
over him, he told me. He ran away in terror of himself.

"I have turned my back on all my old memories and even my
ideals," he wrote in a letter to a friend about that time. He did
not have a cent in his pocket, only a metal medallion of Karl
Marx. He was arrested and thrown into prison because he had
been observed so often in the company of anarchists. During his
sojourn in Switzerland he became acquainted with the insides of

eleven different prisons. This experience made such a deep psychic impression on him that long afterwards in Milan when he used to wander alone in the evening through the public park he often shuddered when it came to closing time and he heard the gatekeeper's key turn the bolt.

"Hunger is a good trainer," he said to me once; "almost as good as the prison or a man's enemies. My mother was a schoolmistress and earned fifty lire [about $10] per month at her job. My father was a blacksmith with an uncertain earning capacity. We lived in two rooms. We scarcely ever had any meat on the table. We used to have heated discussions and quarrels and then we would indulge together in the illusions of hope. Because he was a socialist agitator my father was imprisoned. When he died thousands of his comrades in the Socialist Party followed his remains to the grave. All this had the effect of creating a strong socialist bias in me. Had my father been different I might have turned out a different sort of person. But my character was definitely moulded by these early experiences at home. Anyone who knew me intimately at that time when I was only sixteen years old would recognize that I am the same today as I then was, with all the light and shade. All the trump cards for life's game were put into my hands by the fact of my proletarian origin."

He spoke in a dark muffled tone that sounded like the ringing of a distant bell. I have heard that voice of his in two very different tone qualities. Sometimes when speaking in the open it has a military hardness that reminds me of Trotsky speaking to the crowd. On other occasions the tone is soft and gives one the impression that the speaker is definitely and consciously reserving his nervous resources. And he speaks in this quiet reserved way not merely indoors; for I have heard him speak thus also when addressing a group of twenty workmen who stood around him in a circle. This restraint is indicative of Mussolini's character.

He nurses his energy generally so that he may be able to display it all the more forcefully in public when the occasion arises.

Two events in his life are responsible for detaching Mussolini from the dour nihilism of his early days. He became a soldier and he became a journalist. When he returned from Switzerland at the age of twenty he had to do his military service. This he accepted after the manner of a born fighter and utilized the course of military training as a school wherein to learn the technique of attack and defence.

"As a soldier I was really a model. And I never felt any conflict between military service and my socialist convictions. Why cannot a good soldier be also a protagonist in class warfare? Even today Italians are very critical in their attitude towards those who order them about. That is an excellent control signal. It is a constant warning that a man must learn to obey before he can command."

I suggested that it was difficult to discover any stage of his life at which he had learned to obey.

"As a soldier at any rate," he replied. But he could not discover any other occasion.

"And today, after the passing of fifteen years, do you still look upon war as a means of personal training, as if it were a duel?"

I noticed him scrutinizing me because I had put the question somewhat sharply. He turned a little on his chair and put his fingers together—a favourite gesture of his. Mussolini has well-shaped hands and I have noticed this same characteristic in other dictators.

"The school of war," he replied, "is undoubtedly a great experience. It brings a man up against naked realities. Each day and each hour of the day it is a question of whether he is to live or die."

He also became a journalist at an early age; but he used journalism only as a weapon of battle. He has sketched out some dramas on social questions but never finished them. He wrote a novel for a small paper and had to continue it in instalments from day to day because the readers liked it. He also wrote a history of the Hussite revolt in Bohemia and some essays on French and German literature. But his real passion was for the daily editorial article in which he dealt with the growth of socialism, criticized and attacked it for its failings, as he criticized and attacked conditions in Italy and throughout the whole of Europe. In this way he gradually and steadily secured a numerous following among the reading public.

"For me," he said, "my newspaper was my weapon and my standard. It was my very soul. I have even called it the child of my heart."

"And today," I replied, "if you think journalism so important a school, why do you shackle the press?"

"Today things are no longer as they were before the war," he said decisively. "Most of the newspapers nowadays serve interests rather than ideas. How then can they be a means of moral training for those who read them? Today I read more newspapers than I ever did before and I sometimes think that the average ass's bray is better done. I have that feeling especially when I read newspaper attacks against somebody or other."

"And when you write an article today are you somewhat more moderate than in the old days?"

He looked at me mischievously and said:

"I can only write fiercely and without qualification."

3

Why do people sneer when they see a man who was a revolutionary in his early days turn out in later years to be a champion

of the established order? Isn't the life of each individual an example of the same thing and isn't it quite natural? With a big
NO the strong man starts on his road of life. He kicks traditional
customs aside and in the strength of his youth he is always
over-destructive. But when he reaches the middle thirties and
brings up children and builds himself a home and changes his
lawless and formless visions for a fixed plan of life, he then
finds that the services he receives from the established order of
society are for his benefit and he realizes that many of the things
he wished to accomplish as a radical might easily turn out perni-
cious even to his own life. If he reaches forty years of age and
then finds some share of public power placed in his hands, he
suddenly feels that the assumption of power means the assumption of obligations and he knows that he must carefully consider
the consequences of every step before he can take a decision.
The rebel who began by being a party leader and later on
becomes a statesman is like a river that takes its rise from a
mountain spring and flows in an impetuous torrent downwards
over rocks and cliffs, forming a hundred whirlpools and cas-
cades, until it tires itself out and gradually settles down between
fixed banks, flowing onwards quietly and majestically into a
broad waterway which bears on its bosom big ships laden with
men and merchandise, a servant and at the same time a master.

   In Mussolini's character as a young man it is possible to detect
those traits that eventually made him a champion of the established social order, just as you will find revolutionary features
in the Mussolini of today. In 1911 he was brought before a law
court on the charge of inciting the populace to revolt. In his
defence he said to the jury: "There is such a thing as lawful and
such a thing as unlawful sabotage. The destruction of telegraph
wires may have a moral and political purpose. To derail a neutral
train is inhuman." This rather original classification of mis-
demeanours against the state shows that at the age of twenty-

eight this man felt his responsibility to society. He was by no means out for wholesale destruction. His concept of socialism was inspired by the same principle. He called it "the greatest drama which mankind is enacting for the purpose of rising above its animal nature and reaching a humanitarian level." He did not judge socialist principles by ethical standards; for Mussolini is essentially a constructive realist. In spite of all the opposition I feel towards his system of government I believe that in his youth Mussolini was not a mere revolutionary. He yearned, I think, for the establishment of a definitely new order of things. And if he sought power it was not for its own sake but rather that he might help in building up this new order after which he yearned.

Even while he was a socialist he had distinct nationalist leanings which marked him off from the rest of his party. In him, as in so many other socialists, there was a certain line along which international principles were not pushed to their logical conclusions. In 1911 Mussolini was passionately anti-Austrian. He threatened war to "redeem" the Italian Trentino and demanded of the Austrian Government to allow the Italian language to be spoken officially there. Yet in 1919 his concept of Parliament was that it should be "an Italian department of the League of Nations." "Every nation," he said to me, "has a certain X which characterizes its personality and distinguishes it from the great Y of all that it has in common with other nations. At the present time the emphasis of public feeling is on the X rather than on the Y."

These contradictions were quite natural in a young man whose sympathies were being tugged by two opposing forces, the sense of class solidarity in the one direction and the national feeling in the other. When the war broke out this confusion and contradiction expressed itself in Mussolini's declarations just as in those of other socialist leaders. As a socialist he was against the war and in August 1914 he wrote in his own paper: "Down with the War. We remain neutral." But the idea that the Hapsburg Empire must be annihilated soon took hold of his mind, and therewith the inherited antipathy of generations of Italians towards Austria and also the desire to liberate from the Hapsburg yoke those lands beyond the political borders of Italy which were populated by Italians but had for centuries been occupied by the Austrians. In the incalculable consequences that would result from the war he must have foreseen the possibility of a favourable opportunity for his own ambition. War has often been the prelude to revolution. We must remember also that Mussolini is a Latin through and through. At this historical crisis, therefore, when the neighbouring Latin land of France was in danger, Mussolini's Latin nature asserted itself and in the late autumn of 1914 he cried out: "France, we have forgotten everything you contrived against our fleet two years ago. France, we love you." Mussolini's present misgiving about France is not inconsistent with the spirit in which that cry was uttered. We usually quarrel most with our brothers, but we will jump to their rescue at once if misfortune should befall them. If another war comes it will not find Italians and Frenchmen taking the field against each other.

And even his socialist sympathies must have urged him finally to take up arms against the Central Powers. The Hohenzollern régime in Germany and the Hapsburg régime in Austria had been consistently maltreating his socialist comrades for over forty years. Was it not natural then for him to believe, as so many other socialists in the Entente countries believed, that by making war on Hohenzollern Germany he was saving Germany from itself? Mussolini still upholds the Italian monarchy and quite recently he said to me, apropos of my book on Wilhelm II,

"That kind of imperial rule is over for good. It must be relegated to the past."

When I questioned him about his change from the neutral attitude which he took up at the beginning of the war and asked why he did not remain so, he answered:

"Nobody likes a neutral. He is like a person who has to be forced to defend himself.

"But that dislike for the neutral attitude was only the first sentimental urge. More important was the consideration that no matter which side turned out victorious, we, as neutrals, should find ourselves faced by some coalition or other once the war was over. If Germany were victorious, we should never have been forgiven for having stood aside during the struggle. And if we had stood aside, then when the Entente met in Paris at the close of the war they would have treated us more contemptuously than they treated the other members of the old Triple Alliance. We had to reckon with the possibility that we might eventually have to fight against a combination of states, even though these would have been somewhat tired of war. The third motive that urged me from my neutral attitude was personal. I had hoped to see a national resurgence in Italy and I have lived to see that hope fulfilled. Indeed, I have borne a part in the fulfilment of it myself. There were three of us who held out that hope and worked towards its fulfilment: d'Annunzio, Corridoni and myself. When d'Annunzio wrote Il Nave [The Ship] some years previously he aroused a widespread enthusiasm for the fleet. He now spread the fire of militant nationalism throughout the universities and the Italian youth in general. Corridoni, who fell in the war, had organized the working masses in his syndicalist movement. And I transformed the Socialist Party."

"What was the purpose you had before your mind at that time? Was it to transform Italy in the mould of your own ideas?"

"It was," he admitted frankly. "I have never sought an alibi."

And so he broke with the party whose chief press organ he had hitherto conducted. When he was expelled from the party at the meeting which they subsequently held, he shouted from the platform: "You hate me because you love me."

4

That sentence was the cue for his new rôle. It was the dictum of a personality born to command. It expressed pride and contempt at the same time, like the outcry of a defiant woman who is turned out and proudly accepts her expulsion at the hands of a man she has long and passionately loved. From the moment of that cry and from that day onwards this young man, who was only just turned thirty, cut himself away not merely from his former ideas and his former companions but he defiantly committed himself to a new line of conduct for which there was no precedent. Whither it would finally lead him he did not know. It was now that he began to stand alone.

The road before his feet which led the way to the goal he had in view was by no means a safe or an easy one. He began to walk that road when he first organized the venturous spirits of young Italy in the new Fascist Party. Thousands followed him and enrolled in his movement. They had signs and gestures, banners and flags, and black shirts and caps which visibly marked out this young body of men from the rest of the nation. But their leader remained alone. "Live dangerously" is a Nietzschean motto which Mussolini likes to quote. Though he now acquired many new friends and thousands flocked after him and believed in him, he had no longer any trust in his fellow men. That is the penalty such natures have to pay when they take up an outstanding position in the public eye. "I haven't a friend," he said to me. "And I cannot have one. First because of my temperament, and secondly because of the opinion I hold of my fellow men. That is why I dispense with intimacies and conversation."

This contempt of his for mankind in general is the source of that self-approbation which seized him as a mastering passion even before the fate of the struggle in which he was engaged had turned in his favour. This feeling of having a mission to fulfil dominates every man who undertakes a life of action in the grand style. And the feeling for a mission in life is dominant in such men even before they have accomplished any part of their chief design. In the spring of 1922 Mussolini was only the leader of a party which was then in the early stages of its political growth. He was not a cabinet minister, nor did he hold any official political position. Yet at that juncture he said to a friend of mine in Berlin: "At the present time there are only two powers in Italy—I and the King." During three years of faction fighting (1919-1922) between Fascists and Socialists the whole country had become disorganized. The King and his ministers held council in Rome. The Parliament held its usual sittings. The army also seemed to be under constitutional control. In the meantime Mussolini had organized another army from his own followers. It was impossible to hold these troops in leash any longer; for they were mostly made up of young bloods who had nothing to lose.

During that period Mussolini displayed quite a good deal of forbearance which proved him in the circumstances to have the qualities of a statesman. Contrary to the exhortations of his closest followers, he waited for a whole year. It was only when he felt his organization strong enough and had appointed three generals of the regular army at the head of his volunteers that he gave the sign for the march on Rome. During the closing days of October 1922 he sat in his editorial office in Milan, just as a Commander-in-Chief in modern warfare conducts a battle through the telephone at a distance of some hundreds of miles from the actual fighting. The King signed the decree of martial law and at first decided to fight the Fascists. But later on he had to bow to the *force majeure* of circumstances. He withdrew his orders to the army and had Mussolini summoned to Rome by telegram for the purpose of forming a Government.

At that moment Mussolini showed himself the born journalist. When he received the news from Rome he ran into the composing room and called his brother. Instead of announcing that he had won he said: "Get out an extra edition right away."

"What's that you have there?"

"My appointment."

That night Mussolini left Milan where he had been a newspaper editor for ten years. He came to Rome, where he has now been ten years at the head of the Government. Thousands of problems were running through his head and he had no time, he told me, to indulge in any sentimental thoughts.

"I had already prepared my general plan but not the details. I was overwhelmed with a confused mass of things that had to be done. Within forty-eight hours I had to clear fifty-two thousand revolutionary troops out of the capital and prevent these excited young fellows from making any trouble. Within the first few days I had to make all the decisions about how the machinery of government was to be set in working order again. And I had no experience or knowledge of the mechanism of public administration. Some of the high officials I dismissed immediately but I kept most of them on. Within the first few weeks of our régime the men whom you call *Geheimräte* [Right Honorable Privy Councillors] saw that we were not to be trifled with."

5

It was with mixed feelings that I paid my first visit to Mussolini, in the spring of 1929. He had already been in power for six years. He seemed definitely militarist. The murder of the Socialist leader, Matteotti, had seriously damaged Mussolini's prestige. Some of the outstanding leaders of European thought were strongly against him. Everybody knew that some of Mussolini's closest associates were mixed up in the Matteotti murder. Many of the ideals I had grown up with and had worked for since the close of the war were only half-heartedly subscribed to by him and many others were definitely banned from publication through the medium of the press censorship and the silencing of the Opposition. My friends and I thought at that time that if the ideas of this dictator were brought across the Alps into Germany they would there find a classic soil for their growth. For the Germans, and not the Italians, are the people who love Obedience. They are born with a bias towards it and they are educated to it. They are congenitally disposed to follow a leader in blind obedience rather than think out political problems for themselves. For a century of bourgeois rule in Germany, undisturbed by any revolutionary movements, Italy presents the spectacle of a chronically recurrent revolutionary challenge to the old feudal power of the bourgeoisie in the city-states and the principalities. And added to this there was the periodical upheaval of various contradictory elements in Italy against the temporal sway of the papacy. My friends and I were first attracted by the social features of Mussolini's revolution. I mean that part of his programme which established an organization for the protection of the working classes. But of course we were opposed to the policy of shackling the press and prohibiting the free expression of opinion. When I first came to visit him I certainly felt more against him than for him.

The mental picture of Mussolini which is generally formed by the outside public is by no means true to life. As one enters the marvellous hall on which the master craftsmen of four centuries have lavished their artistic genius it appears at first to be quite empty. Soon a man stands up at a desk at the far end about twenty yards distant and approaches the centre of the hall to greet his visitor. He is rather small and of stocky build. At first one is somewhat surprised to notice the delicate and almost feminine hands. But that feeling changes the moment he grasps the hand of the guest. It is a manly and firm shake. The deep black eyes and the large domed forehead are in striking contrast. And here you have an illustration of the basic contradiction that underlies Mussolini's whole nature. Like every man of creative genius, he is a combination of masculine and feminine qualities, the Act and the Dream.

I had long conversations with him, mostly on general problems. When we touched on questions of political science he was very keen and gave examples from his own career to illustrate theories which he sometimes sponsored and sometimes rejected. The first feature that struck me during these conversations was his perfect naturalness and absence of pose. But if one studies him while he is speaking to a crowd of twenty thousand from a balcony, then one realizes at once that he is consciously endeavouring to produce an effect. Great actors are generally simple and natural in private intercourse. But on the stage every great actor must calculate and adopt the means which will secure an effect with his audience. Otherwise he would not be an exponent of his art. The heroes in Homer had to play their rôle. And the kings of olden times had to parade as spectacular figures before the eyes of their people. But that was only one branch of their activities and by no means the most important one. The real work of the statesman is done in his office.

The gigantic size of the office in which Mussolini works is due to the Roman tradition and also to his liking for the antique. He has the Roman taste for massive external proportions and at the same time a gift for effective detail. He is like a painter who outlines an enormous fresco but paints in delicate arabesques with his own hand. "I don't like things to be *à peu près*", he told me. I heard the same from more than half a dozen political leaders and scientific inventors. The simplicity of the black suit, which he usually wears, suggests a striking contrast with the ribbons and medals that the public expects him to wear on special occasions. The public looks for signs and symbols but Mussolini has too much to do to be always acting.

His desk is almost clear of papers; for the complexity of the work he is engaged upon demands the exactness of the pedant. The greater the task a man has to fulfil the tidier his writing desk will be found. Only the bohemian who does not succeed in anything cultivates disorder among his papers and groans that he has no time to do this or that. The man who has much to do is the man who gets through his work effectively.

Because Mussolini has thought for a long time over the problems he discusses he is decisive in his answers. But if he has not an answer ready he looks silently into his interlocutor's face, a gesture which I prefer even to the best answer that could be hoped for. It gives the opportunity to make a sudden transition to another question along a different line. The look which he gives thus is not harsh when he has a stranger face to face. It might probably be otherwise if he were facing one of his forty million Italians. Meeting him alone it seems to be permissible only to strangers who want no favours of him to give expression to out-of-date ideas.

I once saw him decide an official question within a few minutes. I had brought him a request from an Italian peasant who had some complaints to make. His face changed when he took the letter in his hand. It became hard. He conned the lines studiously, stuck out his chin in the usual manner and put on the proud majestic look of a judge. I had brought the written request with me because I wished to study him for a few minutes when he would be engaged on something that had no relation to myself. My purpose was to get an idea of how he worked with his officials. He immediately addressed a letter to the prefect of the province wherein the peasant woman lived, so that an inquiry should be made. After a few weeks I heard the result of this investigation.

"Don't these things bring you pleasure"? I asked.

"Very much. I have dealt with more than a million of such individual cases within the past few years."

"And is not that a better claim to fame than whole colonies like Tripoli?"

There was a long interval of silence. He gave me the silent look and then he suddenly put me a question which led the conversation off in another direction.

Another time I asked him why he made such bellicose speeches in the spring of 1930.

"We had been irritated and I had to convince myself how far the nation would follow me in case of an emergency. When I had ascertained that it would follow me to a man in case of necessity I delivered a speech over the radio which gave assurances of peace in the opening of nineteen-thirty-one. And here again I was convinced that the feeling of the nation was with me. I have never urged people on to war. All constructive men need peace."

There are four reasons why I, as a convinced pacifist, consider Mussolini a guaranty of peace in Europe in spite of his bellicose utterances. The four reasons are as follows: First, he is a constructive statesman, desiring to lift his people to a higher standard of living and give them a more forward place among the nations. In doing this he has to take into account that, even in the event of a successful issue, any war in which the nation might engage would be bound to inflict injury from which it would take innumerable years to recover. In the second place, Mussolini is not a military man himself, and in case of war he would have to confide the destiny of the country to the hands of some general on whose capability he could not infallibly count. Here he is in quite a different position from that of Napoleon. During the last ten years he has taken all decisions on his own shoulders. In such circumstances, is it likely that he would knowingly walk into a situation wherein he would have to surrender his control? On this dilemma he once spoke very dramatically to me. Moreover, every dictator is conscious of the envy and ambition of his rivals and the big opportunities which a war might bring them. Finally, there is the character of the Italian people. Mussolini knows these people and he knows how difficult it is to shake them out of their traditional ways, especially in the South. The sting of his appeal arouses these gay people to work, whereas the same goad might suddenly drive the Germans to war.

"But what happens," I asked, "if the national enthusiasm which you enkindle in the people should urge them eventually into war?"

"Are you a motorist? Good. So long as you feel the brake under your foot you can drive at a speed of sixty miles an hour without any danger."

"I read that on your first official journey, I think it was through Sicily, you always drove your car yourself. If the kings had driven their own horses long ago instead of shutting themselves in closed carriages away from the eyes of the people, they might be sitting on their thrones today."

"Of course. It is well to let the peasant and the villages see that a responsible man can conduct the vehicle in which he travels. I thought of that myself as a boy when one of the big people from the outside world visited our village."

Thus he took his own experience as a guide in mending the mistakes made by former régimes and with that lead he strove to be a social force. Bernard Shaw, the ablest of all European Socialists, said to me once: "In spite of his dictatorship, Mussolini practises more positive socialism than many of his adversaries whose names are inscribed in the party roll. People will keep on wondering where he is driving to."

6

Twenty thousand men filled the Piazza Venezia. A dozen bands crashed in mutual rivalry. Songs and slogans and hurrahs reverberated from the big walls on every side. It was a Fascist festival and they wanted to see the *Duce*. The palace, usually a tranquil building sunk in the dreams of the past, was accessible to me today only with the help of an officer. The staircases and corridors were thronged with men in uniform. In his great hall the Duce was alone, but in uniform. The King of Egypt once told me that the thoughts which filled his mind when he was clad in his uniform were different from those he had when in civilian dress. He meant that they were weaker. I myself have noticed that an officer alone among civilians feels dressed up and therefore uncomfortable, just as a civilian isolated among a hundred uniformed people thinks his position anomalous. Nor have I ever heard two officers in uniform talking philosophy to each other, any more than I have ever seen two philosophers sparring with their fists like a pair of boxers. Each of these anomalies would be possible, however. Though Mussolini looked quite strange to me in uniform, he was in the same frame of mind as always. The noise in the square made the continuance of our more philosophical discussions impossible. So I began to talk to him about Abyssinia. He continued walking to and fro in the room until an officer came to inquire whether the balcony windows were to be thrown open. He called for his cap, told me to watch from the adjoining window and asked me to return to him as soon as the demonstration came to an end. He had not a minute left in which to think over the speech that he was about to make. When he stepped out on the veranda in response to the reiterated shouts of the crowd, I studied his profile and noticed the firmness which he exhibits when he is speaking of constructive work. As he surveyed the throng beneath the balcony and remained for a moment silent, he reminded me of a playwright who comes into the theatre and finds the actors impatiently waiting for him to superintend the rehearsal.

Suddenly he gave a sign and the noise in the piazza ceased. His features became tense. He barked his opening words at the audience in a vigorous staccato. He had uttered no more than thirty sentences when the shouting reverberated again. As the balcony windows closed, rhythmical calls of "Duce! Duce!" came through the doors of the hall. He ordered the doors to be opened and then about sixty Fascists rushed into the room and gathered around his writing table. They were the secretaries of the party from all quarters of Italy. No ceremony or formality intruded on the friendly reception. In a soft, low-pitched voice, Mussolini began to address each of them, not by name, but by the name of the town from which he had come, pointing to the person concerned. Occasionally he hesitated and had to ask which was which. But most of them he recognized without any difficulty. They all looked up to him as to a father although some of them must have been at least as old as himself. Finally they renewed their chanting and cheers and withdrew from the hall.

Mussolini went back towards the desk but stood for a few moments in front of the fireplace. Seeing on the floor an Order which one of the visitors had dropped, he picked it up and sat at his desk. He rang a bell and when the servant entered he called across the space of sixty feet to ask where I was. Whereupon I emerged from the deep window niche where I had been standing out of view. He smiled at me and the thought flashed across my mind that anybody hidden away as I had been might easily have assassinated him. It is not true to say that the Duce is watched like a Czar. Although his speech from the window and his reception of the secretaries had interrupted our talk, he resumed the conversation precisely where it had broken off half an hour earlier, as if nothing had happened.

Mussolini can be understood only if we realize that he is Latin. He is a pupil and admirer of Nietzsche, who always declared himself to be a man of the Mediterranean type. "I am an incorrigible Italian," he told me. "For me the noblest of all the arts is architecture, for it embraces all. Roman architecture, of course. To Greece I was attracted only by its philosophy."

"I will explain the development of my mind to you," he declared to me another time. "In my youth I believed in nothing. In vain I called on God that he might save my mother, but she died. Besides, anything mystic is foreign to my temperament, as were the colours and the sounds in the monastery in which I was educated. Just as Renan did, I admit that once in a million years perhaps a supernatural phenomenon may have taken place and that therefore Nature may be the work of God. But I have never witnessed a spiritual phenomenon. It may also happen that within another million years a similar supernatural phenomenon may happen. That might happen even within the ambit of the laws of nature, like gravity or death. As I grew older the belief became stronger that there might be a divine power ruling in the universe."

"A Christian power?"

"A divine power," he repeated with a gesture which did not answer my question. "Mankind can praise God in many ways. One must leave that to the individual."

"Granted," I said. "What way have you discovered out of the dilemma which the classic dramas dealt with? Why should man take any initiative at all if Fate leads him along a predestined way?"

Mussolini did not seem to see any problem here.

"Fatalism must be countered with the human will power. That is an interesting struggle. The will has to prepare the ground on which the laws of destiny will unfold themselves."

"And what place has the urge to glory or fame in this struggle?" I asked. "Is not fame the strongest motive force for any ruler, the only warrant against death? Has the vision of it not hovered before you since your boyhood days? And has it not inspired your whole work?"

Mussolini remained imperturbed. "Fame did not light my path in boyhood," he said, "and I do not hold with you that it is the strongest of motives. You are right in saying that it is a consolation to think that one will not wholly die. But my work has never been wholly inspired by the desire for fame. Immortality is the seal of fame. But that only comes afterwards." He made a sweeping gesture to indicate the impenetrable distance.

"Recently," I said, "I read in somebody's room here a proverb which made a strong impression on me. It ran *Oltre il Destino* (Beyond Destiny)."

"Was that a man who had already challenged Destiny?"

"Of course," I said, and mentioned the name of one of the great airmen.

"That is not my motto," said Mussolini. "Nobody may challenge Destiny more than once. Anyhow, everybody meets the death that is in harmony with his character."

Naturally a dictator who governs in Rome must try to win the Pope to his side, just as the German Emperors did throughout a long thousand years, unless he is ready to rule as a vassal. So long as the Pope was a prisoner in the Vatican he was powerful. Mussolini's policy was to persuade this prisoner to come out and be free. When he finally succeeded, against the opposition of leading cardinals, nobody knew exactly who was victorious in this trial of wits. Even today you will get contradictory answers from men of quite independent views who are the most competent to give an opinion on the question. The King of Italy, with whom I spoke soon after the healing of the old breach with the Vatican, said, "I think it was fair on both sides." Anyhow it is a unique instance in history that negotiations between two independent rulers in the same city could be carried on for three years without either seeing the other. When Mussolini finally visited the Vatican he did not recognize the Pope as a spiritual ruler in the ceremonial way. When I asked him about this, he said: "Generally I abide by the rules of the country in which I am a guest. But before I went to the Vatican I had arranged that I should be dispensed from the duty of kneeling and kissing the Pope's hand." This action on Mussolini's part can be explained only by the spirit of resentment against the insatiable power of the papacy which is looked upon with misgiving by every statesman. As an accessory factor of leading importance there was also Mussolini's pride, which prevented him from bending the knee to God himself and therefore to His representative on earth.

This pride is one of the strongest traits in his character. Once as a young man in Switzerland an Italian made him a present of five lire. He took an Arabian knife from his pocket and gave it in return to the donor. That little act struck me as more eloquent than any other of his that I had heard of. At the age of nineteen he was arrested by the police in Zürich and treated as a major criminal. While still in their hands, he shouted: "Wait. The day of vengeance will come." A little while afterwards he was arrested in Austria and deported. When he was conducted to the frontier an official allowed him to go free on his own word of honour. Once in Lausanne his employer threw him his week's wages with the taunt that his work had not been satisfactory and that the taking of wages for it amounted to stealing the money. Mussolini immediately sprang at the man's throat.

We see the same trait of character uppermost at a trial of socialists which took place in Milan some time afterwards. Mussolini admitted seven points of the charge against him and opposed only one. This was to the effect that by destroying some telegraph wires he had imperilled the safety of a railway train. It was the same sort of pride that made him look upon the Peace of Versailles as the humiliation of a people rather than a wrong. He gave an example of the same pride when he attended the Conference of Cannes as a journalist in 1922. At the frontier they gave him five hundred francs in exchange for a thousand Italian lire. His pride boiled up and he swore that he would change that. When he came to power and was able to stabilize the lira at a higher level than the French franc his personal pride had to endure a certain amount of humiliation, because the financial authorities held it to be a false step. But the rulers of this earth do not always act wisely. The best of them are led astray by their visions.

This pride had developed a feeling of self-esteem in him long before he achieved any outer success. It has made him feel like a plastic artist. On this point he said to me once: "If I feel the masses in my hands as they think or if I mingle with them and become mobbed by them, then I feel a part of this mass of people. And yet I have a certain aversion to them, as the artist has towards the material he works on. Sometimes the sculptor will smash the marble in rage because it does not lend itself with sufficient pliancy to the shape he wishes to evoke from it. Here the material rebels against the will of the artist. The important thing is to rule the masses as an artist dominates his material." In his first manifesto to the workers, he wrote: "I shall set the example." And he has been giving that example since the first day he took over power. He avoids the Roman society that throngs around him and he spends about sixteen hours a day at work, just as did the great Russian leader whom the Fascist leader resembles in essentials.

Such a life, directed only by energy and pride, can maintain itself free of all skepticism only by faith in its own mission. For this reason Mussolini speaks sometimes of Destiny and of the stars which protected him as a soldier during the war and saved him when he was seriously wounded. In 1920 his motor car came into collision with a train, through a mistake made by the chauffeur, and several persons were killed. Of this incident Mussolini said: "I felt that the hatred of my enemies protected me as a talisman." When he was learning to fly and once fell from a height of one hundred fifty feet, his escape did not make him wonder in the least. Next day he carried on with his lessons as usual.

In the late hours of that night on which he journeyed by train from Milan to Rome to take over power he called to heaven for its aid, in his own way, and spoke of the invisible help his dead mother was giving him. To that extent he is definitely superstitious, as every man is who entrusts his whole life to a certain work and thus seeks to stand in well with the invisible powers. He often spoke to me of mascots and when I asked him why he ran gratuitous risks such as flying, he said: "Life has a prize and it must always be risked. Today I challenged it again."

On another occasion I mentioned the fact that the people and their leaders often speak of war as the work of Fate. He laughed and looked at me mischievously, saying: "It is only their mistakes that they attribute to Fate."

7

A stranger like myself, who has no party affiliations whatsoever and whose point of view is purely historical, must judge contemporary events as if they were a part of history. He must try to estimate them in their general bearing and not be led astray by the complaints of individuals. He must place the positive benefits which accrue to the nation above the personal losses of individual citizens. If I had been born a Frenchman under the Napoleonic régime, I know that I should have hated the Emperor and would probably have fled the country. But a hundred years later I look upon him with admiration as a marvellous historical phenomenon. When Italian friends complain of the coercion that exists under the Fascist régime, I believe all they say and thank my stars that for my own part I am free to write as I wish.

When Napoleon was at St. Helena he read in a newspaper a story to the effect that he had buried invaluable treasures somewhere or other. "What!" he cried out. "Have I buried my treasures? They are open to every man to see them in the light of day. The harbours of Antwerp and Flushing, the hydraulic works at Dunkirk, Le Havre and Nice, the great dock at Cher-

bourg, the harbour at Venice, the highway from Antwerp to
Amsterdam, from Mainz to Metz, the passes over the Simplon
and Mont Cenis. Then there are the bridges in Paris, the Tours
and Lyons bridges. The establishment of new industries, the
new Louvre, the Napoleon Museum, the millions which were
spent on land reclamation and horse-breeding. These are the
treasures which Napoleon amassed. They are worth billions and
they will endure for centuries."

Mussolini might answer in much the same tone, except that
the list of his works would have to be confined to Italy. Within
the first eight years of his régime, that is to say, from 1922 to
the end of 1930, twenty-five milliards of lire (roughly speaking,
$1,300,000,000) were spent on public works. Of this sum 2.5
milliards were expended on the building of roads, 1.7 milliards
for waterworks and aqueducts, 1 milliard for harbours, 1 milliard
for reconstruction after earthquakes, 2 milliards for railways. I
have not been able to compare these with the figures for the
preceding eight years; but a glance at the annual budget is sufficient to show that the former expenditure cannot be compared
with that of the Fascist decade. Anyone who lived in Italy for
several years, as I did, and now goes through the country again,
cannot fail to be struck by the improvements which are everywhere visible and which sometimes bring a sigh into the soul
of those romantics who bewail the passing of the old easy-going
times. But the truth is that nothing has been lost. In the small
towns and villages the men of all ages still gather on the piazza
as they did before and at half past eleven wander around lei-
surely in the sun.

Naturally all these undertakings, the building of new roads
and railways and harbours everywhere, were initiated for an
internal political purpose and the widespread unemployment
made them more or less necessary. It is true, too, that Mussolini

did not think out the general plan of all this activity. He copied much from the Russians. But the actual putting of the work in hand was due to his ardent energy and his faculty for coming to quick decisions and getting things done. Therefore he is entitled to call these works his own.

From north to south many roads have been reconstructed and three new motor highways have been built. New canals have been constructed and others have been widened. In the province of Puglia a huge aqueduct has been erected across the Apennines and a system of waterworks has been established which will bring drinking water to every village in Italy. Seeing that Italy has no coal, a huge system has been implanted for the production of electricity by hydraulic power. New railways have penetrated unknown quarters of the country. The old railways have been improved and the trains speeded up. The harbours have been enlarged and deepened and a new commercial harbour has been built at Venice. In the Pontine marshes gigantic works have been completed which were dreamed of two thousand years ago by the Romans and vainly attempted by several papal governments. Thousands of square miles of territory in which it was impossible for human life to exist have now been reclaimed and made fit for human dwelling. Within the next decade hundreds of thousands will be able to build their homes in a region that has hitherto been a deadly prey to malaria. When I saw all this I quoted for Mussolini the concluding part of *Faust* which runs thus:

Ein Sumpf zieht am Gebirge hin,
Verpestet alles schon Errungene;
Den faulen Pfuhl auch abzuziehn,
Das Letzte wär das Höchsterrungene.
Eröffn' ich Räume vielen Millionen,
Nicht sicher zwar, doch tätig frei zu wohnen.

A swamp extends towards the mountains,
It poisons all that has been up to now reclaimed
To abolish this cesspool
Would be a supreme achievement.
I open a dwelling space for many millions,
Not indeed to live there without risk, but in free activity.

Giant ships of 50,000 tons are now sailing under the Italian flag, carrying men and merchandise across the seas. An entirely new air fleet has been constructed. Three new universities have been founded, the old modernized, and in Perugia a university for foreigners has been established. The standard of all elementary schools has been raised by the dictator, who was first a schoolmaster himself. Attendance fees have been reduced or entirely abolished, and in the South illiteracy has been almost wiped out. In Rome, Ostia and Pompeii excavations have been carried out on a large scale and new archæological treasures have been brought to light. With an energy that rivals the Russian example, the private interests of the worker, his wife and children, have been taken under the care of the state even to the extent of looking after their pleasures. At the same time the worker is insured against times of distress. "We take hold of the citizen when he is six years old and return him to his family when he is sixteen," Mussolini once told me. With this formula he copies the Russian practice, and admits it. We individualists turn with horror from the idea of nationalizing and standardizing human beings. And, while recognizing the dangers of both systems, we are and will remain individualists.

All that I have described could have come only from a man who is dominated by his imagination, but who at the same time directs the activity of that imagination. Mussolini told me that when he took over power he had no prepared plan, but that all these undertakings slowly developed from a resolute

drive towards constructive action. The work a modern statesman has to perform is much more complex than it was in the
days of Julius Cæsar or even of Napoleon. I once said to Mussolini that many people think a leading man is at the peak of
his genius from morning until night. He answered: "Inspiration
comes to a man only twice a year at the most." All the rest is
routine and detailed work. I heard the same words from Edison,
but in a more ironical way: "Two per cent of inspiration," said
he, "and ninety-eight per cent of perspiration." Everybody whose
work is creative can verify this percentage by his own experience.

And yet Inspiration and Imagination are the wings on which
the superior man is lifted so that he can view the whole scope
of his activities from above. When he comes down to earth he
has to work with his hands. This inspired vision may be
discerned from studying a photograph of Mussolini when he
was only nineteen years old. It is the vision of a poet. And it can
be detected in the portraits taken of all great men when they
were young. In later life the head, and generally also the body,
grows larger, not merely through eating and enjoyment but
also through the expenditure of energy and hard work.

Mussolini's head has changed with the passing of time. One
man, however, who does not know whether he ought to call
Mussolini friend or enemy, declares that he has known him since
1915 and that he has not changed a whit since then. This observer, who is one of the outstanding figures in Italy, may have
anticipated in the Mussolini of 1915 the man who took over
supreme control of Italy in 1922. It was the unconscious forecast of his imagination. If I were a painter I should at the
present moment be able to draw a portrait of Mussolini at the
age of sixty.

But no man must forecast how the hand of Fate will work.
If he have his own presentiments, he ought to remain silent.

STALIN

THE RUSSIAN AUTOCRAT

People say that the world is ruled by numbers. This I know, that the numbers teach us whether it is well or badly ruled.

GOETHE

STALIN

THE RUSSIAN AUTOCRAT

LEGENDS have their place and use in the presentation of historical truth. Though they change with the changing generations of men, the variation is to the advantage of the investigator and the object of his research; for it generally affects only particular aspects. When these are altered or even falsified the process helps to distinguish between the inner truth and its external trappings. Legends are the natural growth of time and may do for historical truth much the same service as the passing of time does for certain forms of artistic beauty. We should probably be shocked if we were suddenly presented with a glimpse of the Athenian Acropolis in the dazzling perfection of all its details, as it was in the time of Pericles. And just as the mysterious influences of wind and weather affect only the patina of the bronze and not the main features of the portrait, so the altered perspective in which historical personalities are presented as the times change does not affect the personality itself. But no matter how objectively we may try to study and picture to ourselves men of another epoch, we shall always see them in the perspective of our own epoch and not as their contemporaries saw them.

When we come to deal with contemporary figures, however, the attempt to invent legends about them is a perversion of the natural historical process. And when the subject of the legend is himself an active party to its promulgation he can expect nothing except harm eventually to come of it. In contemporary life the independent observer is too close to the object of his investigation to permit the interference of fictitious data. We have a right to see our contemporaries face to face in the light of our own age. And where there is question of a contemporary public leader the world at large demands a portrait that corresponds to the reality.

I have made these remarks at the opening of the present chapter because when I was in Moscow one of the first things that struck me forcibly was the attempt made by writers and even photographers to give a false impression of the Russian dictator, Stalin. The picture which one sees of him at every turn of the street and those that are sent for publication abroad are as unreal and untrue as the numerous stories that are published about him in books and newspapers and periodicals. In the new Russia there seems to be an overpowering craze for public hero-worship. Under this influence writers and artists strive to transfigure outstanding individuals of the Soviet régime into idealized types or symbols of some subjective emotion of the crowd. Hence we have a wide-spread falsification that in the first instance is detrimental to the individual who is the subject of this legend-mongering. Stalin is a particular victim of this public craze. His own opinion of it will be given later on in this chapter.

From the portraits I had seen of him and from the stories I had heard and read and from the sound of his name, which does not suit him at all, I had expected to meet a Grand Duke of the old régime, stern and abrupt and unfriendly. But instead of this type of person I found myself for the first time face to

face with a dictator to whose care I would readily confide the
education of my children. I had read that he does not show
himself in public because his face has been much disfigured by
smallpox. But as a matter of fact scarcely any traces of the scars
are to be seen. I had also read that he always has an escort of
five motor cars when he makes his daily journey to and fro
between the city and his country home at Gorki, the palatial
residence where Lenin lived during his illness and where he died.
It is said to be guarded day and night by heavily armed Cos-
sacks. One is told everywhere in Moscow that Stalin enters the
Kremlin each day by a different gate and that when he takes
his meals the table is furnished with the gold plate that belonged to the Czar. Popular rumour even goes to the extent of
declaring that he kept his young wife locked up at home, as if
he were a Turkish Sultan.

The truth is otherwise. He has never entered the palace at
Gorki since Lenin died. Until the death of his wife in 1932 he lived
with her and his two children in a modest little house outside
the city. He goes to his office alone in his own car and enters
by the same gate every day, without receiving any special salute
from the sentry on guard. He lives and eats as the average small
tradesman does. He is very orderly and very particular about
the distribution of the working time at his disposal. His tastes
are quite simple and practically the only form of entertainment
he indulges in is that of the ordinary workman who sits down
once in a while to a glass of wine in the company of a few
friends.

He has often been pictured as an aristocratic freebooter from
the Caucasus. But I could see no traces of that character in him.
Nor could I imagine him as the Georgian adventurer who is
said to have taken Ivan the Terrible as his model. Even the
historical insinuation is incorrect here, seeing that Ivan the

Terrible devoted a large share of his time and energy and means to the care of the poor and the sick. When I visited Stalin I found just a lonely man who is not influenced by money or pleasure or even ambition. Though he holds enormous power he takes no pride in its possession, but it must give him a certain amount of satisfaction to feel that he has triumphed over his opponents. I should say that there are two traits which dominate Stalin's character. The first is the habit of patience, which he has cultivated to a supreme degree, and the second is his ability to depend entirely on himself and entrust nothing to his fellow men. These qualities are found generally in men who move slowly and carefully towards their ends. I need not mention here his extraordinary energy, because that is a quality in all constructive men.

Everything about this man is heavy—his gait, his look, even the movements of his will. He has a habit of laughing often as he talks. And when he does it is a slow and sluggish kind of laughter that seems to indicate the inherent mistrust that all dictators have towards the rest of mankind. Stalin is of a dour nature. He lacks that interior cheerfulness of soul which keeps patient people, like the average Russian peasant, human. In him the virtue of patience, the ability to wait, draws its sustenance from his innate mistrust. He can carry through a policy or plan with plodding perseverance to its completion without suffering the slightest discouragement at the hitches and set-backs that occur during the effort. Having no trust in his fellow beings, he has no disappointments. Hence his efficiency. Like all the Bolshevik leaders, he spent years in exile. Naturally he became a hunter of wild game and lived partly on the provisions which his shotgun brought him. On the lonely steppes he became friendly with nature, with the trees and the plants and the beasts. Evening after evening he read by the light of a primitive candle beside the fire, for which he had gathered the wood himself. He longed for his wife and child. He sang folk-songs and came to like that kind of music which appeals to the emotions. And he developed a fierce antipathy towards all kinds of emotional or intellectual dilettantism.

He is now in the mid fifties. He does not see more than three or four Europeans in the year. Therefore he is somewhat ill at ease when a Western visitor first arrives. This astonished me, for I was fully conscious of the fact that I was face to face with the actual ruler of one-sixth of the world. His embarrassment did not affect me very much, however, for I knew he would have his revenge by swearing at me when I had left because of the loss of time I had caused.

If my intuition be correct, Stalin is naturally good-hearted. But his position has made him hard and unyielding. He is not without imagination, but he denies himself the luxury of indulging in its flights. He is not ambitious, but he is ruthless towards his opponents. He is sensitive and melancholy by nature. And the mission to which he has devoted his life has made him cold and reserved. For the past thirty-five years there has been in his mind only a single thought; and to this he has sacrificed youth, security, health, and all the other blessings of life, not that he himself might govern but that there might be a government according to the principles to which he has sworn his fealty.

"My life's task," he said to me, "is to lift up the working classes to another level, not the consolidation of a national state but of a socialist one which will guard the interests of all the workers of the world. If each step in my career did not lead towards the consolidation of this state I should look upon my life as having been lived in vain."

He spoke softly and in his customary muffled tone, almost as if talking to himself. His friends assured me that that is the farthest he has ever gone in the expression of his feelings.

2

What sort of life has this man led? All these modern leaders have risen from the rank and file of the populace. Therefore we must not compare them with the residents of our democracies. We must rather compare them with the leaders of the French Revolution who, like Danton and Robespierre, were lawyers and free citizens in Paris until the Revolution brought them power and danger together.

In Russia, however, at the beginning of the present century, whoever was known to be a Socialist had to give up everything that freedom means. He had to exchange peace and security for a wandering and uncertain existence. He had to give up home and family and possessions precisely because he was engaged in undermining the foundations of the social order to which they belonged. Therefore he could not claim them for himself. In the adventurous spirit of youth a person may enter on such a course of life, but only staunch faith in his principles will enable him to hold out and endure.

Stalin did not become a Socialist because his parents were downtrodden. His father was a shoemaker and at the same time a farmer. Stalin has something of both these classes in his nature. He has no grudge against either class. On the contrary, he became revolutionary because of the experience he went through as a student in the clerical seminary to which his father sent him in the hope that he would be educated for the priesthood. Had this experience not occurred in his life he would probably have remained in much the same position as his parents were. Today he might be either a farmer or a tradesman in some town or other.

"My parents were uneducated people," he said to me in answer to a question I had put. "But they did a great deal for me. The same kind of urge which, you say, changed Masaryk did not make me a Socialist at the age of six or ten or even twelve years. Not until I was in the clerical seminary did I become a Socialist, and then out of opposition to the régime in vogue there. It was nothing but constant espionage and chicanery. At nine o'clock in the morning we were summoned to our tea and when we came back to our dormitories we found that all the drawers had been ransacked. And just as they ransacked our papers they ransacked every corner of our souls. It was unbearable. I would have gone to any length and championed any cause that it was possible to champion if only I could use it as a protest against that régime. Just at that time the first illegal group of Russian Socialists came to the Transcaucasian mountains. They made a great impression on me and I soon acquired a taste for their forbidden literature."

When this was discovered he was expelled from the seminary, to the horror of his parents. At the age of sixteen he inscribed himself as a member of the Socialist Party. Among his comrades he went by various names. He was sometimes known as Zozo, sometimes as David, and sometimes as Kolba. At that time Lenin was publishing Socialist newspapers abroad, sometimes printed with invisible ink, or in very minute letters, so that they could be read only with a magnifying glass. This clandestine literature was smuggled into Russia principally by sailors. Stalin procured it and read it, and thus thoroughly learned socialist doctrines. He carried on socialist propaganda unceasingly among the leather, tobacco, and mine workers. He worked as a bookbinder to earn his own living, while at the

same time he set up and printed his own newspaper in a cellar
or sometimes in a wooden hut. He took part in preparations for
organizing attacks against the Government and for that reason
was constantly watched by the Imperial Police. In spite of his
false beards and other disguises he was discovered again and
again and from his twenty-fourth to his thirty-fourth year he
was imprisoned six times, first in the Caucasus and then in
St. Petersburg. After each imprisonment he was outlawed and
deported to Siberia, but he invariably escaped after a few weeks
or months. During this eighteen years of his existence as law-
breaker and outlaw, constantly in danger, impoverished and
miserable, he left Russia only a few times and each time he
remained abroad for only a little while. He made one of these
excursions at the age of thirty with the aid of false passports.
On another occasion he smuggled himself across the frontier
into Finland in order to make the personal acquaintance of
Lenin. Later on he succeeded in coming to Germany in order
to meet Lenin and his comrades there. In Vienna he played
chess with Lenin. What a pity that nobody thought of taking
a snapshot of that scene.

And yet during all those years there seemed to be no hope
for the work which he and his friends were doing. He was
twenty-six at the time the Revolution of 1905 collapsed. It was
a severe blow to him. Though the crisis of the Russo-Japanese
war occurred at the same period, it brought little consolation to
the socialist revolutionaries. During this first decade as an active
Socialist, from the age of sixteen to that of twenty-six, neither
ambition nor the will to power, nor the desire for action on a
broad scale, nor recognition by his comrades, brought him any
satisfaction. For in all that he did he remained anonymous.
Nothing except the approbation of Lenin, who was generally
slow to praise the work of his lieutenants, brought him recompense. From beyond the frontiers, Lenin directed the socialist

movement in Russia. At the age of twenty-one Stalin became a follower of his, after a friend had given him a personal account of Lenin's ideas. At the London Congress Lenin threw overboard the tactical plan of fighting for better wages and founded the out-and-out revolutionary Bolshevik Party. Stalin was then in prison at Tiflis. He immediately took Lenin's side against the representatives of the more moderate plan, and ever since then he has remained staunchly loyal to Lenin's teaching. Why? At the head of every issue of Lenin's paper, *Iskra* (*The Spark*), was printed the motto: "Not until the lighting of the spark will the movement be afoot."

Such a hard schooling might make an excellent soldier out of any man who is endowed with character and has cultivated the spirit of self-denial. But it could not make a leader. It is merely the love of hero-worship that has led the Bolsheviks of today to invent legends for the Stalin of that time, claiming that he showed wonderful talent in building up secret organizations and that he owed much of his success to the fact that he could speak directly to the workers in their own language and did not have to acquire it as did Lenin and Trotsky, both of whom belonged to the educated classes.

In 1913 Stalin escaped from exile for the sixteenth time. Then the eyes of the police became sharper. He was discovered at a socialist meeting in St. Petersburg. Though his friends hastily dressed him in female clothes after being hurried into one of the rooms at the back of the hall, the police laid their hands on him. He was transported as far as the Arctic Circle and made to live in a hamlet in which only three peasants formed the whole of the population. A special guard was appointed to watch him. There he heard of the outbreak of the war but got little or no news of its progress, though he had looked forward to it for twenty years and had placed all his hopes in it. During this time Lenin was very active abroad. Once he gave orders that communication be opened with Stalin, who then went under the name of Kolba. "Where is our Kolba, the wonderful Georgian?" he said. "I had almost forgotten him. Write to him for me. It is very important." But Stalin received no communication from his chief. Though born in the South and accustomed to the southern sun, he had to pass the dreary years of the war in this arctic North, wavering between hope and doubt, rather weakened in health through long spells of imprisonment, entirely alone, living in a miserable wooden shack amid the snows, shooting wild geese and ducks for his food during winter and fishing for it in summer. He cooked for himself, made his own clothes and whatever implements he needed for digging and shovelling and building, while at the same time he read Marx and Darwin, for under the Czarist régime all political prisoners were allowed to take books with them into exile. For some time a friend lived there with him, until they were together so much so constantly that they began to hate each other. Then they lived alone and waited, always hoping for some tidings of the revolt.

When the Kerensky Revolution took place, in March 1917, Stalin was liberated. Though most of the other political prisoners were welcomed with public demonstrations on their return home, Stalin came back to Petrograd alone and practically unnoticed. He immediately became an editorial writer on the *Pravda*. The first articles which he published were moderate and conciliatory. But two months later, when Lenin came to Petrograd and immediately put an end to liberalist and moderate socialist tendencies in the ranks of the Bolshevik Party, Stalin took Lenin's side and remained a passionate follower of his to the end. I once asked him if he did not look upon himself as a sort of successor to Peter the Great. He brusquely poohpoohed the suggestion and answered: "I am a disciple of Lenin. And my only wish is to be a worthy follower of him. Historical parallels such as that you have mentioned are always some-

what risky, but if you insist upon suggesting this parallel with
Peter the Great, then I should say that Peter brought only a brick
to the building of the temple but Lenin constructed the edifice
himself. I am only his disciple."

3

One is often inclined to forget that the Russian Revolution and
the World War lasted for five years. It was a long period, rich
in crises, catastrophes and triumphs. That period offered a magnificent opportunity for talented and fiery leaders to assert themselves. Therefore we find them rising in increasing numbers.
About a dozen outstanding leaders appeared. So far as we can
judge today, Lenin, Trotsky and Stalin are the most significant.
One has only to look at a portrait of Lenin and to read his
books and speeches to know that he was superior to all his
comrades and rivals. He was the only one of them who was
able to bring order out of chaos during those early years of the
Revolution. He had a fiery temperament but it was always under
the control of his reason. He was a man of action and a man of
thought at the same time. He had a will of iron; and at the same
time, like all great revolutionary leaders in history, he knew how
to bow to circumstances. Some outsiders and some of his followers considered him too moderate; but that was probably because they measured his moderation and coldness by what the
same sort of moderation and coldness would have meant in
themselves. I never saw Lenin. But I met Trotsky a few years
ago on Princes Island, near Stamboul, and I can compare Stalin
with him, for it is only recently that I have been conversing
with Stalin in the Kremlin. They do not in the least suggest the

parallel of Tasso and Antonio, out of whom Nature formed one man. If all their talents were fused together, they could not have produced a Lenin. Except for their energy, they have not a single characteristic in common. Trotsky's head is remarkable for the brow and the eyes, whereas in the case of Stalin these two are insignificant. This does not mean, however, that Stalin is not a thinker and an observer. It means that his head gives a more general impression and seems as if fashioned by Nature, whereas those of Trotsky and Lenin seem to bear traces of the heroic efforts they made and the sufferings they endured. The only thing common to Trotsky and Stalin in their physical appearance is the delicate hands, which seem to be a general characteristic of dictators.

The peculiarities of character which one finds in each of these two are in keeping with the contrast in their physical appearance. As the leading disciples of Lenin, they showed the many-sidedness of their teacher. Trotsky has the same kind of élan as Lenin, Stalin the same kind of perseverance. Trotsky works from above through speeches and the arousing of mass emotion, whereas Stalin works from below by developing the individual. Trotsky is an enthusiast, Stalin a politician. Trotsky is the strategist, Stalin the tactician. Trotsky inspires the masses, Stalin organizes them. Trotsky is frank and expansive and talkative, Stalin reserved and silent. Trotsky is pleasantly witty, Stalin dangerously humorous. In Trotsky everything is quick and brilliant. The Word is his weapon. It is with that he destroys his opponent. He can speak it and write it in several languages. Over against this brilliant and alert and versatile Trotsky, everything in Stalin is slow and ponderous. He annihilates his opponent with the weight of his carefully gathered material. Trotsky is a prophet, Stalin a father. We might compare Trotsky to a high-powered motorcar that can take all gradients on first speed and will win in almost any speed test. And we may compare Stalin to those tractors that he has introduced into Russia and that turn up the earth in their slow plodding movement, preparing it for the seeds of the new state, silently and inexorably breaking through the hardest soil.

Lenin found it difficult to keep these two strong personalities reconciled with each other. Before the Revolution they scarcely were acquainted. Stalin was one of the original founders of the Bolshevik Party, whereas Trotsky joined it twelve or thirteen years later, and then only on the occasion of the war and the break-up of the old régime. Trotsky's generous and humane nature made Lenin rather slow to accept him as a partner and even then Lenin himself was never able entirely to overcome the mistrust which his comrades felt towards Trotsky. Though Trotsky was also a political exile under the old régime, during the six years which he spent in Siberia as a young man he did not experience any great hardships and was able to utilize his time in study. He then came home for six months to Russia, and as he was once again about to be exiled to Siberia he fled the country and spent the decade from 1907 to 1917 abroad. Therefore from his twentieth to his thirtieth year he lived outside of Russia.

It is inherent in the logic of history that Lenin and Trotsky, as typical intellectuals, and both educated in the West, should have come to power first. As in most other cases, this revolution of workers and peasants was led by intellectuals during its initial stages. But today the new state is established and is ruled by the born worker. In the history of revolutions, men of Stalin's type have always followed men of Trotsky's.

For several years there had been a steadily growing antipathy between those who suffered so much at home and those who worked for the Revolution from abroad. The former felt closer to the people and closer to the cause of the people, the devotion of the latter was given rather to the ideals and principles for which they worked. Those who carried on the revolutionary propaganda from the capitals of foreign nations and went about from city to city certainly developed among themselves an intimate comradeship and fellow-feeling because of the common work in which they were engaged and also because they all had given up home and were living in exile, although amid friendly surroundings. But those who remained in Russia gave up their freedom and homes and families again and again and for long periods at a time. They were lodged in the same prisons. The same lice tortured them. Together they lost the health and strength of their youth through long exile in damp and snow-covered wastes that are almost uninhabitable for human beings. Trotsky was typical of the former, Stalin of the latter. Stalin must have looked with disdain on the humanitarian with the twittering eyes, while Trotsky must have secretly despised the human mistrust and the dark, almost animal, glower in the eyes of the Georgian.

Even at the very beginning these two clashed. During 1918-1920, Trotsky was a sort of generalissimo and insisted on employing officers of the old régime because no others were at hand. Stalin was opposed to this and had grave doubts about such a policy. It is not possible to say how far Trotsky is to be credited with the building up of the Red Army, for it is widely said nowadays that this was the work of Stalin's young friend, Woroschilov, who afterwards became Minister for War. Certainly Trotsky's enthusiasm alone would not have been sufficient to ensure the success of the Red Army. Lenin appointed Stalin to take charge of it on the southern front against Denikin. His messages from there to Lenin sound like those of Napoleon's marshals. One of the messages ran: "It is of course understood that for all important movements I shall take the whole responsibility on my own shoulders." Trotsky at that time sent several written orders from Moscow. But when Stalin received them on the southern front he paid little attention to them. On the back of one of these orders he wrote, as he handed it to one of his officers: "Take no notice of this." Trotsky let the matter pass. He realized that Stalin systematically disobeyed his orders.

During the first stormy period of the Bolshevik Revolution the Red Army was still a chaotic force. Several years would be needed before it could become a regular organ of the new state. Therefore there was no organized military staff, as in the armies of the older states. As a result of this, one did not know exactly by whom such and such orders were issued and what authority they had. While the army was fighting against Denikin in the South, Lenin was only in distant and external contact with it from Moscow. He could not deal effectively with the personal rivalries and differences on practical problems which caused confusion in the actual command on the fighting front. Personal dislikes interfered with plans, while differences of opinion about practical plans reacted on personal dislikes and embittered them still more. Lenin sent the President of the Republic to the South to talk Stalin into a better sense of co-operation and obedience. Later he conferred the Order of the Red Flag on both Stalin and Trotsky at the same time. De facto Trotsky succeeded in having his decisive authority recognized on two of the principal problems that dominated the military controversy. Stalin had to give in. But he prepared for his hour of revenge in his plodding, inexorable way.

At that time Lenin was continually receiving official military reports from both Trotsky and Stalin at the same time. Trotsky's reports are known to us from his published memoirs; but up to the present only a few of Stalin's reports have been seen in print. One of these, which was sent in the autumn of 1919 and makes only seventy lines on the printed page, threw over the whole official strategic plan and introduced another. This was accepted by the Government in Moscow. The result of Stalin's seventy lines of print was to change the whole situation in Russia's favour. Denikin was driven into the Black Sea and the Ukraine was liberated. Here was another proof that successful strategy in war does not come from plans thought out by the professors in military academies but rather from the practical man-on-the-spot who understands all the immediate circumstances and has the character and insight to seize the decisive moment.

4

Lenin's death increased the animosity between these two leaders in a moment of crisis for the Bolshevik state. For six years under Lenin, from 1917 to 1923, Stalin had been Commissary for the People of All the Nationalities in the Soviet Union. During the same period he was for three years at the head of the Workers' and Peasants' Commission of Inspection and for three years a member of the Revolutionary War Council. So he often must have come up against Trotsky again and again; for during that period the latter was successively Chief of the War Department and at the head of the Foreign Concessions and Economic Council. Lenin lived for twenty months after his first paralytic stroke. During that time he saw his death steadily approaching and he must have thought about the problem of who would succeed him, just as Cæsar thought. For he knew that if his tremendous vision of the coming Bolshevik state were to be sustained and progressively carried out in practice this would have to be the work of individual power and genius, despite all materialistic theories of history. The fact that his plan had achieved success in Russia, where capitalism was only in a rudimentary stage of development, is somewhat against the Marxian law and was due to an extraordinary convergence of circumstances, the most important of which was that there had been a leader capable of understanding the situation and utilizing it. The well-organized Communist Party was of course a certain guaranty that the founder's plans would be carried out. But what if the best leaders of the party came into conflict with one another after Lenin's death?

The testament that Lenin wrote two years before his death, in the form of a letter to the Central Committee, has never been published in full. The parts which are known to outsiders seem to be apocryphal, but it is certain that though Zinoviev, Kamenev and others were much more famous than Stalin, only Stalin and Trotsky were thought of as possible successors. *The relationship between these two contains in my opinion more than a 50% probability of bringing about a split in the Party. This danger can be avoided by increasing the membership of the Central Committee. As General Secretary, Stalin has tremendous power in his hands and I am not sure that he will always use it with foresight. Trotsky does not merely possess unusual ability. Individually he is undoubtedly the most gifted man in the Central Committee. But he also possesses a far-reaching self-confidence and a tendency to over-estimate the purely bureaucratic side. The difference between these two most capable leaders might lead to a split, even though they themselves did not wish it.*

That paragraph is probably a genuine excerpt from Lenin's letter. But there is another sentence which is admittedly an authentic postscript and which Stalin himself has quoted. It runs thus: *Stalin is too rude and although this failing does not count for very much amongst us as Communists it will not be borne with in the business office of the General Secretary. Therefore I would suggest that we find a way to remove him from this position. These apparent trivialities can sometimes be of decisive significance.*

To this double-sided criticism I must add by way of comment a very important statement which I have on the authority of Radek. He said: "After Lenin's death we, nineteen men of the Executive Committee, sat together and anxiously awaited the advice which our leader would give us from the tomb. Lenin's widow had brought us the letter. Stalin read it aloud to us. As he did so, nobody made a sound. When he came to speak of Trotsky, the letter said: *His un-Bolshevik past is not an accident.* All at once Trotsky interrupted the reading and asked: *What was that?* The sentence was repeated. These were the only words that were spoken during that solemn hour."

It must have been a terrible moment for Trotsky. His heart must have stood still when he heard those six words, words which really decided his life. Lenin had not concealed his misgivings in regard to those two men whom he singled out as his most capable followers. He seems to have ordered in his letter that full power should be given to neither. Each had, in secret, reckoned on being the only successor. Trotsky, as head of the new state, wished to control the direction of its further development. Stalin, as General Secretary of the Bolshevik Party, wished to hold this instrument in his hands as a power above the state. On the basis of Lenin's testament he handed in his resignation but was again elected as head of the party. And now they both stood over against each other. Stalin and Trotsky were to rule together.

Lenin's error in thinking that two could be at the head of affairs at the same time was explained to me in the following way by one of the cleverest members of the party. "Lenin," he said, "did not in the least realize the fact that he was a dictator. He had merely become a dictator in virtue of the course of events. He did not understand that great decisions can be made only by one man, because he himself had always felt that he was acting in council with others. He did not see that the others were merely his working tools."

So after Lenin's death the struggle between the two rivals became inevitable. From the fact that fundamentally both wanted the same thing, namely the building up of an industrial state and the expropriation of the peasantry, externally the difference between the two men was only a question of *tempo*. But the spirits that are called forth during revolutionary movements cannot be easily sent back all at once to their primal abode. The peasants form eighty-five per cent of the Russian population and they had become the owners of the land. That was the greatest achievement of the Revolution. Through the increase in the population and for other reasons, agricultural produce increased from ten to twenty-five millions within ten years. But the export of grain, which was the leading feature of Russian international commerce before the war, now dwindled to relatively small proportions; because the peasant decided to use the grain for himself and his family. He was now feeding much better than under the old régime, when the export was artificially increased by keeping the peasant on small rations. In the year 1927 it was necessary actually to import grain into Russia.

In Lenin's time and under what was called the New Political Economy the peasants were called upon to make the most of their opportunity and pile up their possessions. "Get rich quick" was the cry. After this had been enthusiastically responded to and the *kulak* had extended his holdings at the cost of the poorer peasant, Trotsky challenged Stalin and said: "We have not made a revolution in the towns for the purpose of creating a new kind of capitalist in the country. The Revolution must be extended to all. Who now holds back is a *Thermidorian*." Stalin replied that the ends of the Revolution could not be gained in a moment, that there had to be transitional solutions, that Lenin himself had to allow a temporary return to Free Trade and that

Trotsky in his unreasonable hurry was like a foolish gardener who pulls up the plant in his anxiety to see the sprouting root.

As a matter of fact both men wanted the same thing; but impetuosity and patience, fire and foresight, can never go hand in hand. As head of the party, Stalin was shrewd enough to fill all the important posts with his own followers during those critical years. He was supported by the party press, which was under his own iron rule, and therefore he was able, in the election of 1927, definitely to bring about Trotsky's downfall.

At the time of Lenin's death it was said that Trotsky had only four friends among the eighteen comrades. Yet as the most powerful man in the country, he could have made a most successful *coup d'état* and taken over supreme power in his own hands; but any sort of Napoleonic venture was contrary to his nature. Even his enemies afterwards acknowledged this. In spite of his self-confidence he was always loyal and in the midst of all his activities he remained a great and forceful writer. He liked to use the pen as the instrument of his power and published stirring articles month after month in the party press organs. He had something also of the nonchalance of the *grand seigneur*. While Stalin was carefully preparing the attack against him, Trotsky, like Danton, thought to himself: "They won't dare." So in the final struggle he was deprived of power by the vote of the party.

To me, however, there appears to be a deeper historical reason for this. By the year 1927 the Revolution had come to that stage wherein the new state founded by it had to be ruled by a conservative and very careful progressive leader. But Trotsky was a typical revolutionary and his fiery spirit was not what was wanted in the management of the consolidated Bolshevik state. He was declared a dangerous man and was exiled with his friends to Siberia. Whereupon his enemy and conqueror immediately bowed to the pressure of the progressive workers, who were all being treated as one unit and demanded the same treatment for the peasantry.

In the very moment that Trotsky was dismissed Stalin began to take over his rival's *tempo*. What Lenin had demanded as the first necessity of the Socialist state, namely the electrification of Russia, had already been studied by the experts and a plan prepared. Stalin now took up this and launched it as the Five-Year Plan. The complete transformation of the regions in the Soviet Union into an industrial country was possible only if the millions of larger and smaller farms were combined. But this meant a struggle with the *kulak* who had already amassed private wealth under the Bolshevik state.

Such an undertaking demanded perseverance and energy and patience, combined. Therefore its demands were in accord with Stalin's character. Of all the ministers who had taken part in founding and directing the Government in October 1917, Stalin was then in the least important position. Today the others are all dead or deprived of power. Stalin alone remains and his power is greater than Trotsky's was when the latter was at the height of his glory.

The case of Trotsky is one that may be described as tragic in the classical sense of that term. Radek was dismissed from the party and condemned at the same time as Trotsky. While conversing on this theme, he said to me: "For twenty-five years I have been active in the Labour Movement and then I was condemned to exile by the Proletarian Government. Our inner feelings told us that we were being sent into exile because the party was moving towards the Right. But I took half-a-hundredweight of books with me—all our socialist works in fact, beginning with Marx. I said to myself that I should study the whole development of socialism from the start and think over it. On grounds of principle, are we right or are the others? I asked myself. For three months I studied the writings of Marx and Lenin and

Stal n and then I recognized that the plan of campaign that was being carried out by our comrades was a magnificent conception for the development of the New State. It reminded me of the second part of *Faust*. Whereupon I withdrew my objection to Stalin's plan out of sheer conviction. I agreed to the new line of action and advised Trotsky to do the same."

But Trotsky could not change his attitude so easily as Radek, who had never been a leader in the sense that Trotsky and Stalin were leaders. It was not possible for Trotsky to return home and live under his rival's régime, to edit school-books, like Zinoviev. And so Trotsky was forbidden either to live or to die. He was deported to a foreign island and there nothing remained for him to do except to return to his original vocation. He began to write books which have made a world-wide appeal and will probably cause him to be remembered when Stalin is forgotten.

5

When a visitor enters the inner courtyard of the Kremlin, which is like an elevated fortress in the middle of the Bolshevik metropolis, he is greeted by Napoleon. Thousands of cannons with their breeches turned towards the old red battlements and the towers are like a thousand iron mouths that challenge the stranger. And each is marked with the imperial *N*. The guard that stands at the old drawbridge simply asks the visitor's name and the soldier by his side compares it with his book to see if it is the same name as that which has been telephoned. A passport is not demanded. It seemed to me that almost anybody who had laid a plan for the assassination of the chief personalities in the Kremlin could very simply gain an entrance. At the gate of the building where the Government of the Soviet Union has its headquarters one is again asked the name. It is in this same building that Stalin has his office as General Secretary of the Communist Party. Here we have another instance of how these two powers are welded together even though the Bolsheviks so often deny this, just as the King of Prussia tried to distinguish between himself in that capacity and as Emperor of Germany in the last tragic moments of his rule. The truth is that in this office nine men of the Bolshevik Party decide everything. Here the ministers make their speeches and from here they take their orders.

The three or four rooms and the corridors that we passed through were quite simply but efficiently furnished as offices. A carpet with wide red borders leads to Stalin's door. He received us immediately. My companion was a young journalist who speaks several languages excellently and translates very precisely. Stalin and Mustapha Kemal are the only men with whom I have had to converse through the medium of an interpreter. The room which we entered was long and at the far end of it a medium-sized man in a light brown jacket rose from his chair. He was dressed with painful neatness, just as the room was arranged with the hygienic accuracy of a doctor's consulting room. A large table stood in the middle, as in an ordinary board-room, with plain water carafes and glasses and large ashtrays. Everything was in apple pie order. The walls were coloured dark green. Pictures of Lenin and Marx and several other people unknown to me hung there, but they were all just enlarged photographs. Stalin's desk was also in perfect order and on it was a photograph of Lenin, beside four or five telephones, such as one finds in all these government offices.

"Good evening," I said, in stumbling Russian. He smiled and seemed somewhat embarrassed but he was extremely courteous and began by offering me a cigarette. He assured me that I was at full liberty to say what I liked and to ask whatever questions I liked and that he had an hour and a half free. But when I drew out my watch at the end of that time he made a prohibitive gesture and kept us for another half-hour. A certain degree of embarrassment is as graceful in a man of power as it is in a beautiful woman. In the case of Stalin it did not surprise me at all because he scarcely ever sees people from the West. Few of the present ambassadors or envoys, and scarcely any of the great experts, have ever seen him. The only foreigner who had free access to him was little old Cooper, the American hydraulic engineer, who constructed the cofferdam of the Dnieper. Though my interpreter holds an important position in the Bolshevik press organization, he had never seen Stalin before. Since he had to speak constantly through the medium of the interpreter, Stalin was looking away from me practically all the time and for the whole two hours he kept on drawing figures on a piece of paper. With a red pencil he drew red circles and arabesques and wrote numbers. He never turned the pencil round, though at the other end it was blue. During the course of our conversation he filled many sheets of paper with red drawings and from time to time folded them and tore them into pieces.

The result was that I managed to get his glance straight into my face for only a few seconds and thus I beheld the great betrayer of mankind. His look was dour and the expression veiled. But it was not the glance of a misanthropist. It was the glance rather of a man who has grown suspicious of his fellow men from long experience and has lived a very lonely life. Though it may happen only seldom, I can imagine this man suddenly rising up and advancing slowly to his opponent and deliberately looking him straight in the eye. For as a matter of fact, this plodding man is capable of sudden surprise. In 1919 or 1920, he unexpectedly got a divorce and married the sixteen-year-old daughter of a Georgian friend.

In the long pauses that are necessary for translation and re-translation I had a good opportunity for observing his movements, especially as he speaks so slowly. Such pauses enable an interviewer to introduce a change of theme in the conversation and thus the better to search the mind of his subject. Stalin's habit of sitting absolutely immobile and of scarcely ever emphasizing a word with a gesture made this all the easier. When I am conversing with somebody I have a habit of standing up and walking about. If I had done it here it might have been considered strange.

What completed the picture of Stalin, as I have already described it, was the heavy and muffled tone of his voice. It was the kind of voice that could never speak the word of destiny "I Will" with fiery emotion. He could only let the syllables fall like heavy hammer blows. The chief impression that I got of him was that of a protector. Stalin is a man before whose name many men and women have quaked, but one could never imagine a child or an animal doing so. In a former age such a man would have been called the father of his country.

Since the stranger arriving in the Kremlin is always looked upon as an enemy, I decided to take that attitude in my questions. Stalin gave me an exhaustive answer each time and I shall not shorten it here. He spoke in short clear sentences, not as a man who is accustomed to simplify things before public audiences, but as a logical and constructive thinker whose mind works slowly and without the slightest emotion. This man who is now the exponent of the whole Moscow ideology struck me as a typical disciple of Hegel. In parentheses, I may here call attention to the curious fact that these foreign dictators have been taught their lesson by the Germans. Marx is the apostle in Russia, Nietzsche in Italy, and Hegel in both countries.

Stalin takes the point of an argument immediately, lays it on the table, as it were, talks around it and then comes close to it and carefully brings to bear on it historical data and statistical percentages. When he speaks he seemed to me to be absolutely a contradiction of Prince von Bülow. He scarcely ever gave me the merely party answer, the experience which I have had with most of the other Communists.

Although he could not have been prepared for most of my questions and although he has not had the experience of our European ministers of state, who are asked the same questions week after week, and although he knew that I should publish his answers to the world, he did not correct himself once. He had all the historical data and names at his fingertips. He did not ask for any copy of what my interpreter wrote down and he did not ask for any corrections to be made. I had never before experienced the same kind of self-confidence. In all my conversations with other leaders, I have not taken down what they have said at the moment but have recorded it afterwards and submitted the script to them for authorization. But here I took the stenographic text as it was copied by another person and when I examined it I could not find the slightest omission and yet nothing had been bettered. Outside of one mere private question, he did not ask me to tone down anything or omit this or that. When I recall to mind the habits of our poor ministers, when they are preparing a parliamentary speech or having an interview corrected by the head of their press bureau, I am filled with respect for the shoemaker's son from the Caucasus. He has never had anything like a systematic education and he is today the absolute ruler of such a large section of mankind.

"You have led the life of a conspirator for such a long time," I said; "and do you now think that, under your present rule, illegal agitation is no longer possible?"

"It is possible, at least to some extent."

"Is the fear of this possibility the reason why you are still governing with so much severity, fifteen years after the Revolution?"

"No. I will illustrate the chief reason for this by giving a few historical examples. When the Bolsheviks came to power they were soft and easy with their enemies. At that time, for example, the Mensheviks (Moderate Socialists) had their lawful newspapers and also the Social Revolutionaries. Even the military cadets had their newspapers. When the white-haired General Krasnov marched upon Leningrad and was arrested by us, under the military law he should have been shot or at least imprisoned, but we set him free on his word of honour. Afterwards it became clear that with this policy we were undermining the very system we were endeavouring to construct. We had begun by making a mistake. Leniency towards such a power was a crime against the working classes. That soon became apparent. The Social Revolutionaries of the Right and the Mensheviks, with Bogdanov and others, then organized the Junker revolt and fought against the Soviets for two years. Mamontov joined them. We soon saw that behind these agents stood the great powers of the West and the Japanese. Then we realized that the only way to get ahead was by the policy of absolute severity and intransigence. The illegal campaigns which we ourselves had carried on in the old days were naturally valuable to us as an experience, but that was not the decisive factor."

"This policy of cruelty seems to have aroused a very widespread fear. In this country I have the impression that everybody is afraid and that your great experiment could succeed only among this long-suffering nation that has been trained to obedience."

"You are mistaken," said Stalin, "but your mistake is general. Do you think it possible to hold power for fourteen years merely by intimidating the people? Impossible. The Czars knew best how to rule by intimidation. It is an old experiment in Europe and the French bourgeoisie supported the Czars in their policy of intimidation against the people. What came of it? Nothing."

"But it maintained the Romanovs in power for three hundred years," I replied.

"Yes, but how many times was that power not shaken by insurrections? To forget the older days, recall only the revolt of nineteen-five. Fear is in the first instance a question of the mechanism of administration. You can arouse fear for one or two years and through it, or at least partly through it, you can rule for that time. But you cannot rule the peasants by fear. Secondly, the peasants and the working classes in the Soviet Union are by no means so timid and long-suffering as you think. You believe that our people are timid and lazy. That is an antiquated idea. It was believed in formerly, because the landed gentry used to go to Paris to spend their money there and do nothing. From this arose an impression of the so-called Russian laziness. People thought that the peasants were easily frightened and made obedient. That was a mistake. And it was a threefold mistake in regard to the workers. Never again will the workers endure the rule of one man. Men who have reached the highest pinnacles of fame were lost the moment they had got out of touch with the masses. Plechanov had great authority in his hands but when he became mixed up in politics he quickly forgot the masses. Trotsky was a man of great authority, but not of such high standing as Plechanov, and now he is forgotten. If he is casually remembered it is with a feeling of irritation." (At that point he sketched something like a ship with his red pencil.)

I did not intend to mention Trotsky to Stalin but since he himself had broached the subject, I asked: "Is the feeling against Trotsky general?"

"If you take the active workers, nine-tenths speak bitterly of Trotsky."

There was a short pause during which Stalin laughed quietly and then took up the thread of the question again: "You cannot maintain that people may be ruled for a long time merely by intimidation. I understand your skepticism. There is a small section of the people which is really afraid. It is an unimportant part of the peasant body. That part is represented by the *kulaks*. They do not fear anything like the initiation of a reign of terror but they fear the other section of the peasant population. This is a hang-over from the earlier class system. Among the middle classes, for example, and especially the professional classes, there is something of the same kind of fear, because these latter had special privileges under the old régime. Moreover, there are traders and a certain section of the peasants that still maintain the old liking for the gentry.

"But if you take the progressive peasants and workers, not more than fifteen per cent are skeptical of the Soviet power, or are silent from fear or are waiting for the moment when they can undermine the Bolshevik state. On the other hand, about eighty-five per cent of the more or less active people would urge us further than we want to go. We often have to put on the brakes. They would like to stamp out the last remnants of the intelligentsia. But we would not permit that. In the whole history of the world there never was a power that was supported by nine-tenths of the population as the Soviet power is supported. That is the reason for our success in putting our ideas into practice. If we ruled only by fear not a man would have stood by us. And the working classes would have destroyed any power that attempted to continue to rule by fear. Workers who have made three revolutions have had some practice in overthrowing governments. They would not endure such a mockery of government as one merely based on fear."

"When I hear repeatedly about the power of the masses," I said, "I am surprised at the hero-worship that is more prevalent here than anywhere else, for this is the last place one would logically expect to find it. Your materialistic conception of history—which is what separates me personally from you, for I hold that men make history—should prevent leaders and symbols from being shown in the form of statues and pictures on the street. You are the very people who, logically, ought not to revere the Unknown Soldier or any other individual. Now how can you explain that contradiction?"

"You are mistaken. Read that part of Marx where he speaks of the poverty of philosophy."

Above Stalin's head hung a portrait of the white-haired Karl Marx. And every time the conversation turned to the great socialist, I had to look at the portrait.

"There," continued Stalin, "you will find that men make history. But not in the way that your fancy suggests. Men make history rather in their reactions to the definite circumstances in which they find themselves placed. Every generation has a new set of circumstances to face. In general it can be said that great men are of value only in so far as they are able to deal with the circumstances of their environment. Otherwise they are Don Quixotes. According to Marx himself, one should never contrast men and circumstances. So far as my opinion goes, it is history that makes men. We have been studying Marx for thirty years."

"And our professors interpret him differently," I suggested.

"That is because they try to popularize Marxism. He has himself never denied the importance of the rôle of the hero. It is in fact very great."

"May I therefore conclude that here in Moscow also one man rules and not the Council? I see sixteen chairs around the table."

Stalin looked at the chairs: "The individual does not decide.

In every council there are people whose views must be taken
into account, but wrong views also exist. We have had experience
of three revolutions and we know that out of one hundred decisions made by individuals ninety are one-sided. Our leading
organ is the Central Committee of the party and it has seventy
members. Among these seventy members are some of our most
capable industrialists and co-operatives and our best tradesmen,
also some of our ablest authorities on agriculture and co-operative
farming as well as individual farming, finally some men who
have a first-class knowledge of how to deal with the various nationalities that make up the Soviet Union. This is the Areopagus
in which the wisdom of the party is centred. It gives the individual the possibility of correcting his partial prejudices. Each
contributes his own experience for the general benefit of the
Committee. Without this method very many mistakes would be
made. Since each person takes his part in the deliberations, our
decisions are more or less correct."

"So you refuse to be a dictator," I said. "I have found these
same tactics are used by all dictators. In Europe you are painted
as the bloodthirsty Czar or the aristocratic freeholder from
Georgia."

He laughed in a genial way and blinked at me as I continued:
"Since there are stories going around of bank robberies and other
burglaries which you organized as a youth in order to help the
party, or at least countenanced, I should like to know how much
of all these we are to believe."

The peasant instinct in Stalin now came to the fore. He went
across to his writing desk and brought me a pamphlet of about
twenty pages which contained his biographical data in Russian
but naturally nothing in answer to my question.

"There you will find everything," he said, obviously pleased
at this debonair way of giving a negative answer.

I began to laugh and asked: "Tell me if you do not feel yourself to be the follower of Stenka Rasin, the noble rapparee whose legendary deeds I have heard recounted on the Volga, where they were done?"

He returned to his constructive, logical way of talking.

"We Bolsheviks," he said, "apart entirely from our national origin, have always been interested in personalities like Bolotnikov, Stenka Rasin, Pugatschev, because they emerged spontaneously from the first elementary uprising of the peasantry against the oppressor. It is interesting for us to study the first signs of that awakening. Historical allegories, however, are out of the question and we have not idealized Stenka Rasin. Individual uprisings, even when organized with the rapacity that characterized these three leaders I have mentioned, lead to nothing. A peasant revolution can attain its ends only when it is united with the revolution of the workers and led by the latter. Only a revolution integrally organized and welded together in all its parts can lead to its goal. This you cannot have among the peasants, because they alone form an independent class. Moreover, the three insurrectionary leaders that I have mentioned were all Czarists. They were against the landed gentry but *for our good Czar*. That was their battle-cry."

The hands of the watch that I had placed before me on the table showed that our time was growing short. I put another question in an innocent way as if I did not know about America in Russia: "Everywhere in this country," I said, "I find that America is respected. How is it possible that a state whose aim is to overthrow capitalism can pay its respects to a country in which capitalism has reached its highest development?"

Without a moment's pause, Stalin gave a magnificent answer: "You are overstating things. Here there is no general respect for everything that is American. There is only a respect for the American sense of practicality in everything, in industry, in literature, and in business; but we never forget that it is a capitalist land. They are sound people, or at least there are many sound people there, sound in mind as well as in body, sound in their whole attitude towards work and towards everyday facts. The practical business side of American life and its simplicity has our sympathy. In spite of its capitalistic character, the customs which are in vogue throughout the industrial and economic life of America are more democratic than in any European country, for in Europe the influence of the aristocracy is not yet obliterated."

"You do not know how true that is," I said in an undertone. But the interpreter heard me and translated it for Stalin.

"Yes, I know," answered Stalin. "In spite of the fact that the feudal form of government has been wiped out in many European lands, the feudal spirit still remains and is powerful. From the aristocratic hang-over many technicians and specialists carry on the tradition of their origin. That cannot be said of America. It is a land of colonists without a landed gentry or an aristocracy, and hence the simple vigour of its customs. In industry and business they are simple, and our workmen who have become leaders of industry here notice that fact immediately when they go to America. There it is difficult to distinguish between the engineer and the simple workman while they are at their job."

Here Stalin had formulated with simplicity and sureness of insight the parallel between those two utterly different nations, America and Russia. All at once and without any signs of making a transition and before I could put a question, he said:

"But if we feel friendly towards any one nation as a whole, or towards a majority in any nation, our friendship is for the Germans. There is no comparison between this friendship and our kindly feelings for America."

"And why the Germans?"

"It is a fact."

Stalin uttered these four words with such conclusive emphasis that he seemed to forestall any further questions on that point, but the spontaneous expression of his sympathy had so much behind it that I did not wish to lose the opportunity. Without mentioning the World Revolution, I said: "I think you are deceiving yourself in your hopes of Germany. The Germans love order more than freedom. That is why we have had no revolutions or at least no revolutions that were successful."

"As to the past you are right in what you say about the Germans," he answered. "When I was living in Berlin in nineteen-seven I was often amused by the spirit of obedience which our German friends displayed. I was told that once the leaders of the party had announced a demonstration to which the Communists from the various parts of Berlin were to come at a given hour. About two hundred had come from one suburb. When they reached the railway gate where the tickets had to be handed over the ticket collector was not there. The Russians who were with them urged them to pass through the open gate as they all had their railway tickets but they would not budge an inch and it looked as if they would have remained there for hours if the ticket collector had not come. When I was in Dresden and Chemnitz between nineteen-five and -seven, I found the law was respected there like frost or thunder or some other force of nature against which the will of man is of no avail. In Vienna in nineteen-twelve when I went with my Russian friends into the park at Schönbrunn, we noticed the sign *Verboten* everywhere but we were not used to such things and we must have paid a fine of a crown apiece over twenty times for the pleasure of having broken the law. Our German friends laughed at us for the pleasure we had taken in that form of amusement. So it was in those days.

"But today? Where is the German sense of order today? Where is the respect for the law? The National Socialists break the law whenever they find it in their way. They shoot and bludgeon all round. In Germany today workers go out of the city and dig up other people's potatoes. Everything is changed since the old days." He was silent for a while. Then I said to him:

"So far as I know you were only a few months in Europe, whereas Lenin was there for twenty years. Which do you think was the better preparation for a revolutionary leadership—at home or abroad?" He neither answered yes nor no; but gave a general explanation.

"For Lenin," he replied, "I would make an exception. Very few of those who remained here in Russia kept themselves so closely in touch with what was happening here as Lenin did while he was abroad. I visited him several times abroad, in nineteen-seven, nineteen-eight and nineteen-twelve, and I generally found that he daily received sheaves of letters from Russian politicians and that he knew more of what was happening in Russia than people who actually lived here. And yet he looked upon it as a great misfortune that he had always to remain abroad. As regards the others who remained in Russia and whose number was of course much greater, they certainly helped the movement excellently. The number of those abroad who helped the movement was only as one to two hundred in comparison with those who carried on the work at home. And in the Central Committee today, out of seventy members, there are only three or four who have been abroad."

"But did you not highly appreciate the knowledge of Europe that Lenin had?"

"What do you understand by the word *Europe*? You know many of those who have sojourned as immigrants in Europe. Anybody who desires to study Europe can certainly do so better in Europe than outside of Europe. In this sense those of us who have been there for only a little while have certainly missed something. But that lack is of no decisive importance when we come to the question of acquiring a knowledge of European economics, industrial technique, the education and training that take place in the centres of leadership, the whole range of literature, belles-lettres and science. Everything else being equal, it would of course be better to study these in Europe itself; but the minus quantity here is not of striking significance. I know several comrades of ours who spent twenty years in Europe, somewhere or other in Charlottenburg, but you might put a concrete question to them about Germany and they could not give an answer."

Somewhat later I brought the conversation round to the surprising change of front that communism had made in abandoning the old theory of equality and introducing piece-work in its place, thus giving the energetic worker a chance to earn more than his companion. "We were astonished," I concluded, "when you yourself characterized equalization as the remains of middle-class prejudice."

Stalin answered: "A completely socialized state where all receive the same amount of bread and meat, the same kind of clothes, the same products and exactly the same amount of each product—such a socialism was not recognized by Marx. Marx merely says that so long as the classes are not entirely wiped out and so long as work has not become an object of pleasure—for now most people look upon it as a burden—there are many people who would like to have other people do more work than they. So long then as the distinction of class is not entirely obliterated, people will be paid according to their productive efficiency, each according to his capacity. That is the Marxist formula for the first stage of socialism. When socialism has reached the complete stage everyone will do what he is capable of doing and for the work which he has done he will be paid according to his needs. It should be perfectly clear that different people have different needs, great and small. Socialism has never denied the difference in personal tastes and needs either in kind or in extent. Read Marx's criticism of Stirner and the Gotha programme. Marx there attacks the principle of equalization. That is a part of primitive peasant psychology, the idea of equalization. It is not socialistic. In the West they look upon the thing in such a primitive way that they imagine we want to divide up everything evenly. That is the theory of Babeuf. He never knew anything about scientific socialism. Even Cromwell wanted to level everything."

Although I thought him mistaken in regard to Cromwell, it was not my business to enter into a historical argument with Stalin. I preferred to revert to the problem of stories and legend-mongering and, since he had asked whether the cigarette he had just given me did not please me—for I had stopped smoking —I said:

"You are supposed to be against the manufacture of legends. And yet surely nothing has made you so popular as the legend that you always smoke a pipe."

He laughed. "You see how little need I have of it. This morning I left it at home."

"But are you really against legends?"

"Not when they are folk-legends."

"It is late. Will you kindly autograph this pamphlet you have given me?"

He nodded. But he seemed bewildered because he was not used to this European custom. "Yes, of course, but what shall I write?"

"Your own name, and that of Herr Ludwig," said the translator. His shyness at that moment attracted me to him very much. He raised the red pencil with which he had been drawing and wrote on the pamphlet. I looked at three sheets of paper which were completely filled with his pictures. I took none of them away because I felt that some disciple of Freud would have taken them from me later on and written an essay from them on calligraphy. I stood up and asked:

"Would you be surprised at a question?"

"Nothing that happens in Russia could surprise me," he said.

"That frame of mind is international. In Germany also nothing that might happen could surprise us. Do you believe in Fate?"

He became very serious. He turned to me and looked me straight in the face. Then, after a tense pause, he said: "No, I do not believe in Fate. That is simply a prejudice. It is a nonsensical idea." He laughed in his dark muffled way and said in German, "*Schicksal, Schicksal.*" Then he reverted to his native language and said: "Just as with the Greeks. They had their gods and goddesses who directed everything from above."

"You have been through a hundred dangers," I said, "when you were banned and exiled, in revolutions and in wars. Is it merely an accident that you were not killed and that someone else is not in your place today?"

He was somewhat annoyed, but only for a moment. Then he said, in a clear, ringing voice:

"No accident, Herr Ludwig, no accident. Probably there were inner and outer causes that prevented my death. But it could have happened by accident that someone else might be sitting here and not I."

And as if he wished to break through this dense and annoying cloud and get back to his Hegelian clarity, he said: "Fate is contrary to law. It is something mystic. In this mystical thing I do not believe. Of course there were causes why I came through all these dangers. It could not have happened merely by accident. *Schicksal* (Destiny, Fate)! The echoes of that mighty German word were still in my ears as we took our seats in the waiting motor car.

In this citadel the Czars lived and ruled, sometimes wielding a power that had not been arrived at by natural means. And here Death found them. Everything around us gleamed sinister in the dusk—sinister and embattled. And here the son of the Georgian peasant had laughed defiantly when the word *Destiny* was mentioned. The ring of cannons in the forecourt reflected the evening light in a dull sheen. But on each muzzle glittered brightly the letter *N*, embossed in gold—the superscription which a little corporal from a barren island had dared to stamp on the mouth of Death. "What have you to do with Destiny?" Napoleon asked Goethe. "Politics are DESTINY."